Post-Conviction Relief: Secrets Exposed

Kelly Patrick Riggs

Freebird Publishers
www.FreebirdPublishers.com

Freebird Publishers
Box 541, North Dighton, MA 02764
Info@FreebirdPublishers.com
www.FreebirdPublishers.com

Post-Conviction Relief: Secrets Exposed
By Kelly Patrick Riggs

All Freebird Publishers titles, imprints and distributed lines are available at special quantity discounts for bulk purchases for sales promotions, premiums, fundraising educational or institutional use.

ISBN: 0-9913591-5-1
ISBN-13: 978-0-9913591-5-8

Printed in the United States of America

appear in these court filings. Finally, while all provided information was up to date at the time of publication, we cannot guarantee that all information is still current at the time you read this.

FOREWORD

I can only speak to those in federal prison who have chosen to pick this book up and read it. That action alone suggests that you have some type of vested interest, or that there is some type of injustice imposed upon you in your case, or that you're seeking some relief that will get you out of prison. Trust me, as a federal inmate who is fighting back, I have been in your shoes. I know the emotional rollercoaster the plague of injustice in this system forces you on. In some cases, inmates get discouraged and give up. It is my desire that you don't give up. You will find hope, if you put in the work to get relief.

This book is designed to help inmates with little-to-no knowledge of the judicial rules and the affect they have on a case. It gives you knowledge of what a "writ of *habeas corpus*" is, the process by which it is implemented, and how to apply it to benefit your case in court. The book's author, Mr. Kelly Riggs, has broken the *habeas corpus* process down into layman's terms, so that the average inmate can get a clear understanding of how to apply it to his case. Like *Computers for Beginners*, this book could be titled *Habeas Corpus for Prisoners* – it will provide you the knowledge to hold the federal court accountable to their own laws through the *habeas corpus* procedure, so that you may receive your just due process of law.

I'm sure that you've heard of the old "jailhouse lawyer," right? I'm also sure some of you have been skeptical of seeking legal advice about your case from these so-called lawyers. In most cases, these guys are simply running a scam to make a buck. Yet my experience working with Mr. Riggs, and meeting others he has helped over the years, has convinced me of his vast knowledge of the law and genuine compassion to help people. The following is my testimony of how Mr. Riggs helped me utilize the *habeas corpus* process:

I was convicted in 2008, of a drug conspiracy charge and sentenced to 150 months in federal prison. I was then transferred to state custody and sentenced to ten years in Texas and 12 years in Georgia. After serving five years in state prison, I was released on parole. Over two years into my parole, I was picked up by the U.S. Marshals and told that I owed federal prison time. The BOP (and lesser-equipped jail-house lawyers) told me that I had to start my federal prison time (150 months) all over, and the time I served in state prison would not be counted towards it.

I felt a little discouraged at first, but I was determined to fight what I felt was an injustice imposed on me. I met Mr. Riggs a few months after I arrived at the federal institution I am currently assigned to. At first, I was skeptical of Kelly and felt that he was arrogant. So, I started researching cases that might apply to my own and asking questions from other jailhouse lawyers. But after a few months went by, the strangest thing happened: I started working in the laundry department, with Kelly Riggs.

To this day I feel it was God's plan that we crossed paths the way we did. Working with Kelly, questioning him about law and my case, I began to see a knowledgeable man of law with a sincere willingness to help as many people as he could get back into court and get actual justice. In my case, through *habeas corpus* 2255, I received five years of federal good-time credit from the state sentence I served.

My advice to the reader is to get involved in the process, whether through legal assistance or doing it yourself. You know your case and can explain it like no other. But you need to learn the judicial process that may have been used to deliver you some type of injustice – an excessive sentence, a denial of an actual innocence, a due-process violation – whatever your case may be. This book is designed to guide you step-by-step through the *habeas corpus* process that will work for you, if you apply it.

I hope life is on your side and that you receive your due justice.

Sincerely,

Carl Regester

OVERVIEW

This publication is geared towards incarcerated people and is written from the prospective an innocent prisoner. Using plain language, this book is designed to aid prisoners in understanding exactly how and why they have come to be incarcerated in a federal prison and what they can do about it. This publication is for – and encourages all who read it to become – fighters, fighters who know they have been wronged and wish to correct the injustice.

In the introduction you see why I am putting my knowledge into comprehensive book form. In chapter one I provide a brief history lesson in civics. In chapter two, I share my own personal feelings, pains, emotions, and passions as a prisoner who is wrongfully convicted. Starting in chapter three and thereafter, it's down to business: I teach, and you learn, step-by-step, how and where to get Post-Conviction Relief.

TABLE OF CONTENTS

INTRODUCTION

Just to be short and to the point, I'm writing this book because of a question that was presented to me last night. Those who have met me know that I gather with several other inmates at the legal library every night to assist prisoners in their efforts to gain freedom. Last night as I walked back from the library with a person for whom I have great respect, I was asked how everything would continue in the event I was to leave. My friend was anticipating me making a visit to the S.H.U., a legitimate concern. I am long overdue. For this reason, I'm putting into writing everything you need to know. It is my intent to explain, in layman's terms, the meaning and procedure of *habeas corpus*.

Chances are if you are reading this book, you are a prisoner in a fine federal establishment, just like I am. If that is the case, you have access to a legal library. In this you will find, on the computer system, a publication named *Federal Habeas Corpus Practice and Procedures*. This is a complicated book about how to find your way through the *habeas corpus* proceedings. I have spent many hours reading through all its information with a dictionary in hand, often spending more time in the dictionary. Imagine doing this night after night, two-hours at a time. Though I was fortunate enough to gain a meaningful education, I still have a hard time following the procedure. I can't imagine what it would be like to try to understand the procedure with a high school education or less. So, I am writing *this book* for you.

Another resource you will need is a dictionary from the commissary. It is a very limited dictionary and some of the words herein will not be found in it. Those words will be found in a glossary in the back of this publication.

You will also find in this book, forms to start the proceeding to gain freedom (*habeas corpus*) very early on. I cannot express to you enough how important it is to read this entire book before you start. I have witnessed many prisoners trigger the process, get to the finish line, and then stumble and fall before they reach their goals – only because they didn't know what to do next. Most prisoners learn what *habeas corpus* gives you (freedom) and believe that is the end of the process. However, a properly executed petition for *habeas corpus* will start a process that moves like a run-away freight train. You don't want to be expecting the caboose, only to meet the engines head on … while you are tied to the tracks.

In this book you will find subjects divided by chapters. The chapters will not be numbered the same as you will find in the library. Each chapter title will have a note under it indicating where you will find it in the procedure manual that is found in the library.

Let me also express that this is not a textbook. You will not find meaningless histories of words or principles that no longer matter. This is, however, a procedural manual. You may or may not use every step in every case but be sure you are familiar with all the steps in the event you need them.

CHAPTER ONE

What is Habeas Corpus

You will find that material in this chapter is also somewhat covered in the second chapter of the *Federal Habeas Corpus Practice and Procedures* manual in the legal library. You are going to find out that I don't like to provide so much material that I confuse the reader, so always check all possible "legal" resources. With that in mind, let's get on with it.

Habeas corpus is a Latin term dating all the way back to 1215. This term was found in the principle foundation of law in England's equivalent to our Constitution. *Habeas corpus* is very specifically translated to mean "you should have the body for submitting." Simply meaning that the Prison has you and the court demands your presence and the Prison will submit or otherwise do as they are told by bringing you to court. What you more commonly hear is that a prisoner is looking for a "writ" of *habeas corpus*. This is where I want you to consider my instructions in the introduction. As you can see, I've introduced a new word, *writ*. The word *writ* is defined as an order or mandatory process in writing issued in the name of a court or judicial officer commanding the person to whom it is directed to perform an act that is specified in the writ. A court order is a writ.

In our modern American legal system, the term *habeas corpus* carries several meanings. The most common being "The right to take legal action to end unlawful detention," or "*habeas corpus ad subjiciendum*." This particular request is that of an order to be brought before the court in person where the government *must* prove that a prisoner is legally detained.

Plainly stated, if you are asking for a "writ of *habeas corpus*" you are not asking to be released. This writ alone will not get you home. It will, however, get you started in the right direction. In making a request for a "writ of *habeas corpus*" you are asking the court to issue an order, to those who are responsible for detaining and transporting you, to have you brought to court. If you are presently in court, you already have what you asked for and the writ of *habeas corpus* was granted and obviously executed. But I caution you, if you ask for nothing further, you will get nothing further, as this is simply another step in the process.

Now that you have been brought to court on a writ of *habeas corpus*, let's go over what is supposed to happen next and why. To do this, a brief history lesson is required.

Declaration of Independence

Prior to the Revolutionary War, the Founding Fathers of America recognized, publicly, your right to be free, your personal liberty, in the Declaration of Independence. This document is widely known to specify America's separation from British Rule, but it also declared the *right* of "*a citizen*"

"Under Natural Law, your personal right to be *free*, your *liberty* is established in this paragraph:

> ***"We hold these truths to be self-evident, that all men are created equal, that they are endowed by their creator with certain unalienable rights that among these are Life, Liberty and the pursuit of happiness. That to secure these rights, governments are instituted among men, deriving their just powers from the consent of the governed."***

As you can see by this paragraph, you are born with some very specific rights. But also note the word "*unalienable*," or in modern English "*inalienable*." This one word is pivotal, because it refers to something that can't be taken from you, nor can you give it away, sell it, or lose it. Inalienable rights are basic rights that automatically belong to every human being and can't be lost. So how does someone become a prisoner if the basic right to liberty can't be lost? That's because of the part of the paragraph that says:

> ***"That to secure these rights, governments are instituted among men, deriving their powers from the consent of the governed."***

It's easy to see that "all men" means everyone; you have the same rights as everyone else. These rights *must* be protected, even one person from another person. In the event you decide to exercise your rights in a way that hurts another person's rights, then the person whose rights have been hurt by you *must* be protected from you. If you are or were a prisoner, then you stand convicted of hurting someone else's rights and your imprisonment is that protection to your victim's rights.

CONSTITUTION AS THE PROTECTION OF RIGHTS

In an effort to bring about a uniform protection of the rights discussed, our Founding Fathers established a government. Just as anything or anyone else, this proposed government needed a set of rules to follow so it wouldn't become a burden on the people's rights itself.

Over the course of two years, 1787-1789, the people debated over everything required to establish a government with a working set of rules. On April 30, 1789, the Constitution of the United States of America took effect with the swearing in of President George Washington.

Under the new government and its Constitution, the right not to be unlawfully imprisoned is protected in Article I, Section 9, which states:

> ***"The privilege of the Writ of Habeas Corpus shall not be suspended, unless when in cases of rebellion or invasion the public safety may require it."***

As the right of *habeas corpus* was put into use, it took very little time to realize that an important part was left out of the Constitution. Even though *habeas corpus* had just become a standardized right among all states throughout the Nation, there was no establishment of what made imprisonment unlawful. Take for example if one state allowed you to be convicted without the benefit of counsel for your defense and another state did not, then the right of *habeas corpus* would be affected by what was considered a lawful imprisonment from state to state.

RIGHT TO DUE PROCESS

As the Federal government was attempting to establish a uniform protection of the right not to be unlawfully imprisoned through *habeas corpus*, it became an increasing challenge to do so based upon laws that differed from state to state. This gave rise to the need for a standardized method of seeking imprisonment. The *only* way to *guarantee* uniformity was to establish a *due process* by which an accused person could be imprisoned.

On December 15, 1791, only three years after the main body of the Constitution was written, the first ten amendments to the Constitution were ratified together and are collectively known as the Bill of Rights. The Bill of Rights is commonly known for guaranteeing the basic civil rights of *all* Americans, including or maybe especially someone who is accused of hurting someone else's rights. This includes those accused of committing criminal offenses.

Due process is first demanded in the Fifth Amendment of the Constitution, which reads:

> ***"No person shall be held to answer for a Capital, or otherwise infamous crime, unless on a presentment or indictment of a Grand Jury, except in cases arising in the land or naval forces, or in the militia, when in actual service in time of war or public danger; nor shall any person***

> ***be subject for the same offense to be twice put in jeopardy of life or limb; nor shall be compelled in any criminal case to be a witness against himself, nor be deprived of life, liberty, or property, without due process of law; nor shall private property be taken for public use, without just compensation."***

Now that an accused person is guaranteed due process, we need to define it. You can't know if your right has been fulfilled if you don't know what it is. Many of your due process rights are laid out in the Bill of Rights but that's only the beginning.

In 1884, the Supreme Court defined due process as:

> ***"Any legal proceeding enforced by public authority, whether sanctioned by age and custom, or maybe devised in the discretion of the Legislative power; in furtherance of the general public good, which regards and preserves these principles of liberty and justice, must be held to be due process of law."***

This could be simply understood to mean proper procedures as established by anybody with the authority to pass laws. In 1914, the United States Supreme Court gave a shorter definition of:

> ***"The fundamental requisite of due process of law is the opportunity to be heard."***

In my humble opinion, you can't go wrong by studying the Bill of Rights, United States Code and *Federal Rules of Procedure* (Criminal, civil, Appellate, Evidence and § 2255).

THE NEED FOR *HABEAS CORPUS*

quality control – *habeas corpus* can best be illustrated as the quality control of the American justice system and the reason for things such as the Bill of Rights and the laws passed to fulfill the obligations set out in the Bill of Rights to prevent unlawful convictions and imprisonment. On February 10, 2016, USA Today, a nationally recognized newspaper, released an article concerning the American justice system. This article made clear that "*According to national registry, 149 convicted defendants were exonerated last year in the U.S.A., a record ...*" Without getting too deep into the how it happens just be aware that many *innocent* people are imprisoned each year, most of which are too poor to pay for a fair review.

It is important, however, that you understand why this happens and why it happens so often. Think about the justice system as any other business, they need to make money to survive. Any business that doesn't make money goes bankrupt. The American justice system is paid to fight crime. If they produce no convictions, they would have nothing to show for their efforts. You should be able to see by this why it's important to have an effective quality control system.

As with any other business, and any other product, it's important to reduce cost to be efficient. Just as a fast food restaurant wants to produce a cheaper hamburger, the judicial districts want to produce cheaper convictions. When reducing production costs of hamburgers, food engineers reduce costs by cutting corners in the preparation process by; leaving out unnecessary ingredients, cooking for shorter periods of time, or cooking on a lower heat, all of which would give some savings. But, while cutting cost, product quality must be reasonably the same. Yes, you must still produce a good tasting hamburger. For instance, even though you and the manager agree that if you have to leave out the salt, it won't make a big difference, the true test is the little child on the other side of the counter. As a father myself, I can assure you that if that hamburger doesn't taste exactly like the last one my child ate, she will tell the world, and will do it loudly. That is true quality control. I'm sure I don't have to tell you how it's going to roll downhill if a child in a public restaurant is not happy with a bad hamburger.

Now consider your judicial district as the restaurant. The judge and the Lawyers (for both sides) are the cooks trying to pull the wool over your eyes,

Your right to *due process* is the ingredient. That bad tasting hamburger is your conviction, you are that pissed off child, and the *habeas corpus* process is a protective parent wanting to know what they are trying to pull. Being a parent myself for over 25 years, I can assure that any three-year-old knows how to get their parents attention when unhappy. One loud scream in the open lobby of any public restaurant will instantly transform my peaceful demeanor into the raging protective instinct of a mother bear seeking to destroy the discomfort of my precious child.

Now, in continuing our comparisons, you can look at your new conviction of guilt, probably by Plea Agreement, as a hamburger coming across that counter that those two lawyers cooked up for you, using only about half of your rights and waiving the rest of them. The judge, sitting on high, is patiently waiting to see if you notice if anything's wrong and fully convinced that you don't know how to make hamburgers or understand your rights under the law. Well no tears, seems all is well as the child retreats to a table to dine. It's not until that hamburger gets unwrapped and the child takes the first bite she realizes that this thing tastes like *dirt*. As you have probably discovered at your sentencing, this conviction is clearly not what you bargained for.

This is where you find the difference. That child who hates that foul-tasting hamburger, even at three years old, speaks his mind with screaming and crying causing his parent to take notice of a problem who then seeks who dared to commit such an act of treachery. You on the other hand are in a court room in front of the manager of the restaurant (judge) and the two cooks who prepared the *dirt*-burger (Lawyers) so even if you speak your mind, it falls on deaf ears. Later you discuss this with the lawyer who the government most likely gave you. I'm sure you shared with him or her how you didn't get what was expected and maybe you're not even guilty at all. You tell all about how you feel that your trust has been betrayed and so on.

Well, let me explain, you are telling all your concerns to one of the cooks who is covering his ass and would just as soon have you quietly eat a *dirt*-burger so he or she may get on to the next screwing.

Just one last comparison, if you will. The purpose of the book you are holding is to teach you to scream at the top of your lungs to get the attention of a protective parent (*habeas corpus* proceedings) to make things right. Remember you are the last line of quality control; you are the child they have taken advantage of. Please don't wait for someone else to care, they will not ask to see if you were treated fairly, you *must* scream.

The need for *habeas corpus* is to correct unlawful imprisonment and I can assure you that a lot of that is going around. And please remember to read the whole book before asking for *habeas corpus*. If need be, ask for an extension of time to file because once you start this train, it won't stop until it reaches a destination good or bad, so let's be prepared.

In this book I'm writing in simplest form the steps to take to get *habeas corpus* relief from a Federal Conviction. I'm going to cover as many aspects as possible from a prisoner's point of view. I'm providing forms and letters needed at all steps as are available to me now, so please remember to check and recheck everything you can. The history and civics lessons are over so let's talk about *habeas corpus* and you.

CHAPTER TWO

HABEAS CORPUS VS. § 2255 PROCEEDINGS

Before we begin challenging our minds with this question that has troubled courts for over 60 years, I would like to help you with the issue of timely filing. Since some of you may be close to your filing deadline you may want to consider asking the court for more time to file. You will find a generic motion for extension at the end of this chapter with instructions. It asks the court to extend your filing deadline by an extra 90 days. That will give you some time to read this book before you start the process.

If you are now in a prison, or you have a loved one who is, you have heard the term *habeas corpus* and of course you have heard about all its "*mystical*" powers. Although *habeas corpus* is not as mystical as a unicorn, the myths and misconceptions are as plentiful as the myth about the unicorn. Upon arriving at your place of imprisonment you are going to discover a whole new class of people. These people will be known by a wide range of titles such as: paralegals, friends, jailhouse lawyers and of course the hustler.

These people are all very similar; every one of them is competing for the opportunity to take advantage of the misery you and your family are now suffering. You are going to hear a lot of technical terms and Numbers that you don't understand such as: 2241, 2254, 2255, and Rules 59, 60, and 33. Although every one of these has the potential to provide relief, not one of them has any mystical power – there are no magic motions. Truth be known, the people telling you all about these motions don't know any more about them than you do.

If you continue, you are going to learn that all avenues of *habeas corpus* require a complete proceeding and not one of them happens, or even begins for that matter, with, the simple filing of a motion. It is for this reason that I consider this chapter one of the *most* important; this is where you are going to learn to begin with, that you are very limited on how many times you may file for *habeas corpus* relief. If you're wondering, the answer to that is, *once*! All others, without special circumstances, will be considered "abuse of the writ." You are also going to learn the difference of various *habeas* motions and which will apply to your particular problem.

HABEAS CORPUS UNDER § 2255

As discussed earlier, there are many types of *habeas corpus* writs that apply in a federal court. There is, however, only one that concerns most federal prisoners: *habeas corpus* and *subjiciendum.* Its purpose is to determine if a prisoner is unlawfully imprisoned. There are only two vehicles, to request *habeas* review, available to a federal prisoner to obtain *habeas corpus* (28 U.S.C. § 2241, and 28 U.S.C. § 2255). This section is specific to those who of you that can seek relief under 28 U.S.C. § 2241.

You are going to find that a federal prisoner has a very limited number of subject-matter over which he may invoke the process under 28 U.S.C. § 2241. Federal prisoners are allowed to resort to the traditional form of *habeas corpus* § 2241 *only* when the § 2255 remedy is found to be ineffective or otherwise inadequate to test the legality of the prisoner's detention, or courts have found that the *habeas* relief provided by § 2255 is inadequate to challenge the following actions:

1) Administration of parole.
2) Computation of pretrial detention credit, good time credit, and other means of shortening a sentence that are determined by prison officials.
3) Prison discipline actions, transfers, and changes in the type of custody, i.e. S.H.U.

4) Prison conditions.
5) Extradition.
6) Deportation.
7) Court Martial proceedings.

If for some reason you feel that § 2241 is more appropriate for your issue than § 2255 and it's not in this list of issues, I strongly suggest you study more. Remember that the limitations to second attempts are extremely unforgiving. Also remember that you as the petitioner/movant bear the burden of proving that you can't get relief under § 2255. You may also be required to file all administrative remedies available before requesting that a federal court become involved. Another important consideration is that 28 U.S.C. § 2241 is *not* affected by a time limitation and therefore gives you the opportunity to seek relief through all other avenues. You may very well proceed all the way through a § 2255 proceeding and then still file for relief under § 2241. It is for this reason that the remainder of this book, even though the principles apply to § 2241, will be focused on those seeking relief in a § 2255 proceeding.

CORRECTION UNDER § 2255

Ever since the beginning of this country, Congress extended *habeas corpus* to federal prisoners as a means by which federal prisoners may challenge the lawfulness of their incarceration. It was a required practice that federal prisoners file for *habeas* relief in the federal district in which they were incarcerated. This meant that just a few federal courts bear almost the entire *habeas corpus* case load of federal prisoner petitions. Prior to the prison industry becoming *big business*, the *only* districts affected were in California, Georgia, Kansas, and Washington, D.C.

Once the judicial districts discovered that convictions and imprisonment could be *very profitable*, the courts began convicting American citizens for anything and everything possible. The courts began to impose convictions and sentences that were *clearly* beyond any possible federal police power. The number of *habeas* petitions, due greatly to the *fact* that many people knew the convictions were against the law, tripled annually between 1937 and 1945. It was because of these problems that the United States judicial Conference designated 28 U.S.C. § 2255 as a method of managing cases. § 2255 was designed as a device that would divert most federal prisoner petitions away from the district of incarceration and send it back to the district that created the problem in the first place.

In consideration for the differences between § 2255 and § 2241, it is very important to realize that a motion under § 2255 is a further step in the petitioner's/movant's criminal case rather than a separate civil action, such as in a petition for *habeas corpus* under § 2241. For these reasons, the § 2255 Motion is considered more related to an appellate step than *habeas corpus*.

If you consider for a moment that you can go to any prison law library in America and find a stack of § 2255 Motions waiting to be filled out, you must also consider that this comes at the expense of millions of tax dollars. *Clearly* Congress wouldn't demand that such money be spent if unlawful convictions didn't exist. The TRUTH is nearly 91% of Federal convictions have one error or another. Many sentences are imposed upon *innocent* American citizens, possibly *just like you*!

Please read and consider the wisdom of Congress when you read the following statute. This is the way 28 U.S.C. § 2255 reads:

§ 2255. Federal custody; remedies on motion attacking sentence

a) A prisoner in custody under sentence of a court established by Act of Congress claiming the right to be released upon the ground that the sentence was imposed in violation of the

1) Constitution or laws of the United States, or that the court was without jurisdiction to impose such sentence, or that the sentence was in excess of the maximum authorized by law, or is otherwise subject to collateral attack, may move the court which imposed the sentence to vacate, set aside, or correct the sentence.

b) Unless the motion and the files and records of the case conclusively show that the prisoner is entitled to no relief, the court shall cause notice thereof to be served upon the United States Attorney, grant a prompt hearing thereon, determine the issues and make findings of fact and conclusions of law with respect thereto. If the court finds that the judgment was rendered without jurisdiction, or that the sentence imposed was not authorized by law or otherwise open to collateral attack, or that there has been such a denial or infringement of the Constitutional rights of the prisoner as to render the judgment vulnerable to collateral attack, the court shall vacate and set the judgment aside and shall discharge the prisoner or resentence him or grant a new trial or correct the sentence as may appear appropriate.

c) A court may entertain and determine such motion without requiring the production of the prisoner at the hearing.

d) An appeal may be taken to the court of appeals from the order entered on the motion as from the final judgment on application for a writ of habeas corpus.

e) An application for a writ of habeas corpus on behalf of a prisoner who is authorized to apply for relief by motion pursuant to this section, shall not be entertained if it appears that the applicant has failed to apply for relief, by motion, to the court which sentenced him, or that such court has denied him relief, unless it also appears that the remedy by motion is inadequate or ineffective to test the legality of his detention.

f) A 1-year period of limitation shall apply to a motion under this section. The limitation period shall run from the latest of –

1) the date on which the judgment of conviction becomes final;

2) the date on which the impediment to making a motion created by governmental action in violation of the Constitution or laws of the United States is removed, if the Movant was prevented from making a motion by such governmental action;

3) the date on which the right asserted was initially recognized by the Supreme Court, if that right has been newly recognized by the Supreme Court and made retroactively applicable to cases on collateral review; or

4) the date on which the facts supporting the claim or claims presented could have been discovered through the exercise of due diligence.

g) Except as provided in section 408 of the Controlled Substances Act [21 USCS § 848], in all proceedings brought under this section, and any subsequent proceedings on review, the court may appoint counsel, except as provided by a rule promulgated by the Supreme Court pursuant to statutory authority. Appointment of counsel under this section shall be governed by 3006A of title 18.

h) A second or successive motion must be certified as provided in section 2244 [28 § 2244] by a panel of the appropriate court of appeals to contain –

1) newly discovered evidence that, if proven and viewed in light of the evidence as a whole,

would be sufficient to establish by clear and convincing evidence that no reasonable fact finder would have found the Movant guilty of the offenses; or

2) a new rule of constitutional law made retroactive to cases on collateral review by the Supreme Court, that was previously unavailable.

WHEN CAN I FILE?

It was my intention to answer this question in chapter eleven. The only problem with that is for all of you who will not be excluded by the one-year time restriction. At that point, believing that their time to file often ended, and who believe that they are no longer eligible, because of time limitations, stop reading and never make it to chapter eleven.

Now that you have read § 2255 you will find the part that says, "[A] 1-year period of limitation shall apply ...." The two most relevant parts most people miss are the parts that specify the beginning of the one-year clock. In (f)(1) it states: "The date on which the judgment of conviction becomes final."

This gives for different times as determined by the Supreme Court.

1) From the date of sentencing;
2) From the date of mandate if you appeal;
3) From the date or resentencing if you win appeal; or
4) From the date of expiration of time to seek certiorari (90 days after appeal).

As you can see, the idea of "becomes final" is a moving target.

Please note that this one-year limitation is what is considered a statute of limitations. Most statutes of limitations have exceptions and the above are some of them. If you are over your one-year limitation, it is important for you to relax and learn about the exceptions that apply.

If you are currently engaged in an appeal, I recommend you wait until the final outcome of your appeal to file a § 2255 Motion. If you don't, it will be denied any way for being too early ("becomes final"), but you will also likely fail in developing your claims concerning the appeals process, like *ineffective assistance of counsel* at appeal.

You will find in the text of § 2255 (f)(4) a clause that reads: "The date on which the facts supporting the claim or claims presented could have been discovered through the exercise of due diligence." This means, very clearly, that the one-year time limitation does not start to run until after you learn of the claim, if you are putting forth a reasonable effort to learn of the claim.

Take for instance that your trial and/or appeals lawyer[s] were Ineffective for failing to make you aware of what the law really means. Then one day, you and some fellow inmates are walking around the track in your favorite prison and someone explains the law to you and suddenly you realize that it didn't really apply to what they accused you of doing. This new knowledge gives rise to you being "*actually innocent*" of the charged offense. Now, here is your problem, you have exactly one year from this day to file for relief. "*Actual innocence*" will always overcome procedural barriers if properly presented (covered in other chapters). It is often the case that inmates discuss the law amongst each other in hopes to find relief. The effort of discussion and hope for relief is in fact what's called "*due diligence.*" Remember that a lawyer, with a meaningful degree, has seven years of higher learning at a university. You, however, having merely one year to learn the law in an unstructured environment are fundamentally disadvantaged in comparison.

When considering the timeliness of a § 2255 Motion, you must consider its purpose. § 2255 is filed, in most cases, to correct a fundamental Miscarriage of Justice, or the incarceration of *innocent* people. Once people learned that most Federal Convictions were unlawful, they began filing for relief en masse. Remember, the Federal government has no *police power* that is not in Article I of the Constitution, and that the *Commerce Clause* does not provide a police power to Congress.

Once prisoners discovered that they had been fooled into a conviction by federal courts for the commission of state offenses, or most commonly plead guilty to conduct that is not an offense at all, they filed for relief under § 2255, which states in part that: "may be made at any time ..."

This created a great financial hardship on the judicial districts. You are probably just learning that you and your conviction are rooted in commerce (trade and money). Your judicial districts are investing hundreds of thousands of dollars in convictions just like yours. This investment is made because once you are convicted and sentenced; the judicial district begins collecting over $28,000 a month for your conviction. You can imagine that once you are released because you were *actually innocent*, Congress stops paying the bill. That would be like buying a car that didn't run. You should be able to see their loss if you are released. No business in the world can make money by paying hundreds of thousands of dollars for a product that only sells for a fraction of the cost.

These financial losses are the sole purpose of the Antiterrorism and Effective Death Penalty Act of 1996. This Act (The A.E.D.P.A.) set a one-year limitation that was also added to § 2255 as an additional procedural bar to relief. Actual innocence, however, overcomes nearly *all* procedural defaults such as failure to raise the issue in earlier proceedings and timely filing, when recently discovered.

The A.E.D.P.A. has and continues to fool many prisoners into believing that they only have one year from sentencing to raise the claim. The truth is, if you committed a state crime and you are in federal prison, you are *actually innocent* and you have one year from the time you realize this *fact* to file for relief under 28 U.S.C. § 2255, providing your affidavit as new evidence.

The passing of the A.E.D.P.A. simply delays or stops you from getting relief which allows your judicial district to recover a larger portion of their investment. Please note almost every federal criminal statute list "In and Effecting Interstate Commerce" as an essential element of the charged offense. When you research the *Commerce Clause* you will discover that the statutes are all related, and you are convicted by a court conducting business for a profit.

MOTION FOR EXTENSION (FORM)

In the motion that follows you will find many blank lines. Each contains a number, use the information in this list to fill in the blanks. This motion as printed in this publication will do nothing. Please do not tear it out and file it.

During my time as a prisoner, I have handwritten many motions, and if need be, you should do the same here. You will need to write slowly and clearly. Remember you have a First and Fourteenth Amendment Right to access the court.

1) This is often the region of your State (i.e. Northern).
2) This is ordinarily the name of the State.
3) This is a subdivision of your region (optional)
4) This is your criminal case number.

Note: Answers 1 through 4 can be found on any order from your Court. You can also ask your Case Manager.

5) This is the actual number of computers in the law library where you are confined.
6) Almost any inmate can give you an approximate number of inmates at your facility.
7) This is the name of the prison you are in; it's in your return address. Check your prison handbook.
8) The calendar day of signing the motion.
9) The calendar month of signing the motion.
10) The present year of signing the motion.
11) Your signature.
12) Your printed name and "in *PRO SE*."
13) Your registry numbers.
14) The return address of your prison facility.
15) Full name of your prison facility (i.e. Oakdale Federal Correctional Institution).

UNITED STATES DISTRICT COURT

IN THE [1] DISTRICT OF [2]__________

______[3] DIVISION

[YOUR NAME] Movant/Defendant vs. UNITED STATES OF AMERICA, Respondent	Civil Case No.: [LEAVE THIS LINE BLANK] Criminal Case No.: [4]

DEFENDANT'S MOTION FOR EXTENSION OF TIME TO FILE HIS MOTION TO VACATE, SET ASIDE, OR CORRECT SENTENCE, PURSUANT TO 28 U.S.C. § 2255

COMES NOW the Defendant/Movant, ________________________ in *PRO SE*, in necessity, and hereby MOVES this Honorable Court to ISSUE an ORDER granting a ninety (90) day extension of time to file his motion to vacate, set aside, or correct sentence pursuant to 28 U.S.C. § 2255.

The Movant/Defendant avers that he has just recently become aware that his Conviction/Sentence was obtained under a Constitutional violation that resulted in the Fundamental Miscarriage of Justice and/or incarceration of an ACTUALLY INNOCENT Defendant. In Support, the Movant/Defendant shows the Court the following:

1) The Movant's/Defendant's A.E.D.P.A. deadline has not yet been reached but rapidly approaches.

The Movant/Defendant has just recently discovered a Constitutional violation in the criminal process that produced his Conviction/Sentence and wishes to file his request for relief, in GOOD FAITH, pursuant to 28 U.S.C. § 2255.

The Movant/Defendant currently has no other choice but to represent himself in *pro se*, in necessity. The Movant/Defendant has no training in the field of law and needs the additional time to research his recent discovery.

The Movant/Defendant has access to a limited law library as it contains [5] computers to facilitate [6] inmates here at [7] . What's more, after waiting his turn, the Movant/Defendant is limited to ONLY two (2) hours to research and then must wait his turn again.

This motion is made in GOOD FAITH, in the Interest of Justice, and not meant to delay the proceedings. The United States nor any other adverse party will be prejudiced by a ninety (90) day delay.

WHEREFORE NOW, above premises considered, the Movant/Defendant respectfully MOVES this Honorable Court to GRANT him a ninety (90) day extension of time to file his 28 U.S.C. § 2255 motion.

Done This [8] , Day of [9] , 20 [10] .

Respectfully Submitted,

[11]

[12]

[13]

[14]

CERTIFICATE OF SERVICE

I, the undersigned, do hereby certify that I have served a copy of this motion upon the Clerk of this Court, via U.S. mail, properly addressed, First-Class postage prepaid, placing into the internal mailing system as made available to inmates for legal mail, at the [15] . The Movant/Defendant further requests that a copy of this [his] pleading be forwarded to all interested parties via the CM/ECF system, as he is detained, indigent, and has no other means.

Done This [8] Day of [9] , 20 [10] .

Respectfully Submitted,

[11]

[12]

[13]

[14]

CHAPTER THREE

BASIC CLAIMS

Contrary to popular belief, all successful *habeas corpus* § 2255 petitions begin with a claim of error or Constitutional violation, your petition, to be successful, *must* start with your claim.

In the chapter that covers *basic motion writing*, I will be discussing the difference between "*fact pleadings*" and "*notice pleadings*." For now, beware that a § 2255 Motion is a *fact pleading*. Any claim you can raise *must* be based upon *facts only*. That means *no* theory, *no* case law, *no* legal arguments – *facts only*, and *only* the *facts* of *your* claim. And you must leave out *all* the humor, history, and civics lessons. The rest of this book is all about constructing an *affective* § 2255 Motion and guiding you through the procedures to follow. So, let's get started.

As I said, you *must* start with a claim of error or claim of violation of constitutional right. Your claim *must* be an error that changed the outcome of your proceeding that has not been ruled out by the court and is supported by evidence that was not previously presented to the court.

Because there is such a huge variety of claims capable of being determined by a court in a Federal *habeas corpus* § 2255 proceeding and the unlimited number of factual combinations possible with regard to each claim, any list of possible grounds I could make would be incomplete. Instead of trying to make a list and possibly failing you by missing the one that would make a difference in your case, I'm going to refer you to my favorite law library publication.

STARTING YOUR LIST

In the main menu of the law library at any federal prison, you're going to find a listing for the "Federal *Habeas Corpus* Practice and Procedure." Click on this selection and scroll down to chapter eleven. Once open, you'll want to select "C, Examples of federal *habeas corpus* claims that have prevailed." You need to sit at the computer, with pencil and paper, and read every case in this section. As you read these cases you will start to remember little things that seemed harmless when they happened to you. These little things could have made a serious impact in your case. Take for example; your lawyer may have failed to interview and present available *alibi testimony*. That is a serious violation of your Sixth Amendment Right to counsel. Using some commonsense here is also very helpful. Let's say for instance you decided to enter a Guilty Plea. In this event, you don't need to read the cases concerning trial. Just continue on to the next section that pertains to you until you reach the end of the cases in Section "C." Take your time and write down word for word every case you feel is similar to yours. As you do this, list the category it was found in such as "(e) Ineffective assistance of Appeal." and the case as "*Evitts v. Lucey, 469 U.S. 387 (1985).*"

REFINING YOUR LIST OF CLAIMS

If you remember reading the Introduction, then you know my intention is to write this book in *layman's terms*. However, when the government responds to you, you will quickly figure out that the United States Attorney will *not* be so helpful. So, what I'm going to do is reduce the impact on you by slowly introducing you to legal terms and words. When I introduce a new word or phrase, it will be in bold italicized print, and the definition will be found at the bottom of the page in which it is first introduced. These words will also be defined in the glossary.

There will be several steps in refining your list of claims. This first step is reducing your list to cognizable claims. You will find that 28 U.S.C. § 2255 defines ***cognizable*** [1] claims as to include a wide variety of errors. These errors include claims that "the judgment was rendered without ***jurisdiction***[2], or that the sentence imposed was not authorized by law or otherwise open to collateral attack, or that there has been such a denial or infringement of the constitutional rights of the prisoner as to render the judgment vulnerable to collateral attack." This language defines four large categories of possible claims that a court will hear: (1) That the court that determined and delivered the criminal judgment lacked either personal or ***subject-matter***[3] jurisdiction; (2) The conviction or sentence is unconstitutional; (3) The conviction or sentence violates other Federal Law; and (4) The sentence or judgment is otherwise open to ***collateral***[4] Attack because it resulted in a ***fundamental***[5] miscarriage of justice. The last two categories are limited to errors that amount to a violation of the Constitution or "*a fundamental defect which* ***inherently***[6] *results in a complete miscarriage of justice,*" or "*an omission inconsistent with the* ***rudimentary*** [7] *demands of fair procedure.*"

To further explain by category:

This category is for claims that the Court did not have the authority to cast judgement upon you, because it lacked one of two types of jurisdiction.

a. Person Jurisdiction is the power to control your conduct because of who you are. Such as if you are a Government Employee, Military Personnel, or an American Citizen living or visiting outside the United States. The Court very rarely asserts this type of jurisdiction and is usually not a concern.

b. Subject-Matter Jurisdiction, however, is a fairly common issue. This means that what you are accused of doing is not against Federal Law. Take for example if you get caught speeding in Alabama. The Court does not have the authority to convict you of murder when you are only guilty of speeding. If you get caught in Birmingham with a gram of Crack Cocaine that you intend for personal use, the Federal Court does not have the authority to imprison you under a Federal Law against Possession with the Intent to Distribute Crack Cocaine in Interstate Commerce.

This category is for claims that the Court did not follow the rules directed by the United States Constitution, more particularly, the Bill of Rights (amendments one through ten). This one can be a bit tricky because of the wording difference between the Constitution and the Laws that were passed to carry out the requirements of the Constitution. For example, the Sixth Amendment *guarantees* you "assistance of counsel." That means you must have a lawyer at trial. The law, however, demands you have adequate representation. The law 18 U.S.C. § 3006A demands effective assistance of counsel and the Constitution

[1] *Cognizable* – 1) Capable of being known 2) Capable of being judicially heard and determined.

[2] *Jurisdiction* – The legal power, right, or authority to hear and determine a cause considered either in general or with reference to a particular matter: legal power to interpret and administer the law on the premises.

[3] *Subject-Matter* – Matter presented for consideration: as **a:** the essential facts, data, or ideas that constitute the basis of spoken, written, or artistic expression or representation; often: the substance as distinguished from the form esp. of an artistic or literary production **b:** a subject of thought or study; often conveyable material (as information, knowledge, skill) actually made available by a branch or course of study: the available factual content of a branch or course as distinct from technique or method of instruction or factors inherent in the individual learner **c:** the topic of disparate in a legal matter.

[4] *Collateral* – Placed or regarded as side by side: parallel, coordinate, corresponding in position, order, time or significance.

[5] *Fundamental* – Of central importance; forming a sustained or recurring element: servicing as a background or starting point: forming the underlying pattern.

[6] *Inherently* – Structural or involved in the constitution or essential character of something: being by nature or settled habit: intrinsic, essential.

[7] *Rudimentary* – Consisting in first principles, fundamental, concerning the most basic. In layman's term, and my personal opinion, rudimentary is defined as very basic principles of right and wrong.

only guarantees assistance of counsel; this is not the category under which to raise an *ineffective assistance of counsel* claim.

This category covers a wide range of claims, probably the largest of all four categories. This category is the one under which you would raise a claim that the court did not follow the Federal Rules of Criminal Procedure, any of the laws in the United States Code and Code of Federal Regulations or Federal Rules of Evidence. This is where you find an Ineffective assistance of counsel (I.A.C.) claim as 18 § 3006A requires that the court make available adequate representation to indigent defendants, the list is too long to list here, so study the applicable laws and rules.

This category is reserved for errors that the conviction was based upon. Meaning serious structural errors, and/or *actual innocence*.

In the case of *actual innocence*, the government claims you engaged in unlawful conduct, but the *fact* is that you either did not engage in such conduct or the conduct you were engaged in did not reach the *essential elements* of the charged offense as they relate to *fact* and *law*. So you may be engaged in a certain conduct, but you must be engaged in the conduct as described by the charging statute. Otherwise, you are "*actually innocent*."

We as a community are just now starting to address similar and wide-spread problems, like where drug users were being charged as drug traffickers, which are now being released from prison by our current President.

A structural error on the other hand, is another moving target. In truth it is any error committed by anyone other than yourself that makes the trial process unreliable. Consider errors like beating a confession out of a defendant, the government withholding evidence proving someone else committed the crime, your court appointed lawyer working with the U.S. Attorney to get you to plead guilty ... just to name a few common errors.

CHAPTER FOUR

Procedural Defenses to Your Claim

After you file your § 2255 Motion and it survives the scrutiny of rule 4 (four) review (covered in chapter 12), the government will be ordered to "*show cause*" as to why you should not be granted your requested relief. This may seem out of place now, but it is easier to consider the probable defenses you will encounter during your claim development rather than waiting until you are finished and then deciding that the claim is not good, requiring you to start over.

In any response from the government you can expect to see the reasons why the court should not even review your claims presented first. Look for statements such as "ineffective assistance claims, most were waived by his decision to Plead Guilty ..." or "know the charges against him were also waived, is procedurally defaulted, and is meritless." These statements are quotes taken from the government's response in my own case. These statements, in that response, were found in the first twelve lines, and even before the Assistant United States Attorney (A.U.S.A.) presented his "*background*." I hope you can see the reason to consider the procedure so early. This is the first thing the government will attack.

It's important to realize that the government often lacks jurisdiction to present a federal charge for a state crime leaving many § 2255 claims quite valid. If the government were to meet the merits in a § 2255 Motion head-on, the government would in most cases lose. This is the reason for attacking the procedure first. That's why knowing what to expect is very important. Remember also that the court in most districts will assist the government in its efforts by holding you to tight procedural scrutiny. The government also has the assistance of Congress who passed new laws specifically to bar meritorious claims from gaining review. Take for example the enactment of the Anti-Terrorism and Effective Death Penalty Act of 1996, (A.E.D.P.A.), which put in place an elaborate procedural obstacle course that stumps most lawyers. Its purpose is to obstruct federal *habeas corpus* review by adding layer after layer of new ***preliminary***[8] steps, limitations, and exceptions.

These defenses are used by the government to postpone consideration of *habeas corpus* § 2255 petitions and to stop the court from considering the merits of particular claims in your petition. Once again remember the purpose: The court is a business, you are a product, and your incarceration is profitable. They want you to stay so everyone profits except you and your family/community. This situation is further aggravated by the disposition of Federal judges to hold a movant to an overly complicated procedure harshly and strictly, without considering either the fair or correcting purpose of a § 2255 Motion filed in *pro se*.

The need to understand these defenses to *habeas corpus* § 2255 petitioners are obvious. Even the slightest misunderstanding, misstep, or error in the federal court, by your lawyer or even you, a prisoner proceeding in *pro se*, might cause you to forfeit a very good Constitutional claim of *actual innocence*. Remember, they get paid to do this, justice and innocence is of *no concern*.

Even though *habeas corpus* § 2255 defenses are a stacked deck in favor of the government, they are also so overly complicated that they also provide some procedural consequences for the Federal government. The Supreme Court has repeatedly ruled that *habeas corpus* § 2255 defenses are not jurisdictional and can be waived, either on purpose, or for failure to preserve the defense (neglect). In the A.E.D.P.A., Congress once again attempted to make it harder for *innocent prisoners* to get relief by changing the waiver standard that applied to the state non-exhaustion defense, requiring that this kind of waiver be expressed in the record thereby stopping the states from wavering by default. By Congress choosing to limit this requirement of an express waiver to the exhaustion defense, signals Congress' desire to maintain the practice of finding

---

[8] *Preliminary* – Preceding the main discourse or business.

waiver by default with respect to other state defenses and "*all*" Federal defenses. The Circuit courts that have considered the issue have held that the defenses that the A.E.D.P.A. created are waivable, including by default.

For these reasons, you *must* know the common procedural defenses and be aware of the ones the government doesn't raise in its response. You *must* also point out these waivers even by default to the federal court because fundamental fairness requires a federal court to treat the litigants on both sides of a lawsuit the same. Most courts have recognized the need to apply waiver doctrines as strictly against the government as against *habeas corpus* § 2255 petitioners proceeding in *pro se*.

COMMON DEFENSES

This section contains a list of common defenses I've encountered in my practice of assisting prisoners with § 2255 filings. Although I have read probably hundreds of responses, I can guarantee you that this list can't possibly be all encompassing. Just as there is always a faster car out there or soon will be, there is also a more cleaver prosecutor, or there soon will be – so be alert.

This list contains five (5) common defenses the government likes to raise and directly following is my most effective counter defense or "*reply*." If you use one of these "replies," always support it with *facts* from your case to clarify it.

Defense 1) The Petitioner's filing of § 2255 motion is untimely.

Reply 1: The Movant is proceeding in *pro se* and is a layman at law. This motion is filed outside of the one-year statutory limitation because the Movant has just recently discovered, through DUE DILIGENCE, the FACTS supporting this claim. The Movant provides his affidavit and other exhibits as newly discovered evidence.

Defense 2) The claim was not previously raised before, or at trial, or on Direct Appeal.

Reply 1: Ineffective Assistance of Counsel claims are not waived by failure to raise in Direct Appeal as issues may not be fully developed until after appeal.

Reply 2: Challenge of jurisdiction of convicting Court not waived by failure to raise on Direct Appeal.

Reply 3: Challenge to plea when Movant is ACTUALLY INNOCENT not waived by failure to raise on Direct Appeal.

Reply 4: Challenge to plea when Movant failed to raise on Direct Appeal not waived because Government did not assert procedural default as defense.

Reply 5: Challenge of Movant's competency to stand trial is not waived by failure to raise in a Direct Appeal.

Reply 6: Challenge by *pro se* Movant based on *Apprendi v. New Jersey* argument allowed on first-time § 2255 appeal.

Defense 3) Petitioner did not show both cause and prejudice from the alleged errors.

Reply 1: The Movant seeks § 2255 relief based on a Constitutional violation that resulted in a fundamental Miscarriage of Justice, such as the conviction of this INNOCENT American Citizen.

Reply 2: The Government failed to object and/or otherwise dispute the consideration of this newly raised issue.

Reply 3: The § 2255 motion raises certain Constitutional claims that may be adequately addressed only on collateral review.

Defense 4) The Movant's § 2255 raises claims that were previously decided on Direct Appeal.

Reply 1: The Movant files this § 2255 motion based upon newly discovered evidence.

Reply 2: The Movant files this § 2255 motion based upon a new rule of Criminal Procedure, and it falls within the exception to the non-retro-activity Rule of Teague v. Lane.

Defense 5) The Movant waived his rights to appeal and/or collateral attack his conviction and/or sentence under the terms of his Plea Agreement.

Reply1: [I will not be providing a reply to this one here; it will be covered throughout the rest of this book in length.]

Always consider how to present *factual innocence* through jurisdictional failure.

CHAPTER FIVE

Documents: What You Are Going to Need to File

Again, as pertains to moving targets, and depending on how far you went through the judicial procedure, will dictate what all you need to file. Of course, your needs are relevant to your need to investigate your case. Let's just say get everything that you can.

Ordinarily, you have a right to get everything in your case from your lawyer. That's ordinarily. On average I get a case file for about 60% of the people I file for. Most of those are because I prompt the court to order the lawyer to do so. I'll cover that better later.

This aspect of preparing your case for post-conviction relief cannot be stressed enough. It's through what you obtain in this step that will reveal the most issues. The more information you have to analyze, the better your chances of discovering issues, arguments, and errors in your case. Just a few prime examples why you need to obtain all you can get are:

- You may learn by reviewing your Criminal Docket that your lawyer never gave Notice of your ALIBI DEFENSE. This one happened to me personally. Lawyers in my case said that they gave Notice of an Alibi Defense and Issued 10 witness subpoenas. When I reviewed the Criminal Docket, I discovered that the lawyer NEVER filed a single motion in my defense.
- Studying your Change of Plea Transcripts may reveal, more times than not, that the Trial Court at Change of Plea failed to follow the *mandated*[9] requirements of Federal Rules of Criminal Procedure, Rule 11. In this same transcript you may discover that you were "RUSHED TO JUDGMENT."
- Studying your Sentencing Transcript may reveal that your lawyer failed to argue for a Departure you deserved, or he didn't argue against an enhancement you didn't deserve.
- The Indictment may, when compared with the charging statute, show that the Government was without SUBJECT-MATTER Jurisdiction to charge you, or that the Court was without jurisdiction to precede over the case to start with.
- A D.E.A. 6 report or an F.B.I. 302 report may contain an unreasonable description of you upon which the identification was based.

This is a Basic documents list:

1) Police reports; F.B.I. 302's; D.E.A. 6 reports; etc.
2) Witness complaints if used.
3) Search or Arrest Warrants and the Affidavits used to support them.
4) Indictments, Superseding Indictments, and/or Information.
5) Pretrial Investigations reports from Probation and Parole Officers.
6) All pretrial motions, orders, and answers.
7) All communications your attorney had with the prosecution.

---

[9] *Mandated* – an authorized command, order, or injunction: a clear instruction, authorization, or direction.

8) All proposed Plea Agreements, and stipulations.

9) Presentence Reports, objections to the Presentence Report, and the Addendums.

10) Docket Sheet.

11) Proposed Jury instructions from both sides.

12) Trial Transcripts; Jury Selection, Opening Arguments, Trial Motion Hearings held before, during, and after trial, Jury Charge and Instructions, and closing arguments.

13) All Verdict Forms.

14) Transcripts relating to New Trial Motions.

15) Sentencing Transcripts, Judgment and Commitment Order.

16) Notice of Appeal.

17) Appellate and Appellee Briefs.

18) Orders from Court of Appeals.

19) All correspondence between you and your lawyer.

20) All witness affidavits who were not called detailing what their testimony would have been if called.

21) Affidavits from Experts Witnesses that weren't used during trial, but whose testimony would have made a difference if they had testified.

This is not a complete list of everything that may be available such as your Original Discovery Items. This list is relating to documents and other such reports produced by government Personnel. Don't be too concerned if you don't get everything because it will contribute to your *ineffective assistance of counsel* claim.

Most of the other books on the subject of post-conviction relief will tell you at this point that your investigation of your case should be just like your Pretrial Investigation. The *only* problem is that you have probably never performed one and your Attorney probably hasn't either. Hence your current tenure. It's for this reason that I'm going to teach you all I know about investigation in the next four chapters. This is important; if you don't pay extra attention here you will likely have more difficulty than necessary. I recommend re-reading these chapters the whole time you're going through everything you get.

DOCKET SHEETS

When you receive your docket sheet from the district court or from the court of Appeals, the first thing you will see at the very top is where it is from. For example, "U.S. DISTRICT COURT" on the third or fourth line down from that you will see, for instance, "CRIMINAL DOCKET FOR CASE #:" Okay, now you can see you have what you're looking for. Now let's see who it belongs to. On the left side of the front page you will see a column labeled, "DEFENDANT[S]." Your name should appear in this column, if not, then it's not yours. This may sound strange, but this has happened in cases I've assisted in more times than I care to count. ***Personal advice***[10] in cases like this and in my own personal case, I keep a meticulous mail log. My mail log contains a column type list where I can record my incoming and outgoing mail. Your log should

[10] *Personal Advice* – advice given, stemming from one's own individual experience(s).

include space for: who it's going to, subject, date sent, if you're expecting a reply, and the date you received the reply. From now on save *everything*.

Okay, back to your docket sheet. When you look at the right column, you will find all the lawyers who represented you. If you see your own name, don't be alarmed, that means you filed something in ***pro se***[11]. Further down and to the right, you will find in the "PLAINTIFF" column the United States, everyone who represented them and your prosecutors.

Below all of that, or on the next page perhaps, you will find the meat of your docket. What you will see is a table of lines that contain a space for a date. Then to the right of that, a small block for the docket entry number. Then in the big box, there will be a space for the title and description of the filing. Once you learn to read legal filings, you will find it makes reference to other filings, especially in responses and orders. These will be referred to by either that date, which is self-explanatory, or by a "DOC. #." This is found in the little block, very useful.

Though you will find a variety of entry titles, those that will concern you most are: Complaint, Minute Entry, Notice of Hearing, order, Motion, and Sealed. First off, an order can only be filed by either the Magistrate judge or the district court judge; this is VERY IMPORTANT. The next is a motion. These can be filed by you, your counsel, or the Prosecuting Attorney. This is where I most often first discover an APATHETIC Defense lawyer who provided *ineffective assistance of counsel*. In the large box, you will find also the subject of the entry and who filed it. Example:

6/12/2012	5	Motion for release from custody by Kelly Patrick Riggs. (John Doe) [2:12-MJ-00756-PWG] Entered 6/12/2012

As you can see in the entry, the lawyer is in parenthesis and the judge is in brackets.

The next VERY IMPORTANT entry is a "MINUTES ENTRY for PROCEEDINGS." This means transcripts. This entry is made by the Clerk of court only. For every minute's entry, there is a transcript and you want them all. As soon as this arrives highlight every minute's entry. The next important entry title is the "RESPONSE." This entry is from the Opposing Party. It's made as an answer to a motion. Ordinarily, you will see a "MOTION," "RESPONSE," then an "ORDER." Pay close attention to the pretrial or pre-plea motions filed by Defense counsel. If you don't see motions to suppress or motions to challenge by your lawyer, then he was *constitutionally ineffective* for lack of either investigation or adversarial testing.

DISTRICT

Getting your docket sheet from your district court is relatively easy in most cases. On the next page is a very standard letter I use. Write this letter and send it *now* and read the rest of this book until you get it.

[11] *Pro se* – Self-representation; for himself or herself; acting alone as in defending oneself in a Court of Law

[Your Name]

[8 Digit Prison Number]

Federal Correctional Institution

[Prison Address, i.e. P.O. Box]

[Town, State, Zip Code]

[Date]

To: United States District Court

Attn: Clerk of the Court

[Court Address]

[Town, State, Zip Code]

RE: UNITED STATES v. [Your Name]

Case No: [Case Number]

Dear Clerk,

At this time, I am requesting a copy of the Criminal Docket Sheet, in the above styled case. Please find enclosed S.A.S.E. for your convenience.

Thank you in advance for your continued assistance.

Sincerely,

[Your Signature]

[Printed Name]

cc: P/file

Cert. mail no.: ____________________

APPELLATE

In the event you did make it to an appeal, you will want to get the Appellate Docket also because you may also have a claim against your Appeals lawyer.

[Your Name]
[8 Digit Prison Number]
Federal Correctional Institution
[Prison Address, i.e. P.O. Box]
[Town, State, Zip Code]

[Date]

To: United States Court of Appeals
In the [Number] Circuit
Attn: Clerk of the Court
[Court Address]
[Town, State, Zip Code]

RE: UNITED STATES v. [Your Name]
Appeals No: [Case Number]

Dear Clerk,

[Same as before just replace the words "Criminal Docket" with "Appellate Docket"]

CASE FILE

A case file, as it is ironically called, is a collection of everything that pertains to your case. Every scrap of paper is important. For example, a Louisiana state prisoner was recently released from custody as *actually innocent*, because of a handkerchief. Most good case files wouldn't fit in a six-foot cabinet. Lucky for you, your criminal case file probably isn't that big.

If you followed my instructions, you started a mail log and sent off for your docket sheet. This is the beginning of your civil § 2255 case file. This case file is going to be different and larger than your criminal case file. It will contain most of your criminal case file within it. You will also need to keep copies of everything you write and/or file. If you write a letter, make a copy and file it. This is important because you will need to show proof that you did send a letter when someone is denying that they received it. This is probably the most common problem and these types of problems usually concern your lawyer and your criminal case file.

AFFIDAVITS

In my humble opinion, affidavits are probably the second most important aspect of your new § 2255 case file. Affidavits throughout the proceeding will be a record of your testimony of the *facts* that have probably never before been heard. All your affidavits must be copied and saved in your new § 2255 case file.

The word *affidavit* is commonly defined as "a sworn statement in writing made especially under oath or an affirmation before an authorized Magistrate or Officer." That said, I can't stress enough how important it is to be truthful. Providing a False statement in an affidavit is the same as providing false testimony while under oath in court. You can be charged with an additional criminal offense. It's very important, in an affidavit, to state that you" allege" or "believe" something is fact. When you cannot base something on fact, but you know it to be true, you can "allege on information and belief, and believe them to be true."

The following is a sample of a case affidavit. Of course, it goes without saying that you need to replace all generic information. Always include your criminal case Number, and where appropriate, space for a civil Number for when you get one.

UNITED STATES DISTRICT COURT

IN THE [the District] of [the state]

[the Division (if you have one)]

JOHN J. DOE, Petitioner vs. UNITED STATES OF AMERICA, Respondent	Civil Case No.: ________________________ Criminal Case No.: [your criminal case number]

AFFIDAVIT OF JOHN J. DOE [PETITIONER]

I, John J. Doe, depose and state that the following FACTS are True and Correct under penalty of perjury, TO WIT:

2) I, John J. Doe, state that I was appointed Counsel by the Clerk of Court on July 19, 2012, pursuant to the Criminal Justice Act.

3) I, John J. Doe, state that I allege, based upon information and belief, that Court Appointed Counsel was CONSTITUTIONALLY INEFFECTIVE.

[Tell your story, use as many paragraphs as necessary]

I, John J. Doe, declare under penalty of perjury, pursuant to 28 U.S.C. § 1746, that the above stated FACTS are True and Correct to the best of my knowledge and belief.

Executed on This [the date] Day of [the month], [the year].

Respectfully Submitted,

____

[Your Name], *PRO SE*

[8 Digit Prison Number]

Federal Correctional Institution

[Prison Address, i.e. P.O. Box]

[Town, State, Zip Code]

CHAPTER SIX

Building Your Civil § 2255 Case File

If you are following instructions, you have already started building your civil § 2255 case file. Now let's add some more materials to your case file. Your criminal lawyer started a criminal case file very early on. Regardless of whether you hired an attorney, and he made a memo of your initial call, or he was a dead beat who waited around the court room waiting for an appointed meal ticket, he made record of it to bill someone. This information is in your criminal case file, and now it's time for you to go get it. It is yours, your property.

Getting Your Case File From Your Lawyer

First off, you need to understand that having your criminal case file delivered to you and sent by your Defense counsel is your *constitutionally protected right*. This is *not* a gift or an added burden upon your Attorney. Providing you with your case file is his *duty* and *obligation* under American BAR Association Standards.

In most cases this is easy enough, a simple phone call, (record the day and time of call), and twenty-one days later, give or take, you're on the call-out to R&D or your counselor has CD's in hand. If this is successful well, you can move on to chapter Seven, unless you're using this information to help others.

As much as I hate the thought of telling you this, it is important to say that, if you have an obvious claim, that lawyer will not want to give up your case file.

So, you made the call ten minutes ago and politely enough your lawyer tells you that you don't need your case file. That lawyer knows he did something wrong or that he did nothing at all to help you. You will discover that fact when your docket sheet gets to you soon enough, but he just confirmed your suspicions.

So let's start writing letters to show him you're serious. The first letter shouldn't be too rough. He just needs to realize that you are serious about obtaining a copy of the entire case file from him that is in his or her possession. Send your letter by certified mail if possible. I always stick the certified mail Number on my mail log. Customize the following sample letter by using your Criminal and/or Appellate Docket Number and parties' names as appropriate to your case.

[Your Name]

[8 Digit Prison Number]

Federal Correctional Institution

[Prison Address, i.e. P.O. Box]

[Town, State, Zip Code]

[Date]

To: [Your Attorney's Name]

Attorney at Law
[Your Attorney's Address]

[Your Attorney's Town, State, and Zip Code]

RE: CRIMINAL CASE FILE FOR:

UNITED STATES v. [YOUR NAME]

CASE NO.: [YOUR CASE NUMBER]

Dear [Your Attorney's Name],

This letter is to inform you that I am seeking to obtain from you my ENTIRE Case/Work File where you represented me in the above referenced action. At this time, I am hereby asking that you or your office *forward to me* the ENTIRE Case/Work File in your possession to include but not limited to all discovery materials, pretrial motions, responses, and orders.

I have a Constitutional Right to receive my Case/Work File under the Sixth Amendment to the Constitution. Neither you nor your office currently represents me, and I plan to pursue a *habeas corpus* petition attacking the Constitutionality of the conviction and/or sentence. As you are aware, a motion under § 2255 has a statutory limitation of one year.

Hopefully, you will act consistent with the American BAR Associations Standards and refrain from impeding my right to challenge the Constitutionality of my conviction and/or sentence. That said, I'm requesting you forward the Case/Work File to me.

Please forward the Case/Work File to me in large envelopes addressed to me and CLEARLY MARKED as Legal Mail. OPEN ONLY IN PRESENCE OF THE INMATE, at [Your Institution],

[Address of your Institution].

Thank you in advance for your cooperation in this matter.

Sincerely,

____

[Your Name]

cc: P/File

The letter you just wrote is direct enough to get what you want. You should have a case file within 21 days. Be sure that you record in your log the date of this letter and keep a copy. This subject is where it's important.

If you're still in this chapter that means that your civil case file has gotten a little fatter and you still don't have your criminal case file. At this point of the game, if I'm helping in the case, Dr. Jeckle has painfully transformed into Mr. Hyde, and he is in a *really bad mood.* Where other people will tell you to take your time, be patient and submit the next three steps consecutively. I, however, believe time is precious, and you shouldn't waste any of it in fulfill your rights – not even 90 days. I personally submit the next three steps on the same day.

First, I write a letter to the state BAR Association to report the attorney for his misconduct.

Second, I write a letter to the attorney, so he knows I know my rights.

Third, I file a motion with the court to compel the attorney to send the file.

So, let's write the remainder of the letters and the motion to the court today. You have already lost 21 days from your last letter, and time counts.

SAMPLE LETTER TO THE STATE BAR

[Your Name]
[8 Digit Prison Number]
Federal Correctional Institution
[Prison Address, i.e. P.O. Box]
[Town, State, Zip Code]

[Date]

To: The [Your State] Bar

Attorney/Client Assistance Program (A.C.A.P.)
[Their Address]

[Their Town, State, and Zip Code]

RE: [Your ATTORNEY'S NAME]

Dear A.C.A.P. Representative,

This letter is concerning the above referenced Attorney's refusal to release my Case/Work File created during his representation of me in the case of the *United States v.* [Your Name], case no.:

[Your Case Number] (Date of sentence), and his impediment of my Constitutional and Statutory Rights to file a timely petition for Post-Conviction Relief.

On or about the [The date of the call where you called the Lawyer] I called Mr./Ms. [Attorney's Name] at approximately [Time you placed the call], in which I requested that he/she send me my Case/Work File.

On or about [The date of your second request], I made a second request by mail to Mr./Ms. [Attorney's Name] requesting that Case/Work File in his possession, created during his representation of me be mailed to me. Once again, he refused by failing to comply with my second request.

I am hereby requesting the assistance of this Honorable [The State] BAR Association to obtain my Case/Work File. Mr./Ms. [Attorney's Name] no longer represents me and has no need to retain the Case/Work File and I am entitled to the Case/Work File. See *Maxwell v. Florida*, 479 U.S. 972, 93 L. Ed. 2d 418, 107 S. Ct. 474 (1986).

I thank you in advance for your assistance in this matter.

Sincerely,

____

[Your Name]

cc: P/File

LETTER TO YOUR ATTORNEY

[Your Name]

[8 Digit Prison Number]

Federal Correctional Institution

[Prison Address, i.e. P.O. Box]

[Town, State, Zip Code]

[Date]

To: [Your Attorney's Name]

Attorney at Law
[Your Attorney's Address]

[Your Attorney's Town, State, and Zip Code]

RE: CRIMINAL CASE FILE FOR:

UNITED STATES v. [YOUR NAME]

CASE NO.: [YOUR CASE NUMBER]

Dear [Your Attorney's Name],

This is my second letter to you concerning my Case/Work File. I have also filed for an ORDER to Compel and a request for assistance with the State BAR Association. Once again, I am encouraging you to forward my ENTIRE Case/Work File to me. I am in need of ALL materials in your possession, or that reasonably should be in your possession, concerning my Case/Work File, to include but not limited to: All Discovery Materials, Pretrial Motions, Responses, Orders, Telephone records/recordings, CD's and Video tapes.

I am entitled to my Case/Work File, as you know, for several reasons. First, the Case/Work File was created during the period of time you represented me, it is my property. See *Hiatt v. Clark*, Ky. No.: 2002-SC-455-MR (6/15/06).

Second, both the law and the American BAR Association recognize that you have a duty not to obstruct my efforts to seek Post-Conviction Relief. See *ABA Standards for Criminal Justice, Defense Functions Standards and Commentary* ("The resounding message is that defense attorneys, because of their intimate knowledge of the trial proceedings and their possession of unique information regarding possible post-conviction claims, have an obligation to co- operate with their client's attempt to challenge their convictions.") In *United States v. Dorman*, 58 M.J. 295 (C.A.A.F. 2003); *Haitt v. Clark*, supra; *Maxwell v. Florida*, 479 U.S. 972, 93 L. Ed. 2d 418,

107 S. Ct. 474 (1986) ("The right to effective assistance fully encompasses the client's right to obtain from trial counsel the work files generated during and pertinent to that client's defense. It further entitles the client to utilize materials contained in these files in any proceeding at which the adequacy of trial counsel's representation may be challenged"); *Spivey v. Zant*, 683 F. 2d 881, 885 (5th Cir. 1982)(*habeas corpus* petitioner is entitled to former trial attorney's file and the work-product doctrine does not apply to situations in which the client seeks access to documents or other tangible things created during course of attorney's representation).

As you know, I'm gathering records and documents to support my § 2255 motion attacking the Constitutionality of my conviction based upon several issues to include, but not limited to Ineffective Assistance of Counsel. You are currently impeding my right to file a meaningful § 2255 motion within the one-year statutory limitation.

Hopefully, you will act with consistency towards your obligations. I expect to have my Case/Work File within ten (10) days of the delivery of this Certified Letter.

Sincerely,

____

[Your Name]

cc: P/File

MOTION TO YOUR CRIMINAL COURT

At this point, if you are diligent, you have called your lawyer asking for your Case and Work File or attempted to do so. It's possible that he agreed over the phone and didn't deliver. So on the outside; you may now be 42 days into trying to get documents. I cannot stress enough that time counts. That's why you are filing all three of these items at once. You've been nice, now that's over. With this motion you will be getting the court involved. It's also important to realize this should be the last motion you file in your criminal case. This will also be the last motion you find outside of the appendix. I want you to read the rest of the book before you start anything else. Remember, chance favors a prepared mind. Let's file this motion, and then read the rest of the book until your paperwork gets here.

UNITED STATES DISTRICT COURT

IN THE [Your DISTRICT] DISTRICT of [Your STATE]

[Your DIVISION] DIVISION

UNITED STATES OF AMERICA, Plaintiff vs. [Your NAME], Defendant	Criminal Case No.: ______________

MOTION TO COMPEL DEFENSE COUNSEL TO SURRENDER THE CASE FILE IN THE ABOVE STYLED ACTION TO THE DEFENDANT OF THIS CASE

COMES NOW the Defendant, [YOUR NAME] in *PRO SE*, in necessity, and hereby MOVES this Honorable Court to ISSUE an ORDER, Compelling Defense Counsel of record, [His/Her NAME]. to surrender the Case/Work File he/she created in representing the Defendant. The Defendant hereby avers that the portions of his Case/Work File, that he has been denied by Defense Counsel of record, include but are not limited to:

1) Transcripts he reviewed for appeal advice.

2) All discovery available by Standing Court Order.

3) All Court filings, motions, responses, and orders.

4) All other notes, letters, correspondence, plea agreements, emails, and/or any other tangible thing associated with this case.

The Defendant hereby avers that he intends to file a motion to vacate, set aside, or correct a sentence pursuant to 28 U.S.C. § 2255. For such motion to be timely, the Defendant must file within one year of his Criminal Conviction becoming final, or from other events according to statute. The records that the Defendant seeks are necessary for preparation of such pleadings and are the Defendant's property. In support, the Defendant shows the Court the following:

1) The Defendant has made attempts to call and/or has made written requests to Defense Counsel of record in hopes that he would act professionally and responsibly by turning over the Case/Work File of the Defendant to him.

2) To date, Defense Counsel of record, has failed to surrender Defendant's ENTIRE Case/Work File to the Defendant, the Defendant asserts that, based on the FACT that Counsel is CLEARLY aware that the Defendant seeks these records to pursue Post-Conviction Relief, Counsel is attempting to frustrate his (Defendant's) attempts to prepare a meritorious § 2255 motion attacking Counsel's INEFFECTIVENESS during all crucial points of proceedings.

3) The Defendant seeks the ACTIVE PROTECTION of this Court through a Court ORDER directing Defense Counsel of record to surrender the Case/Work File to the Defendant.

4) The Court may ORDER Defense Counsel of record to surrender the Defendant's Case/Work File. First, the Defendant is entitled to the Case/Work File because it was created during the time period that Counsel represented the Defendant. Second, both law and the American BAR Association recognize that Counsel has a duty not to obstruct the Defendant's attempts to challenge his conviction and/or sentence. See *ABA Standards for Criminal Justice, Defense Functions Standards and Commentary* ("The resounding message is that defense attorneys, because of their intimate knowledge of the trial proceedings and their possession of unique information regarding possible post-conviction claims, have an obligation to cooperate with the client's attempt to challenge their convictions."); *United States v. Dorman*, 58 M.J. 295 (C.A.A.F. 2003); *Hiatt v. Clark*, Ky. No. 2005-SC-455-MR (6/15/06). See also *Maxwell v. Florida*, 479 U.S. 972, 93 L. Ed. 2d 418-420, 107 S. Ct. 474 (1986) ("The right to effective assistance fully encompasses the client's right to obtain from trial counsel the work files generated during and pertinent to that client's defense. It further entitles the client to utilize materials contained in these files in any proceeding at which the adequacy of trial counsel's representation may be challenged."); *Spivey v. Zant*, 683 F. 2d 881, 885 (5th Cir. 1982) (*habeas corpus* petitioner is entitled to former trial attorneys file and the work product doctrine does not apply to situations in which the client seeks access to documents or other tangible things created during course of attorney's representation.)

5) Finally, it's clear to Defense Counsel that the Defendant is diligently seeking to obtain his Case/Work File and other Tangible things. Counsel recognizes that the Defendant has a right to his Case/Work File and seems to be attempting to stall the Defendant until his statutory limitation has expired.

WHEREFORE NOW, above premises considered, the Defendant, hereby MOVES this Honorable Court to ISSUE an ORDER compelling Defense Counsel of record to surrender the complete Case/Work File to the Defendant as pertains to the Defendant's Criminal case, furthermore, that Counsel place these materials in large envelopes, CLEARLY MARKED: "*LEGAL MAIL, OPEN ONLY IN THE PRESENCE OF THE INMATE*" and mail the large package to:

Done This [Date] Day of [Month], 20 __.

Respectfully Submitted,

____

[Your Signature]

[Your NAME]

[Your PRISON NUMBER]

[The INSTITUTION]

[ADDRESS]

[TOWN, STATE, and ZIP CODE]

CERTIFICATE OF SERVICE

I, the undersigned, do hereby certify that I have served a copy of this foregoing instrument upon the Clerk of this Court, via properly addressed U.S. mail, with first-class postage prepaid affixed thereto, by placing into the internal mailing system as made available to inmates for legal mail, at the Federal Correctional Institution [Your INSTITUTION NAME]. The [Defendant/Petitioner/Movant] further requests that a copy of this [his/her] motion be forwarded to all interested parties via the CM/ECF system, as [he/she] is detained, indigent, and has no other means.

Done This [Date] Day of [Month], 20 __.

Respectfully Submitted,

____

[Your Signature]

[Your NAME]

[Your PRISON NUMBER]

[The INSTITUTION]

[ADDRESS]

[TOWN, STATE, and ZIP CODE]

CHAPTER SEVEN

WHAT TO EXPECT IN YOUR CASE FILE

As mentioned in an earlier chapter, your attorney has maintained a file in your case. Please note the quality of assistance will determine the content of your case file. I've seen some case files with attached sticky notes where an attorney's secretary took the initial phone call. This is the type of case file that is most useful. Your case file should be a road map leaving little guess work. When reviewed, it should tell an accurate story of everything that occurred in your case, from its inception to completion.

When evaluating a case for ineffective assistance of counsel, the story told by your case file can and will establish your claim. Take for example that if, like in most public defendant's cases, you get arrested and your attorney approaches you with a form, for you to sign, that waives your right to a preliminary hearing. This one act provides the government the opportunity to present any evidence it wants, to a judge, to proceed before a grand jury. When you waive this right, you give your ***acquiescence***[12] to every piece of evidence presented. You probably signed the document unknowingly and unwillingly. When waivers are signed, the content of your case file diminishes exponentially. Many cases in federal court are premised upon waivers. Waivers are a defense lawyer's method of minimizing evidence (content of case file) of wrong doing or evidence needed to prove your case against him.

INDICTMENT

In the Fifth Amendment of the Constitution of the United States it's guaranteed that:

"No person shall be held to answer for a capital, or otherwise infamous crime, unless on a presentment or indictment of a Grand Jury ..."

A fair Criminal Justice system must inform an accused person of exactly what charges he or she is facing. An Indictment by a Grand Jury is that notification. An Indictment is normally based on a statute (law passed by Congress). It is essential in the interest of Justice that the statute is clear. The clarity of the statute and the conduct you're accused of that violates the statute should both be set out with particularity in the Indictment.

An Indictment will look a lot like any other court filing. It will set out in the caption the court name, the names of the parties (yours and the U.S.), the case number and the word "Indictment."

In the event you don't find an Indictment, you will probably find that you were tricked into waiving that also. In that event, you should look for a similar filing that is titled as an "Information" instead. In this case search also for the waiver of Indictment. If you have a "Bill of Information" and no waiver, bearing your signature, you have a claim and you can start your list of claims now.

ROUGH NOTES

In any investigation and/or arrest you will find rough notes by officers, agents, private investigators, and lawyers.

Rough notes are the first basic thoughts of any individual who is investigating your criminal case. I find it helpful to seek out the appropriate reports to consider with the rough notes you have discovered.

[12] *acquiescence* – the act of accepting or complying tacitly or passively, as in, accepting something as being inevitable, true or indisputable; acceptance through silence.

Reports include basic police reports from local authorities, DEA 6 reports, F.B.I. 302 reports, warrants, search warrants, arrest warrants, and affidavits used to obtain those warrants.

CORRESPONDENCE WITH THE A.U.S.A.

A.U.S.A. is short for Assistant United States Attorney, your prosecuting attorney. It's very important for your attorney to speak with the A.U.S.A. It's also very beneficial for your attorney to speak on your behalf. Unfortunate that is also very rare. Usually the A.U.S.A. and your attorney discuss the path of least resistance to getting you quickly convicted. They often speak of the most effective method of intimidation to use on you to coerce a guilty plea. Your lawyer must also seek plea agreement when appropriate. If your lawyer takes the first offer that comes down without resistance, or what's called adversarial testing, then your lawyer is constitutionally ineffective, (ref. *Cronic*). You want all these conversations, e-mails, notes, and letters.

MOTIONS AND ORDERS

As discussed in an earlier chapter, your criminal case is executed in a public court record. The court clerk will record these proceedings in an official court docket. In this setting, all events are initiated by motions. These motions are often responded to by the opposing party. Then the court settles the argument with an order. You will also find filings such as plea agreements, proposed plea agreements, presentence reports, objections to presentence reports, and addendums. There are many other types of Docket entries and you want them all, or all you can get.

DISCOVERY

Discovery is the bulk of the ***tangible***[13]evidence against you. There are many items that you will not be able to obtain; in that case you want pictures of all unavailable tangible objects. Say for instance, you were convicted of possessing ten kilograms of cocaine. Well, you're not going to get that back, but you are entitled to a picture of it. Often in a simple possession charge, if the item you were alleged to have possessed can't be produced, then the evidence won't support the conviction.

You want pictures of any surveillance footage involving the alleged conduct. Also, you want any recordings of alleged conversations etc.

WITNESS LIST

In any criminal proceeding, the court requires that both sides provide it with a list of witnesses. You will find a filing from both sides titled "Witness List" in the docket. If the defense filed no witness list and witnesses were available to you, once again, you have a claim against counsel.

These lists are important to have because they identify who was providing testimony against you. There will also be affidavits from these witnesses and/or interviews. In the event you have a long witness list and no affidavits or interviews you may have a case for threat and coercion, which is often accompanied by collusion of the attorneys.

WITNESS AFFIDAVITS

Affidavits are sworn testimony. They must speak the truth. Anything less is perjury. The government uses perjured testimony more often than not. See *United States v. Arthur Anderson LLP.* (5th Cir.) or *United States v. Theodore Stevens*, (Dist. 9th Cir.). In both cases it was proven that the government cheated in the

[13] *Tangible* – Capable of being touched; able to be perceived as materially existent especially through the sense of touch.

proceedings and even lied to produce evidence. It's important to stay diligent because they are very skilled at deception, but also very brazen because they think you will assume, they tell the truth.

CHAPTER EIGHT

Investigating Your Case

Investigating your case is probably going to be the most complicated portion of this whole thing. I can tell you from experience that the most successful case is the most studied. When investigating your case, the first thing you want to do is trim the fat. You would be amazed at how many case files have more useless paper than useable paper. It's not uncommon to receive a case file 16 inches thick, only to throw away 10 inches of blank paper. Start your investigation by:

1) Removing all blank paper
2) Remove all exhibit dividers
3) Remove all duplicate documents
4) Find your docket sheet
5) Put all documents and their supporting evidence in order as indicated by your docket
6) Page number the resulting packet and write the page number of the appropriate document on the docket sheet. This will be your table of contents.

What you will have remaining will be rough notes from counsel, affidavits, pictures and other discovery items, and miscellaneous items. Packet these items independently. It's important to thumb through the second packet daily, at least 20 min a day. This is called studying the evidence.

The first packet you made requires a thorough reading. Don't just thumb through this, read everything and once again, if you can't define a word look it up. As redundant as it may seem, you will need to read over your case a few times. You should do this for at least a month while thumbing through the evidence every day if you can. This practice of study will yield the best results as you will learn something new about your case every time you read it.

Charged Conduct

While investigating your conduct you will have to read your indictment a little closer. Now we are going to read it for conduct. In most Indictments it lists the conduct you are alleged to have committed and that it's all in violation of some statute such as 18 U.S.C. § 2422(b), a crime against the United States. As you can see, by the following example, the language of the statute does not appear. This is a phenomenon found in most federal indictments because most federal convictions are for state crimes. It's important to remember that the United States has no police power unless you are on their property.

This is why most indictments have a clause that states "In and affecting Interstate Commerce" or some derivative of it. All federal statutes mention Interstate Commerce in them somewhere.

Most people indicted by the federal government have never heard of Interstate Commerce.

Charging Statute

At this point, it's important to compare your indictment to the statute you are accused of being in violation of.

For example, take a close look at the conduct it claims you committed and see if it's found in the statute it says you violated. You can find the text of any criminal (federal) statute in either Title 18 or Title 21 of the

United States Code. You can find this in the law library by selecting "United States Code Service" and selecting the appropriate title and scrolling down to your statute.

Investigating the applicability of a federal criminal statute is best conducted as in this example:

Review the wording in your indictment or information. This reading is from an actual indictment as a failed drug investigation, turned into a sexual offense.

> **"Between on or about the 23rd day of May 2012 and including on or about the 26th day of May 2012, in Jefferson County, within the Northern District of Alabama, and elsewhere, the defendant, [name omitted], who was born on or about 1968, while using a facility and means of interstate commerce, to wit: the internet and a telephone, did knowingly attempt to persuade, induce, and entice an individual, known to the defendant as a 14 year old female, who had not obtained the age of 18 years to engage in sexual activity for which the defendant can be charged with a criminal offense, to wit: rape in the second degree ..."**

This ominous statement on its face seems like an honest offense. Remember that the investigation in this case began as a drug investigation, and then an accusation for possession and transportation of explosive materials was made. When all failed, the government charged a sexual offense. When you compare the language of the indictment and the language of the statute, differences are critical to the conviction cooked up by the prosecutor and your defense lawyer. Here is the reading of the charging statute:

> **"Whoever, using the mail or any facility or means of interstate or foreign commerce, or within the special maritime and territorial jurisdiction of the United States knowingly persuades, induces, entices, or coerces any individual who has not attained the age of 18 years, to engage in prostitution or any sexual activity for which any person can be charged with a criminal offense, or attempts to do so shall be fined under this title and imprisoned not less than 10 years or for life."**

In the comparison between this indictment and the charging statute you will find three errors fatal to the indictment.

1) The government provides a definition of interstate commerce that is contrary to law. Here, the government attempts to redefine a "means of interstate commerce," as most phones and computers access the internet as a means of interstate commerce. The Courts have ruled that the internet can be a means, to conclude that every user and every telephone could give rise to jurisdiction under the commerce clause that would create a general police power under the ruse of regulating commerce and completely obliterating all constitutional limitations.

2) The federal statute 18 U.S.C. § 2422(b), was clearly enacted to regulate the enticement of minors to engage in prostitution. In the indictment, the government replaces prostitution with "rape in the second degree."

3) The government replaces the words in the statute "any person can be charged," to "for which the defendant can be charged" in the indictment.

To present such statements to the court is not only unethical; it is also fraud on the court. The government's attorney in the referenced case is attempting to turn a suspected drug dealer into a sexual offender by purposely manipulating the meaning of the statute. In short, you can see the government's attorney changed the wording and definitions in this referenced case. In doing so, the court mistakenly misapplied a prostitution statute over alleged conduct that, if true, would not have even been an offense in the state.

The United States, under this statute, could apply its authority because the statute criminalizes enticing children to engage in prostitution, an activity that "any person," even the minor, can be charged with. But if you're attempting to apply the statute to attempted second degree rape, then the government would have to change the chargeable parties to only the defendant because the victim of rape cannot be charged with being raped. One simply cannot rape one's self.

CONCLUSION

Once again, I urge you to look up words you cannot readily define. While you are investigating your case and reviewing the law library via Lexis Nexus, I suggest you look up these key phrases: *Essential elements* of the *charged offense*, and *alleged conduct* in relation to *law and fact*.

CHAPTER NINE

Determining Your Claim

Claim development will be an ongoing effort. As you may recall, I suggested earlier that you review chapter eleven of the *Federal Habeas Corpus Practice and Procedure Manual*. That's because it contains a wealth of ideas. As we go through this chapter, I'll be giving you some ideas and ways to find errors, but I won't be able to tell you what went wrong in your case. Only you can do that, so use every resource you can find.

What's in Your Docket

Neglect, that's what you will find when reviewing your docket. Most ineffective assistance of counsel claims are based upon what your lawyer didn't do. He may not have hired an investigator. If you're indigent or had a free lawyer, he would have been required to move the court to appoint an investigator. That appointment would be in your docket. If your lawyer claimed in open court, that he filed a Notice of Alibi defense or something else, these filings would be in your docket. If there was an offer of a plea agreement your lawyer didn't present to you, it would also be in your docket. Also check for waivers you didn't sign. I have worked 12 cases to date where the appointed lawyer forged documents, even plea agreements.

What's in Your Lawyer's Notes

Your lawyer's notes are very telling as to how your case was and should have been handled. As in many events or activities, a person's first thoughts are often correct. In most cases, especially first arrest cases, the defendant is talking as fast as he can, and the lawyer is writing as fast as he can, that's why the notes of the initial interview are so important. As the attorney writes in record breaking speed, he often writes the truth because he has no time or reason to lie yet. You will also discover that before the prosecutor tells your attorney what to do, or how he wants your defense handled, he or she is actually preparing to do his best in your defense.

In a recent case, the rough notes of defense counsel provided the pivotal detail that overturned a life sentence in an armed bank robbery case. The case was 12 years old, but upon receipt of the case file it was discovered that the attorney provided his rough notes written upon the note pad from his initial interview. The lawyer's notes, in item five, listed a reminder to compare the ballistics report from the defendant's gun to the report from the victim's autopsy.

A comparison revealed that the ballistics report showed the defendant was in possession of a .40 caliber handgun that had not been recently fired. It also revealed that the slug recovered from the victim's body during an autopsy was a .38 caliber round fired from the security officer's service weapon, as noted in the autopsy report.

In this case, the court appointed defense counsel failed to provide reasonably effective assistance of counsel because he did not conduct "a prompt investigation of the circumstances of the case ...." See *Criminal Justice Prosecution Function and Defense Function Standards*, 4-4.1; *ABA Defense Function Standards*.

In the above-mentioned case, a *habeas* Petition was filed twelve years after sentencing, premised upon his actual innocence concerning the victim's death.

Transcripts

Before you begin scrutinizing your transcripts, I suggest you get a working knowledge of some court rules that apply. It will be helpful to review the Federal Rules of Criminal Procedure and the Federal Rules of Evidence. You can find both of these in the electronic law library.

Upon opening the law library, you should select "court Rules" in the main menu, and then go to the appropriate rules, i.e. *Federal Rules of Criminal Procedure*.

With the rules in mind, you will review a transcript looking for evidence. In another recent case, the transcript of a change of plea hearing provided the appropriate evidence to show a Constitutional violation. In this case, a 70-year-old blind man was convicted for seeing child pornography. The *habeas* Petition was filed 2 years after sentencing and the government contended that he may not have been too blind to commit the charged offense. Upon review of all the transcripts, it was discovered that the district judge questioned the defendant about reading Braille. Once deciding that the defendant was totally blind, the district judge required the defendant to re-sign his typed plea agreement. Defense counsel was prompted to place his hand on the signature line and compel him to plead guilty based upon a typed stipulation he could not read. Afterwards the defendant stated in open court, "I signed it, I think."

In this case, the court didn't read the contract to a blind man and physically forced him to sign. This is clear and blatant violation of the Federal Rules of Criminal Procedure, Rule one. So, keep your eyes and mind open.

Plea Agreement

While compiling your claims, the plea agreement offers a wealth of possible claims. The claims against a plea agreement are also complex because the plea agreement is just that, an agreement; it is not a plea of guilty. A plea agreement is also a contract that is regulated by the basic contract law of your state. In four years I have not yet found a legal contract that takes the place of a plea of guilty. Under this subject it may be best that I provide for you a basic synopsis such as the following taken from an actual, successful petition.

Guilty plea was unknowing and involuntary. The petitioner has, to the best of his ability as a *pro se* litigant, raised his contention that he was not duly informed by counsel or the court as to all the actual effects of the plea agreement the petitioner entered into under duress. The court, at the change of plea hearings, thoroughly questioned the petitioner as to the facts concerning his signing the plea agreement; rather than the alleged guilt he was admitting to in the plea agreement. This plea hearing was nothing more than a dogmatic display concerning appropriate steps to solidify a contract.

In the criminal case from which the petitioner seeks relief, the petitioner was threatened by the very attorney at his side during the change of plea hearing. The petitioner, therefore, recited all required and coached responses in order to avoid having to suffer an unreasonable sentence threatened by counsel. At the time of the plea hearing, that threat was still very real and standing at the petitioner's side. The petitioner was unable to express his concerns to the court without being exposed to the harm that counsel threatened, until after sentencing when counsel's duties were terminated.

The petitioner hereby continues his declaration that the validity of his plea agreement is a "contested factual issue." In the change of plea hearing, the petitioner did not utter a single word concerning the charged offense or the alleged conduct. The trial court determined the petitioner's guilt based upon coached yes and no answers, most of which, concerning Rule 11 steps, the petitioner did not understand. The petitioner hereby avers that his guilt or innocence was never an issue or concern. He simply followed counsel's instructions to the best of his ability to mitigate his sentence.

In considering the validity of a plea agreement, parties must realize that a plea agreement is a contract. See *Santobello v. New York*, 404 U.S. 257, 262-263 (1971). Contracts in federal courts are normally reviewed with the guidance of state law concerning basic contract law. One of the prime objectives of contract law is to protect the justified expectations of the parties and to make it possible for them to foretell with accuracy what will be their rights and liabilities under the contract. In this way, certainty and predictability of result are most likely to be secured.

In federal law concerning contracts, the petitioner's rights are best set out in 42 U.S.C. § 1981. Under the fundamental policy doctrine, a court should not refrain from applying the designated law (42 U.S.C. § 1981) merely because application of that law would lead to a result different than would be obtained under the local law of the state or country, whose law would otherwise govern. (Fed. R. Crim. P., Rule 11). Rather, the difference must be contrary to a public policy of that jurisdiction (court rule) that is so substantial that it justifies overriding the concerns for certainty and predictability underlying modern commercial law as well as concerns for judicial economy generally. Thus, application of the designated law (42 U.S.C. § 1981) will rarely be found to be Contrary to a fundamental policy of the state or country whose law would otherwise govern (Fed. R. Crim. P., Rule 11) when the difference between the two concerns a requirement, such as a statute of frauds, that relates to formalities, or general rules of contract law, such as those concerned with the need for consideration.

In the highly regarded case, *Strickland v. Washington*, 466 U.S. 668, the Supreme Court of the United States asserted a:

> *"Two-part test of effective assistance of defense counsel ... 1) reasonably effective assistance and 2) reasonable probability of different result with effective assistance."*

See also: *United States v. Baramdyka*, 95 F.3d. 840, 844 (9th Cir.1996) United States v. Grewal, 825 F.2d. 220 (9th Cir. 1987); *United States v. Rivera-Ramirez*, 715 F.2d. 453 (9th Cir. 1983), these and many other cases contain additional restrictions that govern a claim of ineffective assistance of counsel that are not found in the plea agreement (contract).

These additional restrictions are well known to those who conduct their business in the legal field. It's absurd to assume that someone outside the legal profession would be aware of such restrictions without being advised of such. The record clearly shows that the petitioner was not made aware of these additional requirements in the contract or at plea hearing. Once again, the assumption is made that counsel must have advised his client, because of the strong presumption of reasonableness; another principle the petitioner was not made aware of. This petitioner has been prejudiced by this very assumption alone.

The petitioner argues that his plea agreement and/or contract is voidable because it was engineered and executed as a misleading device intended to defraud the court, the petitioner, and the public's interest in justice, to wit:

1) ABA standards 1.6 declared that, notwithstanding the acceptance of a guilty plea, the Court should not enter a judgment upon such a plea without making inquiry as may satisfy it that there is a factual basis for the plea. The NAC's position is that the trial judge should refuse to accept a plea from a defendant who asserts facts inconsistent with guilt or is "unable or unwilling to recount facts establishing guilt," even though there may be a "factual basis" for the plea as required by the ABA standard. Thus, the NAC's position is stronger than the ABA's in requiring that, not only must there be a factual basis for the plea, but the defendant must also admit facts consistent with the guilt of the offense to which he pleads. Perhaps, the NAC shared this wisdom with the intent that courts would follow in an effort to prevent clever attorneys from procuring convictions by having a court make a finding that a defendant is merely guilty of being fooled into signing a contract he doesn't understand.

In this context, one must realize the difference between a plea and a plea agreement and/or contract. To plea, means simply, to answer for. Just as at arraignment, a plea is a verbal response to an accusation or indictment. A plea agreement, however, is quite different, it is a negotiated contract in which a defendant agrees to plead guilty or give his answer in exchange for the government's offered consideration. A plea agreement in contract may also set out certain exceptions to such a plea. Please note that Federal Rules of Criminal Procedure, Rule 11, makes no concession for a written plea agreement, or stipulation to facts, to replace the actual plea of guilty. In this consideration, see Fed. R. Crim. P., Rule 10(a)(3), which requires a court to "ask the defendant to plead to the indictment or information." In contrast, Rule 10 has a subsection that allows a defendant to waive appearance, Rule 11 however, makes no reference that allows a defendant to be found guilty without vocalizing the elements that make him guilty.

In the petitioner's plea hearing, he did not admit to a single element of the charged offense. This is easily determined in the Court's record. See United States v. Sylvester, 583 F. 3d. 285, 288 (5th Cir. 2009):

> "When determining whether the factual basis for a guilty plea is sufficient, the district court must compare the conduct which defendant admits and the elements of the offense."; cf. United States v. Marek, 238 F.3d. 310, 315 (5th Cir. 2001) (*en banc*). "The acceptance of a guilty plea is a factual finding reviewed for clear error." The petitioner's guilty plea is obviously voidable and a contested factual issue.

2) In this case, counsel advised the petitioner to enter into an agreement to plead guilty. To solidify this agreement, counsel advised the petitioner to sign a contract agreeing to enter such a plea. The contract in question was based upon omissions of fact and law. This is no different than a real estate attorney executing a closing that had a hidden provision forcing a party to make additional payments after executing the closing or a provision that required the buyer to return the property a month after purchase. This sort of failure would render a real estate contract invalid in any court.

This contractual tactic is fraudulent. A Criminal defendant, who pleads guilty and later discovers his right to adequate representation was denied, would be barred from relief by a hidden and/or extrinsic condition of an agreement that was not annunciated in the contract or plea hearing. This tactic is in violation of basic law for denying justified expectation. Counsel's advice to enter such a contract creates an extrinsic ineffective assistance of counsel waiver, a conflict of interest.

A) Almost every State BAR Association has said in a formal opinion that collateral attack waivers are wrong and cause a conflict of interest between a defense counsel and his client. In fact, the Kentucky State Supreme Court has said that collateral attack waivers "create a non-waivable conflict of interest between the defendant and his attorney." *United States v. Kentucky State BAR Assoc.*, No.: 20013-SC-270-KB (Ky. 2014). The Court also said it is an "ethical breach" by defense counsel. *Id.* When viewed through the lens of conflict of interest, the problem of collateral attack waivers become quite clear.

B) "Counsel owes the client a duty of loyalty, a duty to avoid conflicts of interest." *Strickland v. Washington*, 466 U.S. 668, 688 (1984). The Sixth Amendment of the Constitution's right to counsel includes the "right to representation that is free from conflicts of interest." *Wood v. Georgia*, 450 U.S. 261, 271 (1981), and this "conflict free" representation extends to plea negotiations. *Moore v. United States*, 950 F. 2d. 656, 600 (CA 10 1991). The Supreme Court even said that if a petitioner can show counsel operated under a conflict of interest, he doesn't even have to show that he was prejudiced (that counsel's errors changed the outcome of the proceedings).

Cuyler v. Sullivan, 466 U.S. 335, 350 (1980).

C) It is well established that plea agreements are "contracts." *Santobello v. New York*, 404 U.S. 257, 262-263 (1971). So, if we take a look at how a conflict of interest would affect a contract's validity, we see more issues that are fatal to the plea agreement, or "contract." If a party commits fraud while negotiating a contract, the contract is VOID as if it never existed. *Godly v. United States*, 5 F.3d. 1473, 1476 (Fed. Cir. 1995) ("A contract tainted by fraud ... *is* void *ab inito*"). Such as if the government adds a provision for appeal, or otherwise collaterally attack, the conviction or sentence in which the petitioner relies, in an effort to entice him to agree, only to have an embedded provision that voids the right to appeal that the petitioner relies on to enter the agreement.

The government commits fraud during contract negotiations when it places a provision in the contract it knows will create a conflict of interest between defense counsel and the defendant. A collateral attack waiver creates a conflict of interest between defense counsel because it is unethical for defense counsel to advise his client to enter into a contract (to accept a plea agreement/offer) when the contract has a waiver preventing the client from later challenging his lawyer's advice.

D) "Fraud is a generic term." *Ragland v. Shattuck National Bank*, 36 F.3d. 983, 990 (CA 10 1994). It encompassed a broad range of ways "by which another is cheated." *Id.* There are actually two types of fraud: intentional and constructive. Intentional is when a party intends to deceive the other party. Constructive, though, is broader and covers even unintentional deception. In this case, the type of the plea (contract) allows the petitioner to reserve for himself the right to collaterally attack the conviction/sentence for ineffective assistance of counsel. The petitioner relied on this provision as stated in the contract. Here now, however, the petitioner finds himself defending himself against a procedural waiver that is not expressed in the plea agreement, nor did the petitioner have any knowledge of. Here now, the government's attorney raises new restrictions to the plea agreement that the petitioner had no knowledge of. Additionally, when the government places a collateral attack waiver, intrinsic or extrinsic, in the plea agreement, it creates a conflict of interest. And because the government knows this but fails to say anything, it is fraud because the defendant has "an underlying right to be correctly informed of the facts." Id. Fraud occurs when a party in an agreement has a duty to speak but "fails to disclose the whole truth." Id. at 991. The government, as a party in a contract, has the obligation to say a waiver could cause a conflict of interest. It is constructive fraud when the government *knowingly* remains silent in that issue. Again, any fraud in a contract *voids* the contract, as if it never existed.

E) Also see, *United States v. Shedrick*, 493 F.3d. 292 (3rd Cir. 2007); *United States v. Craig*, 985 F.2d. 175 (4th Cir. 1993); *United States v. White*, 307 F.3d. 336 (5th Cir. 2002) ("The ineffective assistance of counsel argument survives a waiver of appeal only when the claimed assistance directly affected the validity of that waiver or the plea itself") (72 Crl 15, 10/2/02); Davi.11a v. United States, 258 F.3d. 448 (6th Cir. 2001)(69 CrL 556, 8/15/01); *Jones v. United States*, 167 F.3d. 1142 (7th Cir. 1999); *DeRoo v. United States*, 223 F.3d. 919 (8th Cir. 2000); *Washington v. Lampert*, 422 F.3d. 864 (9th Cir. 2005); *United States v. Cockerham*, 237 F.3d. 1179 (10th Cir. 2001)(68 CrL 369, 1/31/01); *Williams v. United States*, 396 F.3d. 1340 (11th Cir. 2001)("There may be a distinction between a claim of ineffective assistance in entering or negotiating the plea versus a claim ... challenging the validity of the plea or agreement")(76 CrL 341 2/2/05).

The synopsis ends here.

In sum, a plea agreement is a contract binding upon both parties and regulated by state laws. As such, if either party breaks the terms of the contract, either openly or deviously so, then the contract can be voided as if it never existed. In this case, even though obligated to do so as the drafter of the contract, the government failed to inform the defendant that the contract he signed would cause a direct conflict of interest between himself and his own attorney. This conflict of interest between client and attorney is an egregious prejudice which irreparably tainted the client's defense. To Wit: Both counsels deprived the defendant of his civil rights to contract as provided in 42 U.S.C. § 1981, all in violation of his 1st, 5th, and 6th Amendment rights.

CHAPTER TEN

Basic Motion Writing

This section is called "Basic Motion writing" for a reason, and that's because there is absolutely no reason to complicate things. Akin to questions, the only stupid one is the one that serves no purpose or is not presented. The most basic element of a motion is the fact that you want the court to do something for you. Just as you may write your family a letter to put money on your account, you're going to write the court a motion to present your request.

Some motions are so basic that they are called "motions in letter." This tool is very helpful when you don't know what to file next. You simply file a "Motion in Letter" and speak concisely and deliberately expressing what you want. Just a reminder, this tactic is frowned upon if used too often.

And just as when you write a letter, you must address it to the appropriate place (address). At this point if you have something from your case, perhaps a motion or memorandum that your lawyer filed, it would be helpful. This is because many courts have local rules that define particular characteristics that your court prefers. Although I have supplied a common structure accepted by most courts, it's always a good idea to comply with the court when possible.

In the event you do something wrong, the judge, in most cases, will be glad to help you out. Take your correction in stride and continue forward.

Don't Talk too Much

I want you to consider back when your English teacher wanted a book report on the most boring book he or she could think of. Or perhaps the owner's manual to a new smart phone. That's right, it's too long or too boring and contains too much useless information. To make it simple, don't do this. If you bore the court or inundate it with useless writing, you only hurt yourself by causing unnecessary delay.

In the title of your Motion, state very clearly what you want, for instance "PETITIONER'S MOTION FOR LEAVE TO EXTEND TIME TO FILE § 2255 MOTION."

In the first paragraph of your Motion you want to direct the court's attention to the law or rule that permits your request.

In the conclusion of your Motion explain the exact action you want the court to take on your behalf. In the instance of this particular Motion, you should request that the court "ISSUE AN ORDER GRANTING LEAVE TO EXTEND THE TIME TO FILE A § 2255 MOTION."

Don't Be Sarcastic

Sarcasm is most often language used to cause pain or irritation; used in retaliation for the emotional attack waged upon you. As satisfying as it may be at this moment, you will find that this is no time to indulge in sarcasm, the courts will respond in kind and they have the authority to, and will, inflict more pain and discomfort upon you.

Keep Events in Order

As you progress through this action you will be required to perfect a "statement of Facts." This is a chronological listing of events in your case. I suggest you start yours now. Once you have yours started, and are reading it over frequently, you will remember additional events you didn't remember the first time. If you get this perfected now, you won't have to scramble for it later.

The most important thing to remember is to keep things in the order as they happened. The biggest mistake you can make is allowing the government, or the court, to guess when, where and how things happened.

ESSENTIAL ELEMENTS OF A MOTION

As we go over this section you may want to open your civil § 2255 case file or review any motion in the appendix of this book as an example to follow.

The first essential entry in any Motion is the caption. It lists the name of the court, the names of the parties and the relevant case number.

The second essential entry is the title (the bold section in my motions). This is where you tell the court what you want them to do for you.

The third essential entry is the opening paragraph. This is where I most often introduce myself by name and status as a party (i.e. the petitioner, JOHN DOE in *PRO SE*). This paragraph also lists what jurisdiction the court has to grant my request. (i.e. the court rule or statute that supports my request).

The fourth essential entry is to express exactly what you want the court to do, often you want the court to "ISSUE AN order."

The last common essential entry is your closing and signature. This is the most important. You can write the most elegant Motion the court has ever seen and invalidate it by failing to sign it. See *Federal Rules of Civil Procedure*, Rule 11(a).

CHAPTER ELEVEN

§ 2255 Motion

By now you have been in a prison long enough to think about fighting your conviction and long enough for this book to arrive. If so, then most certainly, you have been in prison long enough to hear about all the different memorandum and/or briefs of law. Well, let me clear this up for you ... *wrong answer*. Many § 2255 proceedings are lost because of too much notice and not enough facts. The people you are dealing with are well versed in what the law says so they don't need to be reminded. However, they have no idea about things that happened outside of their presence of facts that your attorney didn't raise in court.

To be certain a 28 U.S.C. § 2255 Motion is a *fact* pleading not misconstrued as a *notice* pleading, the court needs to know what happened to you, how it hurt your case, and what Constitutional Issues it is in violation of. So let's get the facts together.

Available Forms

There are many forms available upon which to file for relief pursuant to. 28.U.S.C. § 2255. This aspect is covered in:

"Rules Governing 28 U.S.C. § 2255 proceedings in the United States District Courts."

Rule 2. The Motion

a) Applying for relief. The application must be in the form of a Motion to Vacate, Set Aside, or Correct the sentence.

b) Form, the Motion Must:

   1) Specify all the grounds for relief available to the moving party;

   2) State the facts supporting each ground;

   3) State the relief requested;

   4) Be printed, type written, or legibly handwritten; and

   5) Be signed under penalty of perjury by the Movant or by a person authorized to sign it for the Movant.

c) Standard form. The Motion must substantially follow either the form appended to these rules or a form prescribed by a local District Court rule. The Clerk must make forms available to moving parties without charge.

With that said, let's look at our options. The prison you are presently in is required to have a copy of a § 2255 Motion at your disposal.

Your court is required to provide free forms upon your request. Simply write a letter to your court clerk and ask for a § 2255 Motion.

Of course, the law library has a copy of the Motion you can print off the computer for about $2.

Standard Form

The first blank motion you will find in this book for your use is a standard § 2255 Motion, (refer to page 65). The form you will find in this book substantially follows the form appended to the rules. With the exception that it is printed in smaller size, it may be used if no other forms available.

If you bear in mind that a court must admit that it failed to protect your right to due process in order to grant your § 2255 Motion, then you can realize why a district court loathes the idea of granting you any kind of relief. That's why it's important to make this as easy as possible for the district court.

On most forms you will find inadequate room to convey all the grounds that support your claim. This will cause the need to append additional pages. When you do this, you set a condition where a court has to read a page, then refer to an appended page, then return to the original. If you compile this with numerous pages of evidence and affidavits the court will lose interest quickly.

Please consider your need to be as short as possible as you carefully present all the facts of your claim.

FILLING OUT THE FORM

I suggest that you answer all the questions in the form on a separate sheet of paper. There is nothing more distracting than attempting to think about answers while typing.

For the most part, all questions are self-explanatory except for blocks like "Docket or Case No.:" this block is the third block in the heading, and we will get to that momentarily.

The block that says "district" requires your judicial district such as "Northern district of Alabama," which just happens to have been mine.

The block that says "Docket or Case No.:" you want to leave blank. This is for your court to answer.

Most of the rest of the form is in a "fill in the blanks" format until you get to number 12. If you have followed instructions, you already have a pretty good idea of what your grounds for relief are.

You will list your grounds in the following manner:

> GROUND ONE: The Petitioner was deprived of Constitutionally effective assistance of counsels[14] in violation of the Sixth Amendment and 18 U.S.C. § 3006A.

a) Supporting facts (Do not argue or cite law. Just state the specific facts to support your claim.):
   1) Court Appointed Counsel, John Jackson, failed to conduct a meaningful investigation by which he would have discovered an alibi defense.
   2) Court Appointed Counsel, John Jackson, failed to present the Petitioner's alibi, defense at trial.
   3) Court Appointed Appellate Counsel, John Doe, failed to raise the ground that the Court failed to appoint adequate representation including investigators, at the Petitioner's Direct Appeal.
   4) Court Appointed Appellate Counsel, John Doe, failed to raise plain error as a standard of review in his appellate brief.

This format of listing grounds and supporting facts is used for ground one through four. Please note that there are four types of claims as discussed in chapter three and four under grounds for the petition. There is no need to have the same ground listed twice. Most Petitions only have three grounds, violations of Constitutional rights, lack of authority to sentence, and failure to follow due process of law.

Before answering question 18, I recommend you re-read chapter 41.4(a) of the *Federal Habeas Corpus Practice and Procedure Manual*. I personally use a variety of answers depending on each petitioner's

[14] In most cases, but not all, "counsels" will include both trial and appellate attorneys.

personal circumstances. If you are a first time- filer and within one year of your AEDPA date, you simply state: "This Motion is timely pursuant to 28 U.S.C. § 2255."

The last possible complicated part is the space marked:

"Therefore, Movant asks that the Court grant the following relief."

For this answer, refer to the *Federal Habeas Corpus Practice and Procedure Manual*, chapter 11.8 "Prayer for Relief."

My favorites are:

1) "issue a Writ of *habeas corpus* to have the Petitioner brought before it to the end that he may be discharged from his unconstitutional confinement and restraint."

   (No. one is to overturn the conviction.)

2) "issue a Writ of *habeas corpus* to have the Petitioner brought before it to the end that he may be relieved of his unconstitutional sentence."

   (No. two is for resentencing.)

YOUR AFFIDAVIT

An affidavit in a *habeas* action is an indispensable document. Your affidavits are sworn statements concerning specific events you want the court to consider. Imagine for a moment you and another are in a debate. If you don't speak or present your side of the debate you will lose. The government's response is a sworn statement in which the government presents its position in this matter. Your § 2255 Motion is also a sworn statement of your position. Where you will need affidavits, or where others are involved. Take for example that you intend to tell the court you and your codefendant were present when your attorney said you wouldn't spend any time in prison if you signed a plea agreement. Well, let me assure you that your attorney is not going to admit that. As a matter of fact, your attorney will lie to the court objecting vehemently. For this reason, you will need your codefendant's affidavit to support your claim.

On page 84 you will find a sample affidavit. The affidavit you will find is case specific, so use your specific case information. Keep your affidavits short and simple. Each affidavit should clarify only one issue. If there are several issues, then several affidavits will be needed.

SUPPORTING EVIDENCE

In your file, you have most likely found an enormous amount of evidence to support your claim. You don't need everything because the court also has a copy of your case on hand. You want to use evidence that the court is likely not to have. Attorney notes are hot items here. Always send them copies and always preserve your originals.

PAGE LIMITS

Although you won't find page limits in the *habeas* rules, I like to use common sense. The court will not read a filing that rivals the King James Bible in length. I have witnessed that the court's reject pleadings of only 60 pages.

If you look at the Rules for the court of Appeals and the Supreme Court of the United States, you will find a good rule of thumb to follow. Personally, I like to keep the original fewer than 25 pages and my reply to the government's response under 30.

MEMORANDUM BRIEF

A Memorandum Brief, or Brief in Support, can be a useful tool in many types of litigation even in a *habeas* action. However, timing is critical, and this is not the time. I want you to imagine trying to play poker or spades and showing your opponent your cards before you start.

The rules that govern *habeas* actions in a United States district court require you to show specific and detailed facts. They do not require the initial motion to be supported by a briefing on the law, and I do not recommend it here. With other motions filed in this type of action, you will be filing briefs just not here so let's see what the government has to say first.

NUMBER OF COPIES

In most cases, you will be required to file the original and two copies of your § 2255 Motion in the district court. You will not be required to serve anyone else with this filing.

After this, the government's attorney gets a copy of everything.

I do suggest you check your local court rules concerning the number of copies also. When you file with the district court, remember that the original motion and its attachments are not to be bound in any way. This will assist the clerk in filing. The other two should be stapled in the upper left corner with a single vertical staple. The clerk will forward a copy of the motion and its attachments to the government and another to your district judge.

Make your clerk's job as easy as possible as he or she is not, at this time, your enemy and it's best to prevent them from becoming one.

CHAPTER TWELVE

SUMMARY DISPOSITION

In the Rules Governing § 2255, Rule 4(b) it clearly states in pertinent part that:

> ***"The Judge who receives the motion must promptly examine it. If it plainly appears from the motion, any attached exhibits, and the record of prior proceedings that the moving party is not entitled to relief, the Judge must dismiss the motion and direct the clerk to notify the moving party."***

Summary dismissal is exactly what it sounds like, over before it begins. The key to preventing this from happening is to show that evidence exists to support your claim that the judge cannot see in the record. It helps if the evidence is unavailable because of your attorney's failure to perform professionally.

The best way to prevent summary dismissal is to use evidence to show the court that additional facts are not in the court record.

A witness affidavit is evidence that a witness existed. A witness in your criminal case just now becoming known is proof of the fact that your lawyer didn't investigate your case well enough to determine that a witness was available.

This fact, and the witness's testimony, stand outside of the record. The court cannot rule on the merit of ineffective assistance of counsel without this evidence. You must show this evidence and move the court to grant leave for you to conduct discovery. See page 99

Requesting discovery will prevent the court from summarily dismissing your motion.

CHAPTER THIRTEEN

Show Cause Order

Through diligence and hard work, you have done well and have a meritorious claim in the court awaiting review. If you have followed directions so far, then you have already filed the appropriate number of copies of your § 2255 Motion in your district court. This is the only time you will file a pleading in the court without providing a copy to the government's attorney. That's because the rules governing § 2255 proceedings do not require the petitioner to serve a copy of the petition on the respondent. Instead, *habeas* Rule 4 provides that, once the clerk files the petition, and provided it's not summarily dismissed, the court must serve on the respondent, the U.S. attorney's office, a copy of the petition, any accompanying documents, and any orders in the case.

The service of the motion on the government by itself doesn't obligate the government to respond. The duty to file a response, by the U.S. attorneys, comes only by a court order. See *habeas* Rules 4 and 5(a), under which the court routinely orders the government to "*show cause*."

Now let's consider that you have filed a timely and meritorious § 2255 Motion and justice is due. Even though you want justice quickly, you must also remember that these people get paid for each and every month you serve in prison and as such are in no hurry to serve you. Most, not all, incarcerations have nothing to do with Justice and are unlawfully imposed. Many convictions are nothing more than a method to bill Congress for unearned tax dollars. Understanding this one issue will help you comprehend the next events that follow. Money and not Justice is the reason many of these steps will seem so difficult.

Rule 4 states that "The Clerk must promptly forward the motion to the judge who conducted the trial ..." Ordinarily, and in any other type of proceeding, this act of reviewing your own mistakes would be a direct violation of 28 U.S.C. § 47. In this context the judge who convicted you must be willing to admit that mistakes were made in your case making the judge seem either foolish or corrupt. If you couple this fact with the obvious financial interests at stake you can see why judges are so adamantly against releasing innocent prisoners.

In the last chapter we discussed how to avoid summary disposition. Now we can discuss the remainder of the options the court has before it.

OPTION ONE: The court may opt to do absolutely nothing. This option is chosen about 50% of the time in most judicial districts. If the court issues no order in the case, and you wait patiently for the court to do the right thing, a couple of years are going to pass and then the court will deny the petition for a lack of prosecution. This, in my opinion, is probably one of the most difficult denials to overcome. The appeals court, which also makes money based on criminal convictions, is more often than not of the opinion that if you don't care about justice, then why should they? For these reasons, I chose to address this issue first.

In Rule 12 of rules governing § 2255 it states that:

> *"The Federal Rules of Civil Procedure and the Federal Rules of Criminal Procedure, to the extent that they are not inconsistent with any statutory provisions or these rules, may be applied to a proceeding under these rules."*

Under the *Federal Rules of Civil Procedure*, Rule 12(a)(2) provides that the government "must serve an answer to a complaint ... within 60 days after service ... ." Now is a real good time to realize that your judge works for the government as denoted by the title of the court "United States District Court." In this context you may finally realize that your judge has been an adverse party this whole time. As such when your § 2255 motion has been in the mail for 61 days it's time to file a "Motion for Judgment on the Pleadings." This is otherwise known as a "Motion to Compel the Court to Issue an Order to Show Cause." See page 90 for a sample copy.

Following a "Motion to Compel the Court to Issue an Order to Show Cause" some courts will still refuse to issue an order. This is a rare occurrence and is also a very good sign that you have a serious claim. In the event this happens to you, you will need to file for a Writ of Mandamus in the Court of Appeals. See page 91 for a sample copy.

OPTION TWO: An additional tactic, used by the court, is to give a swift order to the government that includes the defense the court intends to use against your issues. When this is done it puts the U.S. attorney's office on notice concerning what information the court needs to deny your claim, I would like for you to refer once again to the *Federal Habeas Corpus Practice and Procedure Manual*, chapter 11, and realize that not one of the favorable cases listed were granted by a district court. District courts only grant § 2255 motions when it either makes no difference in the monies they will receive, or the district court was ordered to do so by a higher court.

When the court chooses this option it's a good idea to start your research on the issue the court told the government to address. Most often, the court will order the government to address issues like timeliness and/or procedural bars.

OPTION THREE: This option is my most favored. This describes a Judge who is actually neutral. Out of the 94 Judicial Districts throughout the country, and the large number of cases I've been a part of, I can only remember less than ten that were decided by a fair judge. The one common denominator in these cases was a reasonable time for the government to respond and without the court providing clues about how the government should respond.

A reasonable time for a response is between 45 and 90 days. Don't be alarmed about this. Ordinarily, the government uses a prepared response where the assistant U.S. attorney only has to fill in the blanks. In your case however, he is going to have to think about it and perhaps do something original. This is a good sign because (one) the court recognizes that the standardized form will not work; (two) the court sees that you have a novel and fair complaint and (three) the court isn't telling the government how to answer and/or on what grounds the court wants to deny the petition on.

I have in the past encountered other results from the court at this stage, but none of which re-occurred with regularity. It's for these reasons that I suggest you be mindful of anything you have not read about thus far. Remember the interpretation of the law is a living breathing and continually evolving necessary evil that seeks to devour both the guilty and the innocent.

CHAPTER FOURTEEN

GOVERNMENT'S RESPONSE

Well you have just received the government's response, and as most will be, you too are eager to read it to see where you stand. Unfortunately, what you have in your hand is a poor reflection of that. In every case I have ever been involved in, the government has lied and misled the court to the point of fraud. It's time to face reality; you're in the custody of the Federal government, who is the top of the food chain. All the crimes that the government's attorney commits will go unprosecuted because they are the ones who investigate and prosecute exactly what they are doing. Ordinarily I would suggest that you ask people such as former Senator Theodore Steven, from Alaska, former D.C. Prosecutor Nicholas Marsh, or the many others who are mysteriously killed once they prove the U.S. attorney's office is, in my opinion, a corrupt criminal organization.

Instead, I'm going to suggest that you read it once. Put it away in your locker or some other safe place. Go out for a walk in the fresh air and let the reality of the situation soak in.

The reality is that this is only what a cleaver attorney wants to pull over the eyes of you, and the court of Appeals. I want you to remember that you are in prison, most likely, based on the lies told by your defense lawyer to get you there. So, take some time to vent your emotions so you can get back to work.

Now that that is over, you need to get your copy of your § 2255 out. It often helps clear your doubts by remembering your claims, but let's do a bit more. At this point you need to make a fresh list. What you are aiming to do is list your claims in a short concise statement, preferably on a single page of paper. As you're making this list, consider that I'm not talking about your grounds for relief, I'm talking about the supporting facts.

Now back to the government's response. You will have at least 21 days to file a reply to this response so let's not waste time. With a second note pad in hand I want you to read the government's response, but you need to pay particular attention to three things and you want to make a separate list for each of them.

LIST ONE: You will need to list everything the government's attorney lied about. Make just a brief note concerning the content of the lie. You will also list the page and line number of where in their response it appears.

LIST TWO: You will need to list every case reference the government provides along with the page number. Once this list is compiled, you will need to go to the library and check to see that every quote appears as the government states that it does. If you see an ellipsis, that should be a red flag.

LIST THREE: The third and final list is the one that I often find to be the most difficult. In this list, you want to record every claim in your § 2255 motion that the government didn't respond to. Here you will need your first list – the one you made of all your claims. Read your list before you begin this third reading of the government's response. This is important because if you claimed it, and the government did not claim otherwise, then the law states that the fact you claimed is true.

As redundant as this may seem, you need to repeat this list making process at least five times or at least until you can add nothing more to the lists. Also remember to take at least an hour between readings to rest your eyes and absorb what you've just read.

CHAPTER FIFTEEN

Writing Your Reply

Well here we are, we've come a long way from where we started and your about to write your first reply to the government. We just need to discuss a few more things first.

First, you need to know that it's rare that the court orders the petitioner, to file a reply. Most commonly, the courts don't want you to reply to the government at all. Usually the court prefers you wait on the court to issue an order of giving notice of "summary dismissal." When this happens, the court orders the petitioner to answer the court's order rather than the government's response. In such a case, the petitioner often follows the court's instructions and fails to reply to the government's claims. After such a failure, and regardless of how thorough you are when answering the court, the judge denies your § 2255 Motion summarily because you didn't raise any issue rebutting the government's claims. The court, disposing of the action because the petitioner agrees with the government, has concluded the intended magic trick by tricking you to concede. In an effort to forego the preceding events, let's look at the applicable laws and rules.

Prior to 1978 when Congress enacted the *habeas corpus* rules that now govern § 2255 proceedings, the controlling procedural statute provided that ***"the allegations of a return ... if not traversed, shall be accepted as true except to the extent that the judge finds from the evidence that they are not true."*** Accordingly, if the government stretches the truth a bit and its claims are fatal to your claims, the court will dismiss the petition, motion, or claims if you fail to file a "traverse" alleging a contrary fact or principle.

The above principles were changed in 2004, most likely because as written, a petitioner's reply or "traverse" would not be required to produce a fair and just result because the judge is expected to make findings based upon reviewing the evidence. The fact is, if the judge were to have made findings on the evidence, you may not have been found guilty in the first place.

Therefore, you find (as written in the *Federal Habeas Corpus Practice and Procedure Manual*) that:

> "Until an Amendment of the Habeas Rules in 2004, the rules omitted any reference to a traverse or reply.
>
> "Explaining the omission, the advisory committee notes to Habeas Rule 5 stated that a traverse was not required except when the respondent alleged in the answer that the petitioner had improperly filed a successive petition challenging the same conviction and sentence as were unsuccessfully challenged in an earlier *habeas corpus* petition. Although the Habeas Rules dispensed with the requirements of a traverse, they did not forbid such a pleading, and the advisory committee notes endorse a traverse or amendment 'where it [would] serve a truly useful purpose' or was 'called for by the contents of the answer' filed by respondent."

With all this in mind, you should now realize that all the rule changes and court orders are nothing more than a creative way of getting you to miss an important step that the court can use against you.

With a new understanding of this step in the procedure, you should be able to see the importance of the lists that were made in the last chapter. You will find that I have included a standard reply on page 90. This reply has all the standard verbiage required for an effective reply and space for you to insert the information from your list to personalize the reply to your case.

CHAPTER SIXTEEN

FACT DEVELOPMENT

By now you may have learned that the 'outcome of a *habeas* proceeding is most contingent upon how a judge should view the facts rather than dispute over construction of a statute or your interpretation of a line of preceding court decisions. With that in mind, you may need to develop your facts a bit more thoroughly.

You have successfully filed a meritorious claim in the court. You have shown that evidence exists that stands outside of the record. This is the only way you will get relief from your district court if relief is even possible in your district. Remember, the court will not rule in your favor based completely on facts and evidence that is currently in the criminal record and before the court.

Let's go and get your judge good reasons to rule in your favor. This is where I commonly move for discovery and production of documents. I use this step to compel the government and the defense lawyer to cough up all the evidence that they withheld from the judges involved in the case. Remember there is nothing more embarrassing to a judge than incarcerating an *innocent* citizen. So let's not make it his or her fault by relying only on evidence that the court has in its record already. See page 108 for a standard example of a motion for discovery. File also the memorandum brief in support on page 110.

INTERROGATORIES

When you file for discovery and production of documents you must provide all proposed interrogatories. These are important tools in discovery when you are looking for additional evidence. You must be precise.

The interrogatories are exactly as they sound – an interrogation in writing. When considering what you want to know about, especially from the prosecutor, you must keep your questions in relation to some ground that you alleged in your original proceeding. If you claim ineffective assistance of counsel, keep your questions related to communications the prosecutors had with your lawyer. This may establish that your lawyer failed to investigate aspects of your case known to the government and that the government didn't present said evidence to the defense or the court, such as a witness's statement.

You will find a basic construction of an interrogatory on page 114. You will also find an example of two interrogatories I have used as an example of how to ask contradictory questions of the defense and prosecution's lawyers.

CHAPTER SEVENTEEN

MAGISTRATE'S REPORT AND RECOMMENDATION (R & R)

Thus far, I have been very candid with you, the reader, in an effort to minimize the surprises you will encounter. The issues that may arise from the appointment of a Magistrate judge are numerous. In an attempt to be brief, I'm going to hit the high points and refer you to the *Federal Habeas Corpus Practice and Procedure Manual*, chapter 18.1.

Once again, you must remember that 99.9% of *habeas* § 2255 petitions are denied. 99% of those denials are based on procedural bars and not the facts of the case. The appointment of a Magistrate judge to your case is another good sign that you have a very good lawful claim. The downside is that the district judge appointed the Magistrate judge for the sole purpose of adding more procedural requirements in an effort to deny you rather than hear the facts of your claim. Again, keep in mind that the courts and lawyers make money contingent upon you remaining in prison, this is not personal it's just business.

In all Federal Cases, the Federal Magistrate Act allows the district judge to appoint a Magistrate judge to "hear and determine" any ***non-dispositive***[15] matter that arises prior to trial. *Federal Rules of Civil Procedure*, Rule 72(a) requires a Magistrate judge act as follows:

> ***"promptly [to] conduct the required [non-dispositive] proceedings and, when appropriate, issue a written order stating the decision,"***

This rule is not used in your favor in any court I have encountered. Ordinarily, once the order is given, written or otherwise, you the petitioner and/or the government have 14 days after the entry of the order to file objections with the "district judge in the case." Upon concluding that the magistrate judge's order is erroneous or contrary to law, the district court must "modify or set aside" that portion of the order.

Just a few of my own observations:

1) I have never been involved in a case where a district court found the Magistrate's order clearly erroneous or contrary to law.
2) I have never been involved in a case where the prosecution filed an objection to a Magistrate's order. The Magistrate himself was probably at one time a prosecutor.
3) I have never been involved in a case where a Magistrate's order was in favor of a petitioner. I have personally objected to the Magistrate's order one way or another in every case for good cause.

In a *habeas* or § 2255 proceeding, the Magistrate is not authorized to decide a ***dispositive***[16]matter, only the district judge has the power to enter a final judgment. The Magistrate judge is limited to submitting, to the district judge, proposed findings of fact and recommendations for the disposition, by a judge of the court.

This step in the proceeding is where the courts separate the privileged from the poor. A privileged petitioner who can afford counsel will get his, meritorious claim beyond this point because he can pay the cost of Justice. The poor petitioner is prejudiced by the court at this step because; first, an under-privileged petitioner likely has no legal training and doesn't understand the damage of acquiescence, second, without legal knowledge he the petitioner has no idea that a district judge won't review a magistrate judge's Report and Recommendation for accuracy without an objection on file. This is a legal deception A.K.A., a loophole.

---

[15] non-dispositive – the opposite of "dispositive"

[16] dispositive – Being a deciding factor; (of fact or factor) bringing about a final determination.

The controlling doctrine: "*upon concluding that the Magistrate judge's order is clearly erroneous or contrary to law, the district court must 'modify or set aside' that portion of the order.*"

In this context, the word *must* imply a requirement. True as it may be, this does not imply that the district court "must" review the R & R to see if it is "clearly erroneous." The district court sets the stage for this action early on by refusing to appoint counsel. Early in the preceding the district court uses its discretion to determine that your case is not complex to the average attorney, therefore premised upon this opinion you're denied the counsel that would have known to object to the R & R.

Thus, based upon this circular reasoning, the district court can limit any possible relief and/or Justice to those who can afford it. Once again, take note of the demographics of your prison.

When you look around, you should discover that the profit of prison is established by the court's ability to continually deny relief to the underprivileged and minorities.

Neither in my four years of experience with the *habeas corpus* Proceedings or that of the lawyers and paralegals I'm acquainted with have any of us ever witnessed a Magistrate judge recommend that *a habeas* § 2255 petition be granted. Suffice it to say, an objection will be necessary. Simply by objecting in a timely manner, an aggrieved petitioner may secure a de novo review of any aspect of the Magistrate's report.

It's also rare, that upon objection, a district judge will agree with you, but you have secured the claim for the impending appeal. Remember, I have witnessed a court convict a 70-year-old blind man of seeing child pornography and refuse his § 2255 review leaving Justice up to the court of Appeals. So, object and do it in 14 days or less.

YOUR OBJECTION

When objecting to the R & R, you must remember that you are not dealing with the government here. When you object, you must object more precisely than when you replied to the government.

The Magistrate judge's R & R will be one of two types: one that is all bad and one that is only mostly bad. The Magistrates have a habit of including one or two aspects that are favorable to the petitioner. The reason for this is to cause the petitioner's failure in the event he objects to it as a whole.

When objecting to the R & R, read it carefully and object only to the unfavorable aspects and do it with as much precision as possible.

At the end of any objection include a conclusion that sets out that the petitioner is due the relief requested in his petition, see an example on page 129.

CHAPTER EIGHTEEN

HEARINGS

As I mentioned earlier in chapter one, you have a "due process" right to be heard. This right is protected by the Constitution, and of course, just as your rights were at pretrial - ignored by the district court. The right to be heard is your right to a full and fair hearing.

ESTABLISHING A RIGHT TO A HEARING

To establish your right to a hearing, you must present to a district court, and most likely to the court of Appeals through Mandamus, that three required conditions exist in your case:

1) Your petition must allege facts that, if proven, would entitle you to relief;
2) That your fact-based claims survive summary dismissal because their factual allegations are not "palpably incredible" or "patently frivolous or false"; and
3) Because of reasons beyond your control the factual claims were not previously the subject of a full and fair hearing. For example, if you claim your counsel provided ineffective assistance you must state how he was ineffective in order to get your claim past summary dismissal by presenting evidence. Additionally, this must be the first time this claim has been raised. These facts serve for all types of issues to warrant a mandatory hearing.

REQUESTING A HEARING

The most important issue you need to realize in a § 2255 proceeding is that you are the prosecutor and that if you do nothing, so will the court. Once you have your facts developed, and you have presented them in your petition, and have filed your reply to the government's response, you are then ready for what's called fact determination.

You are now ready for an evidentiary hearing on your first fact-based claims. That means you must ask for a hearing. The court and the government would be thankful if you remained silent here, so they could rule against you for a lack of prosecution, so let's stay on our toes.

THE MOTION

You will have to file a simple motion to request an evidentiary hearing. See page 131 for an example. You will also be filing a couple of other things to go along with it that are covered in this chapter. Remember to attach all additional evidence and/or affidavits that were not available at the time of filing your petition to this motion. File also the memorandum brief on page 133.

CHAPTER NINETEEN

YOUR RIGHT TO COUNSEL

As mentioned earlier, in non-capital *habeas* cases, Rule 8(c) of the *habeas* rules makes clear that district courts have the discretion to order "the appointment of counsel at any stage of the proceeding." This also means that the district court has the authority to deny you counsel as is most commonly the case. I do suggest that you move for appointment of counsel at every stage, so you may show the court of Appeals the lengths the district court went through to obstruct Justice.

MANDATORY APPOINTMENT

The district court has its own discretion to order discovery upon request. If discovery is ordered upon the request of an indigent petitioner, and if counsel is "necessary for effective discovery," *habeas* rule 6(a) provides that "the judge must appoint an attorney for a petitioner who qualifies to have counsel appointed."

The right to the appointment of counsel becomes airtight once the court orders an evidentiary hearing.

CHAPTER TWENTY

PREPARING FOR HEARING

You won't find anything on this in the chapters to follow in any publication I have ever reviewed. All that follows are my personal opinions based on the experiences of other *habeas corpus* practitioners and myself.

YOUR NOTES

You will quickly discover, by speaking with others that your record of filings is available to you upon request when you get to court. The most critical things, however, won't be filed. If you remember reading about the importance of notes earlier, then it won't be hard to realize how important even your own notes might become.

I suggest that you organize your notes by category and file them with the court as a memorandum in support. Remember, you must serve the government with this document so don't include anything you want to surprise them with. It's helpful at this point to include any American Bars Association Function Standards you intend to use.

Anything you wish to surprise them with you want to either send it to someone who will bring it to court for you or memorize it.

MEETING YOUR LAWYER

This is where the sifting begins. Your lawyer, in most cases, will attempt to convince you to withdraw your claim, so *don't*.

It's clear, by your being in a holding facility, that your claim is serious enough to bring you to court. Lawyers who are prosecution friendly will at this point threaten you to withdraw your claim by telling you that you will get more time. This is not true. Unless you have charges dropped in your indictment or you have additional conduct you could be charged with, you cannot be given more time unless you agree to it, so *don't*.

WHAT TO EXPECT

A proceeding under 28 U.S.C. § 2255 is often a federal prisoner's last opportunity to ensure that the process by which he is convicted and/or sentenced accords with Federal Law. In all cases, and especially in Capital Cases, court appointed counsel bears the responsibility of ensuring that all reasonable available avenues of legal redress are considered. This responsibility requires counsel not only to explore thoroughly the legal basis for the petitioner's claims, but also to take full advantage of the capacity of Federal proceedings to develop the factual basis for the claim.

Except for a few extraordinary cases, this responsibility will not have been done until after you meet your new attorney the facts are that the court didn't pay this attorney enough to drive to the jail today, much less review your case. Therefore, you must know what to expect and demand your expectations and your rights.

Perhaps I should advise you that not all attorneys are bad, but the numbers, I can guarantee you, are above 80%. That said, try not to be prejudice, you don't want to get off on the wrong foot if you happen to get one of the 20 out of 100 that is a good one.

Meeting Your Attorney

When you meet your lawyer, this will probably be in the late evening, introduce yourself and wait for him or her to start the conversation. In the event he or she begins with the common "withdraw the claim" speech, just listen to what he or she has to say.

Once they are finished, inform him or her that you would like that advice in writing. I also ask him or her for a copy of his or her bar license and malpractice insurance certificate.

When he or she is done yelling and performing all other theatrics, inform your counsel of your rights and his or her liabilities if he or she chooses to provide ineffective assistance of counsel during the post-conviction stage. See *Federal Habeas Corpus Practice and Procedure Manual*, chapter 11(e).

When You Get Counsel to Court

This is where you discover if your lawyer understands you or not. In many cases I have discovered that appointed counsel will talk a good game until he or she gets you into court. Often counsel will become silent when he or she gets you before the judge. I believe, this is a planned tactic that is commonly conducted by the court, the government, and defense counsel.

When this happens, be prepared to speak your mind. The judge will often call upon the defense to present its claim and your lawyer will not speak at all or speak nonsense. Most often the court will simply say "anything from the defense?" At this point, if you say nothing you will lose for failing to make a claim.

If this happens, be BOLD. Don't hesitate to inform the judge that:

> "The petition that was filed contains meritorious claims that warrant relief."
>
> "Judge, it's my opinion that my counsel in this matter is purposely providing ineffective assistance, and I object."

CHAPTER TWENTY-ONE

The Power of an Objection

If warranted, you just made your first objection in a court of law; this is your right to do so. As you may recall, in an earlier chapter, due process is the right to be heard, so speak up.

There are two times to speak the loudest:

1) When the government lies, and they will, this also includes when your government hired defense lawyer does it and,

2) When you don't understand what's being said. I always ask for a plain English hearing which gives me the right to object when something is said I don't understand.

Words of Art

You will discover that the judge and both lawyers will continue to use words you don't understand such as "ex-post-facto." If you speak English only, this phrase would sound strange to you because it's not English, so, OBJECT.

The record is an important tool for your appeal. Just as you want to get the truth on the record for your use, the judge and the lawyers want to get an alternative to the truth on the record and say you agreed by not objecting to it.

Words of art are the court's favorite tool to get your acquiescence. Most people won't speak up when they don't understand due to the fear of seeming ignorant. The court uses this fear coupled with French and Latin in an effort to make the record against you, so *object.*

Rush to Judgment

When you object, you will get a variety of responses in court. The lawyers will be shocked that you have become so bold and often remain silent. Now your real enemy will become known, the judge. He or she will come alive and attempt to stop you from objecting by stating, "That's your lawyer's job." Simply reply, that your "attorney is not acting in your best interests."

Be prepared for three different responses from the judge:

1) Over-ruled, this one is good for you because your claim is preserved for appeal.

2) Is, "noted," this one is bad, you must at this very moment tell the Judge that, "I wish to preserve this issue for appeal your Honor." This statement puts the Judge on notice that you already realize that the hearing is a farce.

3) And the worst for last, no response at all. When the Judge allows the circus to continue after you object, you must continue to object. In most cases the Judge will threaten you with contempt of court or obstruction of justice. Don't be afraid of "the man behind the curtain" this is a hollow threat. When you hear "contempt" or "obstruction" you simply ask the judge "am I being rushed to judgment judge?" As the charade continues, you must ask this question three times, I've never seen a case that went past two, once you have asked this question three times, simply tell the court, "clearly I'm not going to be allowed to be a part of this proceeding." Take your seat and be silent. When the judge asks if there will be anything else at the end of the hearing, politely stand and state that "I am giving a verbal Notice of Appeal."

Objections Generally

I can't think of any aspect of a court proceeding that is more difficult to master that the art of objecting properly. An objection properly made can cripple the government's case. When the government brings up subjects that don't matter or subjects that hurt your reputation, their efforts can often be derailed by a carefully placed objection.

Also, remember that making repeated and/or unnecessary objections will irritate the judge. Objections should be used to give pause to a government witness. Remember the governments witnesses are often laymen at law and will likely say something that is prejudicial and/or irrelevant. Watch for things about feelings or repeating what they heard. Both are objectionable and may plant a favorable seed of doubt in the judge's mind. You may study objections in any law library, see "Criminal Defense Techniques."

CHAPTER TWENTY-TWO

Notice of Summary Disposition

One last thing: I have shared with you as many events as possible that occur regularly in a § 2255 proceeding. However, there are some that occur infrequently. A Notice of Summary Disposition is one of those. This one has only happened once to my knowledge and that's amongst about 25 *habeas* practitioners I share notes with.

A "Notice of Summary Disposition" is an order from a district judge. It's very similar to a Magistrate's R & R except this one will be final with no recourse at appeal. You must file a brief in opposition to this order if you want to appeal.

When preparing your brief in opposition, you must object and/or oppose every issue the judge raises. Most importantly, you must identify any issues the court didn't address in its order.

If you read Rule 4, you will also find that the time for Summary Disposition was before briefing. Meaning that if the court wishes to Summarily Dispose of your petition based upon issues available in the record before briefing, it cannot.

If you have found yourself in this or any similar situation, then you know my frustration. Everything you have been through is merely a dogmatic procedure meant to minimize your appealable issues. You must oppose these actions, see page 138.

You must remember, the first lines of § 2255. "...a court enacted by an Act of Congress ...," the court you are in is the same Article One court that violated your rights in the first place. This court has no inclination to reach for justice or free the *innocent*. This court is *only* interested in securing its conviction quotas and inflating their Christmas Bonus. In the likely event you are denied by the district, you will also be denied any right to appeal. This is not the end of it. Please remember that district courts don't reverse convictions for poor or undereducated petitioners unless ordered to do so by the court of Appeals.

Although I'm not going through the appeals process in this publication, I am including one of the required filings in the miscellaneous section. You *must* start by filing for a Notice of Appeal. You will find this filing on page 152.

Appendix

The following motions and Memorandum Briefs are the same filings that I use in the courts. However, as discussed in earlier chapters, you *must* personalize these filings to your case. If you will refer to chapter Two, you will find the instructions on personalizing if you don't remember.

AO 243 (Rev. 01/15) Page 1

Motion to Vacate, Set Aside, or Correct a Sentence
By a Person in Federal Custody

(Motion Under 28 U.S.C. § 2255)

Instructions

1. To use this form, you must be a person who is serving a sentence under a judgment against you in a federal court. You are asking for relief from the conviction or the sentence. This form is your motion for relief.
2. You must file the form in the United States district court that entered the judgment that you are challenging. If you want to challenge a federal judgment that imposed a sentence to be served in the future, you should file the motion in the federal court that entered that judgment.
3. Make sure the form is typed or neatly written.
4. You must tell the truth and sign the form. If you make a false statement of a material fact, you may be prosecuted for perjury.
5. Answer all the questions. You do not need to cite law. You may submit additional pages if necessary. If you do not fill out the form properly, you will be asked to submit additional or correct information. If you want to submit a brief or arguments, you must submit them in a separate memorandum.
6. If you cannot pay for the costs of this motion (such as costs for an attorney or transcripts), you may ask to proceed *in forma pauperis* (as a poor person). To do that, you must fill out the last page of this form. Also, you must submit a certificate signed by an officer at the institution where you are confined showing the amount of money that the institution is holding for you.
7. In this motion, you may challenge the judgment entered by only one court. If you want to challenge a judgment entered by a different judge or division (either in the same district or in a different district), you must file a separate motion.
8. When you have completed the form, send the original and ____ copies to the Clerk of the United States District Court at this address:

   Clerk, United States District Court for
   Address
   City, State Zip Code

   If you want a file-stamped copy of the petition, you must enclose an additional copy of the petition and ask the court to file-stamp it and return it to you.
9. **<u>CAUTION:</u> You must include in this motion all the grounds for relief from the conviction or sentence that you challenge. And you must state the facts that support each ground. If you fail to set forth all the grounds in this motion, you may be barred from presenting additional grounds at a later date.**
10. **<u>CAPITAL CASES:</u> If you are under a sentence of death, you are entitled to the assistance of counsel and should request the appointment of counsel.**

AO 243 (Rev. 01/15) Page 2

MOTION UNDER 28 U.S.C. § 2255 TO VACATE, SET ASIDE, OR CORRECT
SENTENCE BY A PERSON IN FEDERAL CUSTODY

United States District Court	District	
Name *(under which you were convicted)*:		Docket or Case No.:
Place of Confinement:	Prisoner No.:	
UNITED STATES OF AMERICA	V.	Movant *(include name under which convicted)*

MOTION

1. (a) Name and location of court which entered the judgment of conviction you are challenging: ______

(b) Criminal docket or case number (if you know): ______

2. (a) Date of the judgment of conviction (if you know): ______
(b) Date of sentencing: ______

3. Length of sentence: ______

4. Nature of crime (all counts): ______

5. (a) What was your plea? (Check one)
(1) Not guilty ☐ (2) Guilty ☐ (3) Nolo contendere (no contest) ☐

(b) If you entered a guilty plea to one count or indictment, and a not guilty plea to another count or what did you plead guilty to and what did you plead not guilty to? ______

6. If you went to trial, what kind of trial did you have? (Check one) Jury ☐ Judge only ☐

7. Did you testify at a pretrial hearing, trial, or post-trial hearing? Yes ☐ No ☐

8. Did you appeal from the judgment of conviction? Yes ☐ No ☐

9. If you did appeal, answer the following:
   (a) Name of court: ______
   (b) Docket or case number (if you know): ______
   (c) Result: ______
   (d) Date of result (if you know): ______
   (e) Citation to the case (if you know): ______
   (f) Grounds raised: ______

   (g) Did you file a petition for certiorari in the United States Supreme Court? Yes ☐ No ☐
      If "Yes," answer the following:
      (1) Docket or case number (if you know): ______
      (2) Result: ______
      (3) Date of result (if you know): ______
      (4) Citation to the case (if you know): ______
      (5) Grounds raised: ______

10. Other than the direct appeals listed above, have you previously filed any other motions, petitions, or applications, concerning this judgment of conviction in any court?
    Yes ☐ No ☐

11. If your answer to Question 10 was "Yes," give the following information:
    (a) (1) Name of court: ______
        (2) Docket or case number (if you know): ______
        (3) Date of filing (if you know): ______
        (4) Nature of the proceeding: ______
        (5) Grounds raised: ______

(6) Did you receive a hearing where evidence was given on your motion, petition, or application?

Yes ☐ No ☐

(7) Result:

(8) Date of result (if you know):

(b) If you filed any second motion, petition, or application, give the same information:

(1) Name of court:

(2) Docket of case number (if you know):

(3) Date of filing (if you know):

(4) Nature of the proceeding:

(5) Grounds raised:

(6) Did you receive a hearing where evidence was given on your motion, petition, or application?

Yes ☐ No ☐

(7) Result:

(8) Date of result (if you know):

(c) Did you appeal to a federal appellate court having jurisdiction over the action taken on your motion, petition, or application?

(1) First petition: Yes ☐ No ☐

(2) Second petition: Yes ☐ No ☐

(d) If you did not appeal from the action on any motion, petition, or application, explain briefly why you did not:

12. For this motion, state every ground on which you claim that you are being held in violation of the Constitution, laws, or treaties of the United States. Attach additional pages if you have more than four grounds. State the facts supporting each ground.

AO 243 (Rev. 01/15) Page 5

GROUND ONE: ________________________________

(a) Supporting facts (Do not argue or cite law. Just state the specific facts that support your claim.):

(b) **Direct Appeal of Ground One:**

(1) If you appealed from the judgment of conviction, did you raise this issue?

Yes ☐ No ☐

(2) If you did not raise this issue in your direct appeal, explain why: ________________

(c) **Post-Conviction Proceedings:**

(1) Did you raise this issue in any post-conviction motion, petition, or application?

Yes ☐ No ☐

(2) If you answer to Question (c)(1) is "Yes," state:

Type of motion or petition: ________________

Name and location of the court where the motion or petition was filed: ________________

Docket or case number (if you know): ________________

Date of the court's decision: ________________

Result (attach a copy of the court's opinion or order, if available): ________________

(3) Did you receive a hearing on your motion, petition, or application?

Yes No

(4) Did you appeal from the denial of your motion, petition, or application?

Yes ☐ No ☐

(5) If your answer to Question (c)(4) is "Yes," did you raise the issue in the appeal?

Yes ☐ No ☐

(6) If your answer to Question (c)(4) is "Yes," state:

Name and location of the court where the appeal was filed:

Docket or case number (if you know):

Date of the court's decision:

Result (attach a copy of the court's opinion or order, if available):

(7) If your answer to Question (c)(4) or Question (c)(5) is "No," explain why you did not appeal or raise this issue:

GROUND TWO:

(a) Supporting facts (Do not argue or cite law. Just state the specific facts that support your claim.):

(b) **Direct Appeal of Ground Two:**

(1) If you appealed from the judgment of conviction, did you raise this issue?

Yes ☐ No ☐

(2) If you did not raise this issue in your direct appeal, explain why:

(c) **Post-Conviction Proceedings:**

(1) Did you raise this issue in any post-conviction motion, petition, or application?

Yes ☐ No ☐

(2) If you answer to Question (c)(1) is "Yes," state:

Type of motion or petition: __________

Name and location of the court where the motion or petition was filed: __________

____

Docket or case number (if you know): __________

Date of the court's decision: __________

Result (attach a copy of the court's opinion or order, if available): __________

____

____

(3) Did you receive a hearing on your motion, petition, or application?

Yes ☐ No ☐

(4) Did you appeal from the denial of your motion, petition, or application?

Yes ☐ No ☐

(5) If your answer to Question (c)(4) is "Yes," did you raise the issue in the appeal?

Yes ☐ No ☐

(6) If your answer to Question (c)(4) is "Yes," state:

Name and location of the court where the appeal was filed: __________

____

Docket or case number (if you know): __________

Date of the court's decision: __________

Result (attach a copy of the court's opinion or order, if available): __________

____

____

(7) If your answer to Question (c)(4) or Question (c)(5) is "No," explain why you did not appeal or raise this issue: __________

____

____

____

____

____

____

GROUND THREE: __________

____

(a) Supporting facts (Do not argue or cite law. Just state the specific facts that support your claim.):

____

____

____

____

____

(b) **Direct Appeal of Ground Three:**

(1) If you appealed from the judgment of conviction, did you raise this issue?

Yes ☐ No ☐

(2) If you did not raise this issue in your direct appeal, explain why:

(c) **Post-Conviction Proceedings:**

(1) Did you raise this issue in any post-conviction motion, petition, or application?

Yes ☐ No ☐

(2) If you answer to Question (c)(1) is "Yes," state:

Type of motion or petition:

Name and location of the court where the motion or petition was filed:

Docket or case number (if you know):

Date of the court's decision:

Result (attach a copy of the court's opinion or order, if available):

(3) Did you receive a hearing on your motion, petition, or application?

Yes ☐ No ☐

(4) Did you appeal from the denial of your motion, petition, or application?

Yes ☐ No ☐

(5) If your answer to Question (c)(4) is "Yes," did you raise the issue in the appeal?

Yes ☐ No ☐

(6) If your answer to Question (c)(4) is "Yes," state:

Name and location of the court where the appeal was filed:

Docket or case number (if you know):

Date of the court's decision:

Result (attach a copy of the court's opinion or order, if available):

(7) If your answer to Question (c)(4) or Question (c)(5) is "No," explain why you did not appeal or raise this issue:

GROUND FOUR:

(a) Supporting facts (Do not argue or cite law. Just state the specific facts that support your claim.):

(b) **Direct Appeal of Ground Four:**

(1) If you appealed from the judgment of conviction, did you raise this issue?

Yes ☐ No ☐

(2) If you did not raise this issue in your direct appeal, explain why:

(c) **Post-Conviction Proceedings:**

(1) Did you raise this issue in any post-conviction motion, petition, or application?

Yes ☐ No ☐

(2) If you answer to Question (c)(1) is "Yes," state:

Type of motion or petition:

Name and location of the court where the motion or petition was filed:

Docket or case number (if you know):

Date of the court's decision:

Result (attach a copy of the court's opinion or order, if available):

(3) Did you receive a hearing on your motion, petition, or application?

Yes ☐ No ☐

(4) Did you appeal from the denial of your motion, petition, or application?

Yes ☐ No ☐

(5) If your answer to Question (c)(4) is "Yes," did you raise the issue in the appeal?

Yes ☐ No ☐

(6) If your answer to Question (c)(4) is "Yes," state:

Name and location of the court where the appeal was filed:

Docket or case number (if you know):

Date of the court's decision:

Result (attach a copy of the court's opinion or order, if available):

(7) If your answer to Question (c)(4) or Question (c)(5) is "No," explain why you did not appeal or raise this issue:

13. Is there any ground in this motion that you have not previously presented in some federal court? If so, which ground or grounds have not been presented, and state your reasons for not presenting them:

14. Do you have any motion, petition, or appeal now pending (filed and not decided yet) in any court for the you are challenging? Yes ☐ No ☐

If "Yes," state the name and location of the court, the docket or case number, the type of proceeding, and the issues raised.

AO 243 (Rev. 01/15) Page 11

15. Give the name and address, if known, of each attorney who represented you in the following stages of the you are challenging:

(a) At the preliminary hearing: ______________________________

____

(b) At the arraignment and plea: ______________________________

____

(c) At the trial: ______________________________

____

(d) At sentencing: ______________________________

____

(e) On appeal: ______________________________

____

(f) In any post-conviction proceeding: ______________________________

____

(g) On appeal from any ruling against you in a post-conviction proceeding: ______________________________

____

____

16. Were you sentenced on more than one court of an indictment, or on more than one indictment, in the same court and at the same time? Yes ☐ No ☐

17. Do you have any future sentence to serve after you complete the sentence for the judgment that you are challenging? Yes ☐ No ☐

(a) If so, give name and location of court that imposed the other sentence you will serve in the future:

____

____

(b) Give the date the other sentence was imposed: ______________________________

(c) Give the length of the other sentence: ______________________________

(d) Have you filed, or do you plan to file, any motion, petition, or application that challenges the judgment or sentence to be served in the future? Yes ☐ No ☐

18. TIMELINESS OF MOTION: If your judgment of conviction became final over one year ago, you must explain why the one-year statute of limitations as contained in 28 U.S.C. § 2255 does not bar your motion.*

____

____

____

____

____

____

____

____

* The Antiterrorism and Effective Death Penalty Act of 1996 ("AEDPA") as contained in 28 U.S.C. § 2255, paragraph 6, provides in part that:

A one-year period of limitation shall apply to a motion under this section. The limitation period shall run from the latest of –

(1) the date on which the judgment of conviction became final;

(2) the date on which the impediment to making a motion created by governmental action in violation of the Constitution or laws of the United States is removed, if the movant was prevented from making such a motion by such governmental action;

(3) the date on which the right asserted was initially recognized by the Supreme Court, if that right has been newly recognized by the Supreme Court and made retroactively applicable to cases on collateral review; or

(4) the date on which the facts supporting the claim or claims presented could have been discovered through the exercise of due diligence.

AO 243 (Rev. 01/15) Page 13

Therefore, movant asks that the Court grant the following relief: ______________________________

____

____

or any other relief to which movant may be entitled.

____
Signature of Attorney (if any)

I declare (or certify, verify, or state) under penalty of perjury that the foregoing is true and correct and that this Motion under 28 U.S.C. § 2255 was placed in the prison mailing system on ______________________________.
(month, date, year)

Executed (signed) on ______________________________ (date)

____
Signature of Movant

If the person signing is not movant, state relationship to movant and explain why movant is not signing this motion.

____

____

____

CASE AFFIDAVITS

When writing a Case Affidavit, it is important to construct it as a motion in all aspects. In this Section, you will find two (2) Case Affidavits actually used in a *habeas* Case in the Northern district of Alabama. The facts in these Affidavits are unrebutted in the court and as such are now law of the case.

There are three essential elements to a Case Affidavit:

1) Case caption.
2) The very first unnumbered paragraph, To WIT:
3) "I, [YOUR NAME], depose and state that the following FACTS are True and Correct under penalty of perjury, TO WIT:"
4) The very last unnumbered paragraph, TO WIT:

   "I, [YOUR NAME], declare under penalty of perjury, pursuant 28 U.S.C. § 1746, that the above stated FACTS are True and Correct."

UNITED STATES DISTRICT COURT

IN THE [REDACTED] DISTRICT of [REDACTED]

[REDACTED] DIVISION

UNITED STATES OF AMERICA, Respondent vs. KELLY PATRICK RIGGS Petitioner	CASE NO(S): [REDACTED]

AFFIDAVIT OF KELLY PATRICK RIGGS [PETITIONER]

I, KELLY PATRICK RIGGS, depose and state that the following FACTS are True and Correct under penalty of perjury, TO WIT:

1) I, Kelly Patrick Riggs, state that on October 18, 2013, the United States Magistrate Judge issued an ORDER to terminate the Federal Public Defender's Office as to its representation in my criminal case. New Counsel was needed following my presentment of evidence that, [redacted] and [redacted] were involved in a scheme to coerce me to plea guilty; that [redacted] was aware of this scheme and discussed with me that he would take over my case if I dropped my contentions against [redacted]; and [redacted] providing my name and case information to Mexican Cartel associates after becoming aware of a letter I wrote concerning my testimony against the Cartel involving a shipment of "ICE" into the Northern District of Alabama.

2) I, Kelly Patrick Riggs, state that on October 30, 2013, [redacted] filed Notice of Appearance into the record of my criminal case after being appointed by the Court.

3) I, Kelly Patrick Riggs, state that I advised Court Appointed Counsel [redacted] that I had filed a Motion to Withdraw the coerced guilty plea; that I gave him a list of alibi witnesses, the source of an exculpatory video, the source of a video of impeaching value, and a detailed account of the Conflict of Interest between Court appointed Counsel [redacted] and myself due to his other client murdering [redacted].

4) I, Kelly Patrick Riggs, state that I advised Court appointed Counsel [redacted], that NO LESS than my name was forwarded to the Mexican Cartel from the information obtained by the Federal Public Defender's Office, Northern District of Alabama, by and through Attorney [redacted].

5) I, Kelly Patrick Riggs, state that I advised Court appointed Counsel, [redacted], that previous Counsel, [redacted], had refused to investigate the case for possible defenses, refused to take alibi witness statements, and/or refused to challenge the Government's evidence and witnesses in any way.

6) I, Kelly Patrick Riggs, state that I advised Court appointed Counsel, [redacted], that previous Counsel, [redacted], filed for a waiver of Speedy Trial after the time for Speedy Trial had expired, and that I was under the understanding that this was required to challenge a violation of Speedy Trial.

7) I, Kelly Patrick Riggs, state that I advised Court appointed Counsel, [redacted], .that previous Counsel [redacted], refused to interview alibi witnesses, refused to subpoena video evidence, refused to investigate my criminal case, and/or refused to expose the Government's case to the crucible of Adversarial Testing.

8) I, Kelly Patrick Riggs, state that I advised Court appointed Counsel that the subject matter jurisdiction was in question in this case and that the Court refused to provide to me a Bill of Particulars.

9) I, Kelly Patrick Riggs, state that on December 20, 2013, the Court did set out in the record that I was deprived of my right to compel witnesses, [redacted],. and/or, order his presence for testing on my behalf due to Court appointed Counsel [redacted], failure to file motions on a timely basis.

10) I, Kelly Patrick Riggs, state that on December 20, 2013, Court appointed Counsel was present in the courtroom when, previous Counsel, [redacted], stated that he filed a Notice of Alibi; [redacted] advised a guilty plea in contradiction to SOLID DEFENSE and ACTUAL INNOCENCE; [redacted] admitted she failed to issue subpoenas to alibi witnesses; [redacted] makes personal attack to alibi witness credibility; [redacted] acknowledges that [redacted] had possession and presented to a United States Magistrate Judge, falsified Federal Documents to hamper my defense; and many other issues still not investigated to this day.

11) I, Kelly Patrick Riggs, state that on April 22, 2014, Court appointed Counsel was present in the courtroom when Judge [redacted] stated that: "Any problems that may have existed with prior Counsel and your disagreement with them have been cured by [redacted] representation of you."

12) I, Kelly Patrick Riggs, state that on April 22, 2013, Court appointed Counsel was present in the courtroom when I announced that I intended to appeal the district court conviction based upon many issues to include and not limited to the obvious ineffectiveness of multiple Court appointed Counsel, and the many other objections that were observed by [redacted], "There are plenty objections and they are all through this docket and you may have a very good time at the Eleventh Circuit,"

13) I, Kelly Patrick Riggs, state that on September 8, 2014, Court appointed Counsel, [redacted], filed with the Court of Appeals his "Ander's Brief" and Motion to Withdraw based on his belief that there is not "any issue of arguable merit."

14) I, Kelly Patrick Riggs, state that on September 23, 2014, I submitted my own Appeals Brief, in necessity, which raised Ineffective Assistance of Court appointed Counsel, inter alia.

15) I, Kelly Patrick Riggs, state that on January 29, 2015, Court appointed Counsel, [redacted], submitted a letter to the Alabama State BAR that CLEARLY establishes a Conflict of Interest between his, [redacted], understanding of his obligation in my case, and the expectations that I had of Trial Counsel's obligations to investigate possible defenses in a criminal case. Court appointed Counsel stated in his letter that: "My initial role in his defense was to litigate his *pro se* Motion to Set Aside his guilty plea,

I,Kelly Patrick Riggs, declare, under penalty of perjury, pursuant to 28 U.S.C. § 1746, that the above stated FACTS are True and Correct,

Executed on This 10th Day of November 2015,

Respectfully Submitted,

[REDACTED]

Kelly Patrick Riggs, *PRO SE*
Reg # [redacted]

Federal Correctional Institution
Mailing Address
City, State and Zip Code

UNITED STATES DISTRICT COURT

IN THE [REDACTED] DISTRICT of [REDACTED]

[REDACTED] DIVISION

UNITED STATES OF AMERICA, Respondent vs. KELLY PATRICK RIGGS Petitioner	CASE NO(S): [REDACTED]

AFFIDAVIT OF KELLY PATRICK RIGGS [PETITIONER]

I, KELLY PATRICK RIGGS, depose and state that the following FACTS are True and Correct under penalty of perjury TO WIT:

1) I, Kelly Patrick Riggs, state that on or about April 22, 2014, and prior to final judgment in the criminal case that I declared to the District Court and objected to the United States District Court's "RUSH TO JUDGMENT" in this case.

2) I, Kelly Patrick Riggs, state that on September 5, 2013, that I was in a hearing before Magistrate Judge [redacted], to determine the Conflict of Interest, between Court appointed Counsel and myself. At said hearing and in preparation for trial, I declared that there existed a Conflict of Interest between Court appointed Counsel and myself concerning my reports against [redacted] concerning the murder of [redacted]. I declared a conflict due to [redacted] being a client of Court appointed Counsel, [redacted] also. [Redacted] representation of me was affected by his concerns for his other client. [Redacted], during the hearing, declared that there was no conflict, which in itself is CLEARLY in conflict with my position and/or contention. The Court declared that there was no conflict without further investigation.

3) I, Kelly Patrick Riggs, state that on September 5, 2013, directly after the hearing, I was compelled by Court appointed Counsel [redacted] to give a detailed statement against his client [redacted] to United States Duty Marshal [redacted], concerning threats against Court appointed Counsel and the murder of [redacted].

4) I, Kelly Patrick Riggs, state that on September 5, 2013, and shortly after being returned to County Jail, I was placed back in General Population and confronted by [redacted], who confronted me about providing a statement to the Government. It was at that point that he, [redacted], reminded me that he and/or a gang known as the "Piru" could and would kill my wife and children.

5) I, Kelly Patrick Riggs, state that on September 5, 2013, that I called Court appointed Counsel, on the jailhouse phone, and stated to him that I would have to do what was best for everyone involved.

6) I, Kelly Patrick Riggs, state that on September 5, 2013, at approximately 8:30 PM, Court appointed Counsel [redacted] arrived at the County Jail at which time we discussed in length the protection provided by the U.S. Marshal's Service for my family and myself in exchange for the statement that I provided and how we, Counsel and I, were going to conduct the appeal after the threat of harm had been averted.

7) I, Kelly Patrick Riggs, state that on September 5, 2013, we (Counsel and I) completed and/or

authenticated the Plea Agreement he presented in such haste that we failed to complete the document as required to be done by its own

8) I, Kelly Patrick Riggs, state that on September 6, 2013, at approximately 2:00 PM, roughly 18 hours later, that I was rushed into a hearing, for the Court to accept the guilty plea, in such haste that no one, not the Judge, not either Lawyer, and/or myself detected that the Plea Agreement was not completed properly. (Not initialed on every page).

I, Kelly Patrick Riggs, declare under penalty of perjury, pursuant to 28 U.S.C. § 1746, that the above stated FACTS are True and Correct.

Executed on This 10th Day of November 2015.

Respectfully Submitted,

[REDACTED]

Kelly Patrick Riggs, *PRO SE*
Reg # [redacted]

Federal Correctional Institution
Mailing Address
City, State and Zip Code

KELLY PATRICK RIGGS

UNITED STATES DISTRICT COURT

IN THE [YOUR DISTRICT] DISTRICT of [YOUR STATE]

[REDACTED] DIVISION

[YOUR NAME], vs. UNITED STATES OF AMERICA	CASE NO(S): [LEAVE BLANK] [YOUR CRIMINAL CASE NO.]

PETITIONER'S MOTION FOR ISSUANCE OFSHOW CAUSE ORDER

COMES NOW the Petitioner, [YOUR NAME] in *PRO SE*, in necessity, and hereby MOVES this Court to ISSUE an ORDER requiring the Government to Show Cause as to why the Petitioner's § 2255 motion should not be granted, pursuant to Rules governing § 2255, Rule 4. In support, the Petitioner shows the Court the following:

1) On or about, [DATE OF YOUR § 2255 MOTION], the Petitioner filed a detailed 28 U.S.C. § 2255 motion with exhibits.

2) Rules governing 28 U.S.C. § 2255 proceedings in the United States District Courts, Rule 4(b) states in part:

> "If the motion is not dismissed, the Judge MUST order the United States Attorney to file an answer ..." (Emphasis added).

WHEREFORE NOW, above premises considered, the Petitioner hereby MOVES this Court to ISSUE a Show Cause Order in compliance with Rule 4(b)'s mandatory language.

Done This [DATE] Day of [Month], [YEAR]

Respectfully Submitted,

[YOUR SIGNATURE]

____

[YOUR NAME], *PRO SE*
Reg # [YOUR REG. NO.]
[YOUR FACILITY]
[THE FACILITY'S ADDRESS]

KELLY PATRICK RIGGS

APPEAL NO.:

UNITED STATES COURT OF APPEALS
IN THE [YOUR CIRCUIT] CIRCUIT

IN RE:
[YOUR NAME]
[PRESENTLY INCARCERATED]

ON PETITION FOR A WRIT OF MANDAMUS
TO THE UNITED STATES DISTRICT COURT,
[YOUR DISTRICT] DISTRICT OF [YOUR STATE]
CASE NO. : [YOUR CIVIL CASE NO.]

PETITION FOR WRIT OF MANDAMUS

[YOUR NAME]
in *PRO SE*
Reg # [YOUR REG. NO.]
[YOUR CORRECTIONAL FACILITY]
[THE FACILITY ADDRESS]

UNITED STATES DISTRICT COURT

IN THE [YOUR CIRCUIT] CIRCUIT

[YOUR NAME] APPELLANT vs. UNITED STATES OF AMERICA APPELLEE	Appeals No.: (Appealed from the [YOUR DISTRICT] District of [YOUR STATE]) [YOUR CRIMINAL AND CIVIL CASE NO(s)]

CERTIFICATE OF INTERESTED PERSONS

AND CORPORATE DISCLOSURE STATEMENT

Pursuant to [YOUR CIRCUIT] circuit Rule 26.1, counsel for Appellant, [YOUR NAME], certifies that the following persons may have an interest in the outcome of this case:

1. [YOUR NAME]
2. [YOUR DISTRICT COURT JUDGE]
3. [YOUR MAGISTRATE JUDGE]
4. [YOUR DEFENSE ATTORNEY]
5. [THE ASSISTANT UNITED STATES ATTORNEY ON YOUR CASE]
6. [ANY OTHER DEFENSE ATTORNEYS]
7. [ANY OTHER ASSISTANT UNITED STATES ATTORNEYS]
8. [AND SO ON ...]

KELLY PATRICK RIGGS

UNITED STATES COURT OF APPEALS
IN THE [YOUR CIRCUIT] CIRCUIT

IN RE:
[YOUR NAME]
PETITIONER

PETITION FOR A WRIT OF MANDAMUS

COMES NOW the Petitioner, [YOUR NAME] in *PRO SE*, in necessity, and hereby MOVES this Court to ISSUE a Writ of Mandamus, ordering the United States District Court, in the [YOUR DISTRICT] District of [YOUR STATE] to rule and/or pass judgment in his § 2255 proceeding, case no.: [YOUR CASE NO.]. The Petitioner hereby avers that judgment is due pursuant to Law and Rule provided herein.

In support, the Petitioner shows the Court the following:

I.

JURISDICTIONAL STATEMENT

The jurisdiction of this Court is invoked pursuant to the Federal Rules of Appellate Procedure, Rule 21; Rules governing § 2255 proceedings, Rule 8(c); the All Writs Act, 28 U.S.C. § 1651; and the Constitution of the United States GUARANTEE of a Speedy Trial. The Petitioner avers that he is currently in Federal custody and filing in *pro se* due to financial disability, who therefore, requests that this Court liberally construe his pleadings in light of *Haines v. Kerner*, 404 U.S. 519, 521 (1972).

II.

STATEMENT OF THE CASE

> NOTE: This section is reserved to particularize The events of your case. Be specific and concise. Below is an example.

1) On or about [DATE], the Petitioner filed a meritorious 28 U.S.C. § 2255 motion, in the United States District Court, in the [YOUR DISTRICT] District of Alabama.
2) On or about [DATE], the Petitioner filed a motion requesting the Court to ISSUE a SHOW CAUSE ORDER.
3) Herenow, the Petitioner MOVES this Honorable Court to intervene, and/or ORDER the District Court to ISSUE a SHOW CAUSE ORDER, in compliance with Rules governing § 2255, Rule (b).

III.

ISSUES PRESENTED

4) The Petitioner hereby avers that the District Court abuses its discretion and/or commits PLAIN ERROR by flouting the Federal Habeas Rules and depriving a citizen of his Constitutional Rights to *habeas corpus* and to access the Court.

IV.

FACTS OF THE CASE

[NOTE: the following are FACTS that were used in an actual case. This is ONLY an example]

5) The Petitioner has repeatedly presented the record of the Court's that CLEARLY show that his efforts as a Confidential Informant have collided with CORRUPT PUBLIC OFFICIALS included in MAJOR DRUG TRAFFICKING OFFENSES in and around the Northern District of Alabama, and elsewhere.

6) The Petitioner has shown evidence that the Police Department in Hoover Alabama abducted him while he was shopping for insurance after he provided information to the FBI affecting their local prosecutor.

7) The Petitioner has shown that the United States Chief District Judge, [REDACTED] has and continues to OBSTRUCT JUSTICE by *CONCEALING* evidence in [REDACTED'S] murder.

8) The Petitioner is herenow providing evidence that Court Officers have inadvertently facilitated [REDACTED'S] murder by OBSTRUCTING JUSTICE.

9) The Petitioner has shown that the Court convicted him without SUBJECT-MATTER JURISDICTION.

V.

REASONS WHY THE WRIT SHOULD BE ISSUED

10) The Petitioner has NO other remedy of law in which to compel the District Court to rule on his § 2255 motion. The District Court took JUDICIAL NOTICE of [REDACTED'S] testimony in which he testified that he gave NOTICE OF ALIBI and subpoenaed 10 (ten) witnesses. An Alibi Defense is NOT consistent with guilt; therefore, the Writ of *habeas corpus* is due. The District Court issued an ORDER regarding Summary Disposition on March 17, 2016. The Petitioner requested judgment on August 8, 2016. The Fifth Circuit Court of Appeals in *United States v. Samples*, 897 F. 2d 193, 195 (5th Cir. 1990) held that:

> "In rare instances involving lengthy delays ... Appellate Courts should enforce Rule 8(c)'s Speedy-Trial Policy by means of Mandamus under the All Writs Act, 28 U.S.C. § 1651."

11) Because habeas corpus helps assure that the determination of a prisoner's guilt was "full and fair," delays in processing petitions that are not justified by a need for adequate investigation or preparation interfere with the policy underlying the Constitutional guarantee of a Speedy Trial.

12) "Writ of Mandamus is an order directing a public official or public body to perform a duty exacted by law." *United States v. Denson*, 603 F. 2d 1143, 1146 (5th Cir. 1979). It "is an extraordinary remedy for extraordinary causes." In re *Corrugated Container Antitrust Litig. Mead Corp.*, 614 F. 2d 958, 961-62 (5th Cir. 1980). To obtain the Writ, the Petitioner MUST show "that no other adequate means exists to attain the requested relief" and that his right to issuance of the Writ is "CLEAR and INDISPUTABLE."

WHEREFORE NOW, above premises considered, the Petitioner MOVES this Honorable Court to ISSUE a WRIT OF MANDAMUS directing the United States District Court, in the Northern district of Alabama, to ISSUE its RULING either GRANTING or DENYING the Petitioner's motion for relief under 28 U.S.C. § 2255. The District Court's ruling is OVER DUE pursuant to its "order regarding Summary Disposition" and *Federal Rules of Civil Procedure*, Rule 58(c)(2).

Done This 31st Day of October 2016.

Respectfully Submitted,

[REDACTED]

[REDACTED], *PRO SE*
Reg # [REDACTED]
Federal Correctional Institution
Mailing Address
City, State and Zip Code

BASIC REPLY

This is an actual reply in a *habeas* case. Simply use common sense when constructing your own. Here, I share with you much of my emotion, pain, and issues that really arise in *habeas* cases. I suggest you use more tact than I did, as I can almost guarantee your judge has acted with a great deal more honor than mine did.

UNITED STATES DISTRICT COURT

IN THE [REDACTED] DISTRICT of [REDACTED]

[REDACTED] DIVISION

KELLY PATRICK RIGGS, Petitioner vs. UNITED STATES OF AMERICA Respondent	CASE NO(S): [REDACTED]

REPLY TO UNITED STATES' ANSWER TO MOVANT'S 28 U.S.C. § 2255 MOTION TO VACATE, SET ASIDE, OR CORRECT SENTENCE

1) COMES NOW the Petitioner, KELLY PATRICK RIGGS in *PRO SE*, in necessity, and hereby files this reply to the United States' answer to Petitioner's 28 U.S.C. § 2255 motion, pursuant to Rule 5 governing § 2255 proceedings. The Petitioner hereby avers that he stands firmly on all points raised in his initial § 2255 motion. This reply will address only the points raised in the United States' response that requires a reply. After a review of the Government's response, it became CLEAR that the United States, by and through its Attorney, made many FALSE STATEMENTS tantamount to FRAUD upon this Court. Former Procedural Statute provided that the allegations of a return [i.e. response], if not traversed, shall be accepted as true except to the extent that the Judge finds from the evidence that they are not true. An amendment of the Habeas Rules in 2004, omitted any reference to a traverse. Although the Habeas Rules dispensed with the requirement of a traverse, they did not forbid such a pleading, and the Advisory Committee notes endorsed a traverse or amendment "where it would serve a truly useful purpose" or was "called for by the contents of the answer" filed by the respondent. It's a CLEAR matter of law that the Petitioner MUST rebut FALSE STATEMENTS made by the United States to avoid his silence being construed as his acquiescence. The Petitioner therefore, files this reply in GOOD FAITH as it will serve the "truly useful purpose" of preserving judicial resources. The Petitioner herein presents to this Court the TRUE FACTS of this case and supporting evidence thereto, as follows:

PETITIONER'S REBUTTAL ARGUMENTS

2) The Government's Attorney, has by his assertions of waiver to appeal premised upon Ineffective Assistance of Counsel, has effectively withdrawn negotiated consideration of Plea Agreement, and thereby VOIDS the binding contract.

3) In the Government's response to Petitioner's § 2255, the Government's Attorney states, more than once (page 7 & 8), that: ."..Mr. Riggs waives his right to assert are claims of ineffective assistance of counsel prior to the plea."; "Mr. Riggs waived his right to assert these ineffective- assistance claims when he elected to plead guilty to the charges against him."

4) These contentions by the Government's Attorney have required the Petitioner to purchase additional research materials and books. The Petitioner has been deprived of: essential rights under agreed upon contract; precious resources; time; sleep; peace of mind that the Government would honor its own contract; and has suffered other irreparable damages and harms that are better particularized in the ensuing Bivens action. Furthermore, this act has further burdened the Petitioner beyond his obligations of Strickland by requiring him to first litigate for an agreed upon right of a contractual agreement.

5) The Petitioner contends that the Government has, by its response, withdrawn its considerations in the Plea Agreement and therefore VOIDS the agreement KNOWINGLY breaching the contract.

6) The Petitioner contends that he does have a right to appeal and/or collaterally challenge his conviction and/or sentence pursuant to the very Plea Agreement the Governments Attorney has VOIDED by withdrawing its considerations. See the following:

7) Plea Agreement in question CLEARLY STATES under § IV "**Waiver of rights to appeal and post-conviction relief.**" That the defendant reserves the right to contest in an appeal or post-conviction proceeding any and all of the following:

   a. Any sentence imposed in excess of the applicable statutory maximum sentences; and

   b. Any sentence imposed in excess of the guideline sentencing range determined by the Court at the time sentence is imposed; and

   c. **Ineffective Assistance of Counsel.**

8) In hearing on 9/6/13, a Federal Judge particularizes several characteristics of a Plea Agreement, in pages 6-15 of that transcript as follows:

9) "Where a plea agreement exists and where a defendant is entering his plea of guilty relying, at least in part, upon such a plea agreement. The defendant, his attorney, and the United States Attorney's Office all have the obligation to disclose that fact to the Court and to tell the Court the terms and the conditions of any plea bargain or plea agreement upon which the defendant might be relying at the time he enters his plea of guilty."

10) On page nine (9), the Judge notes that the defendant reserved the right to appeal or collaterally attack his conviction and/or sentence based upon "Ineffective Assistance of Counsel."

11) On page 15, the Judge expressly made known that "the United States Attorney's Office is required to comply with any obligations imposed upon it by the plea agreement."

12) A Plea Agreement that contains a collateral attack waiver is a CLEAR Conflict of Interest because it impinges on a defendant's right to be sure of the Effective Assistance of Counsel under the Sixth Amendment when Defense Counsel advises a defendant to plead guilty and waive his right to allege that Counsel was ineffective at the Plea of Guilty stage.

13) Almost every State BAR Association has said in a formal opinion that collateral attack waivers are wrong and cause a Conflict of Interest between a Defense Counsel and his Client. In fact, the Kentucky State Supreme Court has said that collateral attack waivers "create a non-waivable Conflict of Interest between the defendant and his attorney." United States v. Kentucky State BAR Assoc., no: 20013-SC- 270-KB (Ky. 2014). The Court also said it is an "ethical breach" by Defense Counsel. Id. When

viewed through the lens of Conflict of Interest, the problem of collateral attack waivers becomes quite clear.

14) Court appointed Counsel stated on the record of 12/20/13, that he did advise the Petitioner to plead guilty even after he filed Notice of Alibi and subpoenas for 10 witnesses in support thereof. With the Defense Counsel intimate knowledge of the law and expectation that the Government could raise waiver claims due to pre plea conduct. ("Among the non- jurisdictional defects Mr. Riggs waives his right to assert are claims of Ineffective Assistance of Counsel prior to the plea.") Defense Counsel in effect bound the Petitioner to an agreement characteristic that was not enumerated in the Plea Agreement nor could he, [Petitioner], otherwise have known about. Defense Counsel thereby protected himself from an Ineffective Assistance of Counsel claim, expressly, by advising the Petitioner to plead guilty who was expecting to be able to appeal for Ineffective Assistance of Counsel.

15) "Counsel owes the client a duty of loyalty, a duty to avoid Conflicts of Interest." *Strickland v. Washington*, 466 U.S. 668, 688 (1984). The Sixth Amendment right to Counsel includes the "right to representation that is free from conflicts of interest." *Wood v. Georgia*, 450 U.S. 261, 271 (1981), and this "Conflict Free" representation extends to plea negotiations. *Moore v. United States*, 950 F. 2d 656, 660 (CA 10 1991). The Supreme Court even said that if a Petitioner can show Counsel operated under a Conflict of Interest, he doesn't even have to show that he was prejudiced (that Counsel's errors changed the outcome of the proceedings). *Cuyler v. Sullivan*, 466 U.S. 335, 350 (1980).

16) It is well established that Plea Agreements are "Contracts." *Santobello v. New York*, 404 U.S. 257, 262-263 (1971). So, if we take a look at how a Conflict of Interest would affect a contract's validity, we see more issues that are fatal to the Plea Agreement, or "Contract." If a party commits fraud while negotiating a contract, the contract is VOID as if it never existed. *Godly v. United States*, 5 F. 3d 1473, 1476 (Fed. Cir. 1995) ("A contract tainted by fraud ... is void ab inito"). Such as if the Government adds a provision for appeal, or otherwise collaterally attacks the conviction or sentence in which the Petitioner relies, in an effort to entice him to agree, only to have an embedded provision that voids the right to appeal that the Petitioner relies on to enter into an agreement.

The Government commits fraud during contract negotiations when it places a provision in the contract it knows will create a Conflict of Interest between Defense Counsel and the Defendant. A collateral attack waiver creates a Conflict of Interest between Defense Counsel and the Defendant because it is unethical for Defense Counsel to advise his Client to enter into a contract (to accept a plea agreement/offer) when the contract has a waiver preventing the client from later challenging his lawyer's advice.

17) "Fraud is a generic term." *Ragland v. Shattuck National Bank*, 36 F. 3d 983, 990 (CA 10 1994). It encompasses a broad range of ways "by which another is cheated." Id. There are actually two types of fraud: Intentional and Constructive. Intentional is when a party intends to deceive the other party. Constructive, though, is broader and covers even unintentional deception. In this case, the type of the plea (contract) allows the Petitioner to reserve for himself the right to collaterally attack the conviction/sentence for Ineffective Assistance of Counsel. The Petitioner relied on this provision as stated in the contract. Here now, however, the Petitioner finds himself defending himself against a procedural waiver that is not expressed in the Plea Agreement, nor did the Petitioner have any knowledge of. See *United States v. Fairchild*, 803 F. 2d at 1124, which the Government now relies on and the Petitioner was never advised of. Additionally, when the Government places a collateral attack waiver, intrinsic or extrinsic, in the Plea Agreement, it creates a Conflict of Interest. And because the Government knows this but fails to say anything, it is fraud because the Defendant has "an underlying right to be correctly informed of the facts." Id. Fraud occurs when a party in an agreement has a duty to speak but "fails to disclose the whole truth." Id. at 991. The Government, as

a party in a contract, has the obligation to say the waiver could cause a Conflict of Interest. It is Constructive Fraud when the Government knowingly remains silent on that issue. Again, any fraud in a contract VOIDS the contract as if it never existed.

18) Also see, *United States v. Shedrick*, 493 F. 3d 292 (3rd Cir. 2007); *United States v. Craig*, 985 F. 2d 175 (4th Cir. 1993); *United States v. White*, 307 F. 3d 336 (5th Cir. 2002)("An ineffective assistance of counsel argument survives a waiver of appeal only when the claimed assistance directly affected the validity of that waiver of the plea itself")(72 CrL 15, 10/2/02); Davila v. United States, 258 F. 3d 448 (6th Cir. 2001)(69 CrL 556, 8/15/01); Jones v. United States, 167 F, 3d 1142 (7th Cir. 1999); DeRoo v. United States, 223 F. 3d 919 (8th Cir. 2000); Washington v. Lampert, 442 F. 3d 864 (9th Cir. 2005); United States v. Cockerham, 237 F. 3d 1179 (10th Cir. 2001)(68 CrL 369, 1/31/01); Williams v. United States, 396 F. 3d 1340 (11th Cir. 2005)("There may be a distinction between a claim of ineffective assistance in entering or negotiating the plea versus a claim ... challenging the validity of the plea or agreement")(76 CrL 341 2/2/05).

19) The Petitioner hereby avers that the Government's contention, that entering the Plea Agreement serves as waiver to the agreed upon right to challenge the conviction, is tantamount to conclusive NEW EVIDENCE of Ineffective Assistance of Counsel during plea negotiation. The Government's response serves as an unconditional stipulation that Court appointed Counsel was in FACT Constitutionally Ineffective. This issue alone would serve as sufficient grounds for this Court to exercise sound judicial prudence by issuing a Writ of *habeas corpus* to have Petitioner brought before it to the end that he may be discharged from his unconstitutional confinement and restraint.

20) The Government's claim that Petitioner's "Ineffective Assistance of Counsel claims fail on the merits" is an indicator that perhaps he has not taken his duty serious enough to even review the § 2255 motion and addendum.

21) The Petitioner hereby avers that the Government's Attorney has, by its contention concerning waiver, provided New Evidence of Ineffective Assistance of Counsel. The Petitioner therefore, re-alleges and incorporates by reference paragraphs (3)-(6).

22) The Government's Attorney, in his contentions to the merits of Petitioner's Ineffective Assistance of Counsel (herein after IAC) claim, employs very generalized statements in what can only be considered a shotgun approach. The Petitioner hereby avers that all aspects of his § 2255 motion are TRUE and FACTUAL which are furthermore supported by Witness Affidavits and evidence attached thereto. The Government's contentions are CLEARLY made "IN BAD FAITH" to once again deprive this Court of its ability to pass judgment based on accurate information.

23) The Petitioner hereby reminds this Court that he has attached to his § 2255 motion, the following:

    A) Six affidavits concerning the subject as follows:

    - Alibi Testimony
    - Ineffective Assistance of Counsel
    - Failure to Investigate
    - Falsified Federal Documents
    - Rush to Judgment
    - Threat and Duress
    - Murder of [REDACTED]

- Failure to give Notice

B) A letter to the Alabama BAR Association, from [redacted], admitting she spoke with [redacted] concerning the Petitioner and in turn discussed her findings with her client a Mexican National.

C) A copy of an opinion of the United States Court of Appeals in the Eleventh Circuit that CLEARLY STATES that:

> "Specifically, because Riggs still is 'in custody', he has available to him the statutory remedy of filing a § 2255 motion."

D) [Redacted], although filing a lengthy and overly verbose response, failed to provide this Court with a single affidavit from anyone to contend with the Petitioner's assertions. [Redacted] has admitted to several aspects of the Petitioner's claim of IAC in a section of his response and then denies them in another. [Redacted] claims that "Riggs does not present any new evidence of his innocence" even though the Petitioner has attached sworn affidavits of alibi testimony.

24) [Redacted] states in his response that: "Mr. Riggs does not present any new evidence of his innocence; indeed, he does not appear to assert his factual innocence at all." In this contention, [Redacted] blatantly lies to the Court with the intent to impinge the Court's ability to rule fairly. This Court, in consideration of Fed. R. Civ. P., Rule 60(b)(3), should and could act sua sponte, and vacate this VOID Federal Judgment in the Interest of Justice, issue a Writ of *habeas corpus* to have the Petitioner brought before it to the end that he may be relieved of his unconstitutional sentence, or in the alternative, order that this case be investigated as this behavior is indicative of the Government's Misconduct from the inception of this case. The Petitioner hereby reminds the Court of the following:

A) That the Petitioner is a *pro se* litigant in this proceeding, he is, and should be, deserving of the consideration mandated by: Jarzynka v. St. Thomas Unviversity of Law, 310 F. Supp. 2d 1256, 1264 (S.D. Fla. 2004); Haines v. Kerner, 404 U.S. 519, 520-521 (1972); Powell v. Lennon, 914 F.2d 1459, 1463 (11th Cir. 1990); Albra v. Advan, Inc., 490 F. 3d 826, 829 (11th Cir. 2007). Under such consideration the Petitioner's failure to invoke the words "FACTUAL INNOCENCE" is excusable because he did state that there exists, still to this day, alibi witnesses and exculpatory video footage, that are indicative to a claim of "FACTUAL INNOCENCE."

B) The Petitioner has in FACT attached to his § 2255 motion affidavits from witnesses concerning:

- An alibi defense established by the testimony in the affidavits;
- The existence of exculpatory video footage from the [Redacted] in Trussville, Alabama, which was obtained by Detective [Redacted];
- The existence of impeaching video footage from an Insurance Office that shows the Agents lied about the arrest location to better fit their theory of the staged. crime; ... and
- A letter from [Redacted] that proves she did in FACT discuss the Petitioner with a Mexican National after learning about a letter from the Petitioner that implicates the Mexican cartel in a Major Drug Trafficking Offense.

C) The Petitioner has continually, from the inception of this case, asserted his FACTUAL

INNOCENCE. [Redacted] submits to this Court, in the appendix to his response, an affidavit from the Petitioner that expressly asserts his FACTUAL INNOCENCE.

D) The Petitioner has indeed attempted to show this "FACTUAL INNOCENCE" since the inception of his criminal case by demanding investigation, presentation of witnesses, and fair trial. The record CLEARLY reflects that: \

- The Court has appointed five lawyers;
- The Petitioner has demanded investigation of each of them;
- An Investigator was never appointed;
- The Petitioner moved the Court to order investigation; and
- The Petitioner still to this day seeks to obtain his case file and the video of the second police interview that is alleged to be a confession. Both of which give rise to FACTUAL INNOCENCE.

E) Currently Court appointed Appellate Counsel is refusing to turn over the Petitioner's case file. This act is, in the belief of the Petitioner, an effort to deny the Petitioner materials that prove his INNOCENCE. This assertion, by the Petitioner, is not disputed by the Government who therefore concedes to this issue. See page 17 of Government's response. See also, *United States v. Dorman*, 58 M.J. 295 (C.A.A.F. 2003); Hiatt v. Clark, Ky. no 2005-SC-455-MR (6/15/06); *Maxwell v. Florida*, 479 U.S. 972, 93 L. Ed. 2d 418-420, 107 S. Ct. 474 (1986) ("The right to effective assistance fully encompasses the client's right to obtain from Trial Counsel the work files generated during and pertaining to that client's defense. It further entitles the client to utilize materials contained in these files in any proceeding at which the adequacy of Trial Counsel's representation may be challenged") See also, *Spivey v. Zant*, 683 F. 2d 881, 885 (5th Cir. 1982).

It is CLEAR that [Redacted] is aware that the Petitioner seeks his case file by reference in his response. [Redacted] makes no contention that the Petitioner has been deprived of his case file, but only that:

> "Mr. Riggs' assertion that [Redacted] has to this day refused the Petitioner access to his case file also does not support an ineffective assistance claim."

The Petitioner hereby asserts that this is yet another calculated fraud on the Court as [Redacted's] contention is in DIRECT CONTRAVENTION to the Supreme Court of the United States in Maxwell v. Florida, and others. The Petitioner avers that this Court could and should issue a Writ of *habeas corpus* to have Petitioner brought before it to the end that he may be discharged from his unconstitutional confinement and restraint.

25) The Government on page 18 of its response states that "the Court should reject Mr. Rigg's claim of inadequate notice. "This statement and the following section of the response from III to its Conclusion is nonsense. In yet another attempt to re-direct this Court to the TRUTH of the matter. The Petitioner shows this Court the following:

A) That a Federal Judgment/Conviction is VOID when procured in violation of Federal Statutory Law and/or Federal Rules of Criminal Procedure. The Court of conviction failed to comply with the mandated requirement that "the Court must inform the defendant of, and determine that the defendant understand the nature of each charge to which the defendant is pleading." As mandated by Fed. R. Crim. P., Rule 11(b)(1)(G). Failure to do so is PLAIN ERROR.

B) Petitioner hereby presents to the Court relevant decisions concerning this issue as follows:

- "In accepting guilty plea, Court must comply with Fed. R. Crim. P., Rule 11 and, in particular, address three core concerns by ensuring that: (1) guilty plea is voluntary, (2) defendant understands nature of charges, and (3) defendant understands consequences of plea." *United States v. Brandelmena*, (2006, CA 11 Fla) 177 Fed Appx 929, Cert. Den. (2006) 549 U.S. 922, 127 S. Ct. 280, 166 L. Ed. 2d 214.

- "Trial Court's failure to explain nature of charge render defendant's guilty pleas ... involuntary since elements of statute were never discussed during plea hearings, recital of factual basis was insufficient to satisfy requirement that defendant understand nature of charge." *United States v. Lujano-Perez*, (2001, CA 5 Tex) 274 F. 3d 219.

- "Since guilty plea is more than confession that admits that accused did various acts, but is admission that accused committed crime charged, by him, so that by entering guilty plea accused is not simply stating that he did acts described in indictment but is admitting guilt of substantive crime, defendant must be instructed in open Court on nature of charges to which plea is offered, and plea cannot be truly voluntary unless defendant possesses understanding of law in relation of facts." *United States v. Broco*, (1989) 488 U.S. 563, 109 S. Ct. 757, 102 L. Ed. 2d 927, 1989-1 CCH Trade cases FLW 68393.

- "Entry of guilty plea waives several constitutional rights and since guilty plea admits all elements of criminal charge, it cannot be truly voluntary unless defendant possesses understanding of law as well as facts." *Monroe v. United States*, (1972, CA 5 Fla) 463 F. 2d 1032.

- "District Court committed plain error in failing to inform defendant of nature of charge to which he was pleading guilty; District Court failed to satisfy core objective that defendant understands nature of charge against him, which constitutes violation of defendant's substantial rights." United States v. Quinones, (1996, CA 11 Fla) 97 F. 3d 473, 10 FLW Fed C 478.

- "Guilty plea is not knowingly and voluntarily made when defendant has been misinformed about critical elements of charged offense, even when that misinformation is result of Appellate Court's erroneous prior interpretation of criminal statute; thus, guilty plea ... is invalid without informing defendant that knowledge of ... essential elements of crime." United States v. Brown, (1997, CA 11 Ga) 117 F. 3d 471, 11 FLW Fed C 212.

- In the Petitioner's case, he is indicted fraudulently for attempting to violate Alabama State Law, Rape in the Second Degree (Ala. Code § 13A-6-62) Inter alia. By [Redacted] City Police employing a police informant and a police detective to stage conversations purporting to be the Petitioner. This was conducted between two adults, one pretending to be a child and the other pretending to be the Petitioner. While the Petitioner was with numerous alibi witnesses at his son's birthday party.

- The indictment is CLEARLY based upon Alabama State Law as an essential element. However, the Alabama State Laws in which the Government relies requires an ACTUAL CHILD be involved to constitute a criminal offense in which any one can be charged. See *State of Alabama v. Steve Giardini*, in which Giardini, a 20-year veteran who was prosecuting child sex offenses, case was thrown out for the lack of an actual victim and he continues to practice law today.

- At sentencing on April 22, 2014, the sentencing Judge makes clear on the record that "this case does not involve ALABAMA STATE LAW ..." and "Alabama State Code doesn't apply ..." Making CLEAR that the District Judge not only failed to make the Petitioner aware of the essential elements, but also vehemently denied that the Alabama State Law was an essential element.

- In a recent, Eleventh Circuit Court of Appeals oral argument held on or about August 27, 2015, where two Circuit Court Judges CLEARLY disagreed with the District Judge in the Petitioner's case. In the case of *Freeman Eugene Jockisch v. United States*, case no.: 14-13577C, an appeal filed from Oakdale Federal Prison, "Assistant U.S. Attorney Adam Overstreet down played the importance of the State Rape ... crimes ..." on the contrary, Shields' Defense Counsel said those offenses were essential "elements" of the crime ... Judge Adalberto Jordan states to Overstreet "If what your saying is true, then next time you can confidently say, 'Judge, we aren't required to prove a sex act would have occurred. The enticement is enough'." Jordan told Overstreet, "there is no way on God's green earth that a U.S. Attorney is going to do that after today's oral arguments," During the closing statements, Over- street said the entire issue over State crimes listed in the indictment would have no effect on the crime of child enticement. He said if anything, not knowing which specific crime the Jury believed Jockisch contemplated was a "harmless error,"

  From the bench Carnes did not agree. Judge Julie E. Carnes stated, "It's not a harmless error" You've got to prove he did something that would violate a law."

  As reported by Jason Johnson, Lagniappe, Mobile, AL.

CONCLUSION

The Court should issue a Writ of Habeas Corpus to have the Petitioner brought before it to the end that he may be relieved of his unconstitutional sentence. The Petitioner has presented ample evidence, statements, and matters of law to support all requested relief. In conclusion of the Petitioner's response that Court must presume the TRUTH of any of the Petitioner's FACTUAL allegations that are not affirmatively disproved by records actually before the Court. In the alternative, this Court should expand the record to include all materials, filings, and/or evidence in Petitioner's criminal case in preparation for his appeal. § 2255 provides that "unless the motion and the files and records of the case conclusively shows that the prisoner is entitled to no relief, the Court shall ... grant a prompt hearing thereon, determine the issues and findings of FACT and Conclusions of Law with respect thereto.

Finally, United States Attorney's, like Counsel for other parties to Federal Civil Actions, are ethically barred from moving for Summary Judgment when a FACTUAL DISPUTE CLEARLY is present.

Done This [redacted] Day of [redacted], 2015.

Respectfully Submitted,

[REDACTED]

Kelly Patrick Riggs, *PRO SE*
Reg # [redacted]

Federal Correctional Institution

Mailing Address

City, State and Zip Code

KELLY PATRICK RIGGS

UNITED STATES DISTRICT COURT

IN THE [YOUR DISTRICT] DISTRICT of [YOUR STATE]

[YOUR DIVISION] DIVISION

UNITED STATES OF AMERICA, Respondent vs. [YOUR NAME] Petitioner	CASE NO(S): [YOUR CASE NUMBERS]

PETITIONER'S MOTION FOR DISCOVERY AND PRODUCTION OF DOCUMENTS PURSUANT TO RULE 6 GOVERNING 28 U.S.C. § 2255 PROCEEDINGS

COMES NOW the Petitioner, [YOUR NAME] in *PRO SE*, in necessity, and hereby requests that this Court GRANT him [The Petitioner] Leave To Conduct Discovery and MOVE the Court to ORDER the production of documents pursuant to Rule 6(a) and (b) governing 28 U.S.C. § 2255 proceedings. In support, the Petitioner shows the Court the following:

1) That this District Court has declared that the Petitioner should and can pursue relief pursuant to a 28 U.S.C. § 2255 motion.

2) That the Petitioner hereby avers that he is now prosecuting a § 2255 motion with detailed FACTS concerning his claim that Defense Counsel (i.e. [ATTORNEY'S NAME] provided Ineffective Assistance of Counsel by failing to:

   A) Seek the appointment of an Investigator to take statements from ALIBI WITNESSES. [Use if alibi witnesses were available]

   B) Subpoena exculpatory evidence. [Use if exculpatory evidence exists]

   C) To memorialize alibi witness testimony of available alibi witnesses. [Use if alibi witnesses were available]

   D) To investigate and understand the applicability of the Federal Statute of conviction, and/or its essential elements.

   E) To advise the petitioner of all essential elements of the charged offense so that the petitioner could have a reasonable understanding of law and fact.

3) The Petitioner attached to his § 2255 motion an affidavit detailing the FACTS concerning the

Ineffectiveness of Defense Counsel, relating to [his/hers/their] failure to communicate all essential elements of the charged offense as they relate and/or do not relate to the alleged conduct, and [his/hers/their] overall refusal to investigate the Petitioner's case for possible defenses.

4) This motion seeks Leave To Conduct Discovery, Production Of Documents, and Disclosure from the United States of ALL typed, written, or electronic versions of any and all emails, letters, memos and/or any form of communication from the United States Attorney's Office to any of the Defense Counsel in this case concerning:

   A) Jailhouse phone recordings;

   B) An ALIBI DEFENSE;

   C) Exculpatory evidence;

   D) Other Plea Agreements;

   E) Alibi Witness testimony/affidavits;

   F) [Etc. as necessary]

   Production and disclosure of these documents will prove Petitioner's claim that he was denied Effective Assistance of Counsel. Where Counsel refused to investigate this criminal case for possible defenses and/or offer any resistance to the Government's Witnesses or Evidence in their Case in Chief.

5) Petitioner seeks to have ALL Attorneys answer the attached interrogatories concerning the existence of Exculpatory Evidence, possible alibi witnesses, and/or Failure to Investigate to discover the same. Furthermore, the Petitioner seeks ALL correspondence, in any form, with the United States Attorney's Office, production and disclosure of ALL written, typed, or electronic conversation from the United States Attorney's Office to Defense Counsel concerning ALL evidence, statements, affidavits, recorded phone conversations, interviews, alibi defenses, and/or exculpatory evidence.

6) Good Cause is shown because production of the requested documents will establish the validity of Petitioner's Constitutional claim that Defense Counsel provided Ineffective Assistance for failure to investigate the Petitioner's criminal case inter alia.

WHEREFORE NOW, above premises considered, the Petitioner [YOUR NAME] hereby MOVES this Court to GRANT Leave To Conduct Discovery and for Production Of Documents pursuant to Rule 6(a) and (b) governing § 2255 proceedings.

Done This [DATE] Day of [MONTH], [YEAR].

Respectfully Submitted,

____

[YOUR NAME], *PRO SE*

[YOUR INMATE NUMBER]

[YOUR INSTITUTION]

[INSTITUTION'S ADDRESS]

UNITED STATES DISTRICT COURT

IN THE [Your DISTRICT] DISTRICT of [Your STATE]

[Your DIVISION] DIVISION

UNITED STATES OF AMERICA, Respondent vs. [Your NAME], Petitioner	CASE NO(S). : [YOUR CASE NUMBERS]

MEMORANDUM BRIEF IN SUPPORT OF MOTION FOR DISCOVERY AND PRODUCTION OF DOCUMENTS PURSUANT TO RULE 6 GOVERNING 28 U.S.C. § 2255

COMES NOW the Petitioner, [YOUR NAME] in *PRO SE*, in necessity, and hereby files this Memorandum Brief in support of his motion for Discovery and Production Of Documents pursuant to Rule 6(a) and (b) governing 28 U.S.C. § 2255 proceedings. In support, the Petitioner shows to the Court the following:

Rule 6 of the rules governing 28 U.S.C. § 2255 proceedings entitles litigants to request discovery process available under the *Federal Rules of Civil Procedure*, if GOOD CAUSE is shown and the Court exercises its discretion allowing discovery. *Federal Rules of Civil Procedure*, Rule 26(c) through 36 provides a wide range of discovery devices available which includes but is not limited to: Depositions, Production of Documents or other Physical materials, Physical and Mental Examinations, Requests for Admissions and Interrogatories, Permission tō Enter Upon Land or other Property for Inspection or other purposes. The Court may appoint Counsel for indigent prisoners if necessary, for effective utilization of discovery. See 18 U.S.C. § 3006A.

GOOD CAUSE for Discovery exists under Rule 6(a) governing Section § 2255 cases ("Habeas Relief") where specific allegations before the Court showed reason to believe that the Petitioner may, if the facts are fully developed be able to demonstrate that he is entitled to relief. See *Harris v. Nelson*, 394 U.S. 286, 89 S. Ct. 1082, 22 L. Ed. 2d 281 (1969); *Bracy v. Gramley*, 520 U.S. 899, 117 S. Ct. 1793, 138 L. Ed. 2d 97 (1998); *Payne v. Bell*, 89 F. Supp. 2d 967 (W.D. Tenn. 2000).

The Petitioner has attached to this Memorandum Brief a copy of an affidavit, that is attached to his § 2255 motion, detailing the facts concerning the Ineffectiveness of Defense Counsel as they relate to [his/hers/their] failure to investigate the Petitioner's criminal case for possible defenses, to include but not limited to the availability of alibi defense and other exculpatory evidence. Such unprofessional errors and omissions by Defense Counsel constitute Ineffective Assistance of Counsel and warrants an Evidentiary Hearing to resolve the factual dispute. See *Valentine v. United States*, 488 F. 3d 325, 332-333 (6th Cir., 2007); *Griffin v. United States*, 330 F. 3d 733, 739 (6th Cir.,2003).

The Petitioner seeks Leave to Conduct Discovery, Production of Documents, and Disclosure from the United States of ALL typed, written, or electronic versions of any and all emails, letters, memos, or any form of communications from the United States Attorney's Office to any Defense Counsel and all other information requested in the Motion and Brief concerning the investigations of this the Petitioner's case. Production and Disclosure of these documents will prove Petitioner's claim that he was denied Effective Assistance of Counsel where Defense Counsel failed to investigate the Petitioner's criminal case for possible defenses and/or failed to communicate to the Petitioner all essential elements of the charged offense against him. See list of all cases here:

1) "In accepting guilty plea, court must comply with Fed. R. Crim. P., Rule 11 and, in particular, address their core concerns by ensuring that: (1) guilty plea is voluntary, (2) defendant understands nature of charges, and (3) defendant understands consequences of plea." *United States v. Bandel-Mena* (2006, CA11 Fla) 177 Fed. Appx. 929, cert den. (2006) 549 U.S. 922, 127 S. Ct. 280, 166 L. Ed. 2d 214.

2) "Trial court's failure to explain nature of charge breached defendant's guilty plea ... involuntary since elements of statute were never discussed during plea hearings, recital of factual basis was insufficient to satisfy requirement that defendant understand nature of charge." *United States v. Lujano-Perez* (2001, CA5 Tex) 274 F. 3d 219.

3) "Since guilty plea is more than confession that admits that accused did various acts, but is admission that accused committed crime charged by him, so that by entering guilty plea accused is not simply stating that he did acts described in indictment but is admitting guilt of substantive crimes, defendant must be instructed in open court on nature of charge to which plea is offered, and plea cannot be truly voluntary unless defendant possesses understanding of law in relation of facts." *United States v. Broce*, (1989) 488 U.S. 563, 109 S. Ct. 757, 102 L. Ed. 2d 297, 1989-1 CCH Trade Gases FLW 68393.

4) "Entry of guilty plea waives several constitutional rights and since guilty plea admits all elements of criminal charge, it cannot be truly voluntary unless defendant possess understanding of law as well as facts." *Monroe v. United States* (1972, CA5 Fla) 463 F. 2d 1032.

5) "District court committed plain error in failing to inform defendant of charge to which he was pleading guilty; district court failed to satisfy core objective that defendant understand nature of charge against him, which constitutes violation of defendant's substantial rights." *United States v. Quinones* (1996, CA11 Fla) 97 F. 3d 473, 10 FLW Fed. C 478.

6) "Guilty plea is not knowingly and voluntarily made when defendant has been misinformed about critical elements of charged offense, even when that misinformation is result of appellate court's erroneous prior interpretation of criminal statute; thus, guilty plea ... ***is invalid*** without informing defendant that knowledge of ... essential element of crime." *United States v. Brown* (1997, CA11 Ga) 117 F. 3d 471, 11 FLW Fed. C 212.

7) "Ordinary contract principles govern plea agreements and there must be meeting of minds on all of its essential terms, including nature of charge to which defendant is pleading guilty; where both parties are mistaken as to nature of charge against defendant, entire agreement is invalidated; if court rules that some provision of plea agreement is invalid, it must discard entire agreement ..." *United States v. Bradley* (2004, CA7 Ind) 381 F. 3d 841.

Also see *United States v. Padilla-Martinez*, 762 F. 2d 942 (11th Cir., 1985); *Mitchell v. Mason*, 325 F. 3d 732 (6th Cir., 2003) ("The pretrial period constitutes a 'critical period' in criminal proceedings because it encompasses Counsel's Constitutionally imposed duty to investigate the case.") *United States v. Tucker*, 716 F. 2d 576 (9th Cir., 1983) (The defendant was denied effective assistance of counsel where his inexperienced trial attorney did little investigation, little pretrial, and no impeachment of witnesses.) *Harris v. Wood*, 64 F. 3d 1432 (9th Cir., 1995) (Although police reports listed approximately 32 persons with knowledge of the murder and Harris told him of others, Anderson interviewed only three witnesses. He did not request an investigator to help interview witnesses." "In addition to finding prejudice from individual deficiencies, the district court concluded that the deficiencies it found were cumulatively prejudicial.") *Harris*, 853 F. Supp. at 1274. The exact same scenario applies to the defendant in this case at hand.

Defense Counsel thus far has refused to disclose the case file to Petitioner or any correspondence from the United States Attorney's Office and/or previous Defense Counsel concerning any witnesses and/or exculpatory evidence that was known or reasonably should be known to the United States Attorney's Office and Defense Counsel. The Petitioner has repeatedly reminded Counsel that the cost of such task is paid pursuant to The Criminal Justice Act. Petitioner seeks disclosure of the entire case file in the Defense Counsel's possession, or reasonably could be expected to be in his possession, because it will provide Petitioner with the necessary documentation which supports his claim of Ineffective Assistance of Counsel. Both the law and the American BAR Association recognize that Counsel has a duty not to ***IMPEDE*** Petitioner's attempts to challenge his conviction and/or sentence.

See, *ABA Standard for Criminal Justice, Defense Functions Standards and Commentary* ("The resounding message is that defense attorneys, because of their intimate knowledge of the trial proceedings and possession of unique information regarding possible post-conviction claims, have an obligation to cooperate with their client's attempt to challenge their convictions."); *Maxwell v. Florida*, 479 U.S. 972, 93 L. Ed. 2d 418, 107 S. Ct. 474 (1986)("The right to effective assistance fully encompasses the client's rights to obtain from trial counsel the work file generated during and pertaining to that client's defense. It further entitles the client to utilize materials contained in those files in any proceeding at which the adequacy of trial counsel's representation may be challenged."); *Spivey v. Zant*, 683 F. 2d 881, 885 (5th Cir., 1982) (*habeas corpus* petitioner is entitled to former trial attorney's file and the work-product doctrine does not apply to situations in which the client seeks access to documents or other tangible things created during course of attorney's representation).

Petitioner seeks to submit the proposed interrogatories and production of documents. The documents being the letter/letters from the United States Attorney's Office and/or previous Defense Counsel concerning and/or communications concerning the availability of an alibi defense, exculpatory evidence, and all other *Brady/Giglio* material that the Court ordered the Government to disclose and that the Petitioner can have a reasonable expectation that the United States Attorney's Office did in FACT make Defense Counsel aware of pursuant to *Berger* supra. Production of these documents and answers to the Interrogatories will provide Petitioner with the necessary proof to support his claim of Ineffective Assistance of Counsel. See *Cronic*, and furthermore prove that failing to provide Effective Assistance of Counsel prejudiced the Petitioner by denying the Petitioner of his right to present witnesses and evidence that would have proven his "ACTUAL INNOCENCE" if provided to any reasonable juror. See *Strickland.*

Petitioner seeks to have all Defense Counsel and all Assistant United States Attorneys answer the attached interrogatories concerning the availability of witnesses, exculpatory evidence, and all other *Brady/Giglio* materials that the Government provided to Defense Counsel; who has refused disclosure to the Petitioner; and production and disclosure of all written, typed, electronic communication; and/or any other correspondence from the United States Attorney's Office to any and all Defense Counsel concerning materials requested herein.

GOOD' CAUSE is shown because production of the requested documents will establish the validity of Petitioner's Constitutional claim that Defense Counsel provided Ineffective Assistance of Counsel by failing to investigate the Petitioner's criminal case for possible defenses and/or essential elements of the charged offense. See *Cronic*, *Strickland*, *Harris v. Wood*, et. al.

WHEREFORE NOW, above premises considered, the Petitioner hereby MOVES this Court to GRANT Leave to Conduct Discovery and for Production of documents pursuant to Rule 6(a) and (b) of the rules governing § 2255 proceedings.

Done This [DATE] Day of [MONTH], [YEAR].

Respectfully Submitted,

____

[YOUR NAME], *PRO SE*

[YOUR INMATE NUMBER]

[YOUR INSTITUTION]

[INSTITUTION ADDRESS]

KELLY PATRICK RIGGS

UNITED STATES DISTRICT COURT

IN THE [REDACTED] DISTRICT of [REDACTED]

[REDACTED] DIVISION

UNITED STATES OF AMERICA, Respondent vs. KELLY PATRICK RIGGS Petitioner	CASE NO(S): [REDACTED]

FIRST SET OF INTERROGATORIES FOR [REDACTED]

COMES NOW, the Petitioner, KELLY PATRICK RIGGS in *PRO SE*, in necessity, and hereby presents this first set of Interrogatories to [REDACTED], pursuant to *Federal Rules of Civil Procedure*, Rule 33, to be answered separately in writing and under oath within thirty [30) days. A place for your answer is provided below each Interrogatory. If additional space is needed for your answer use additional paper.

Each of the Interrogatories inclusive deemed to be a continuing Interrogatory pursuant to *Federal Rules of Civil Procedure*, Rule 26(e). The Petitioner, KELLY PATRICK RIGGS, request that [REDACTED], amend or supplement answers to these Interrogatories promptly and fully if at a later date, the Petitioner, KELLY PATRICK RIGGS, obtains additional facts or obtains or makes assumptions or reaches conclusions that are different from these set forth in the answer to these Interrogatories.

INTERROGATORY NO. 1: [REDACTED], are you a licensed attorney who is authorized to practice law in the State of [REDACTED], and did you represent KELLY PATRICK RIGGS in the United States District Court for the [REDACTED] District of [REDACTED]?

ANSWER TO NO. 1:

INTERROGATORY NO. 2: Did you or anybody from your office investigate Mr. Riggs' Criminal case for possible defenses prior to your first appearance in Court as Mr. Riggs' Defense Attorney?

ANSWER TO NO. 2:

INTERROGATORY NO. 3: Did you memorialize witness testimony in Affidavit?

ANSWER TO NO. 3:

INTERROGATORY NO. 4: Did you receive the Case/Work file from Attorneys who were previously appointed to represent Mr. Riggs?

ANSWER TO NO. 4:

INTERROGATORY NO. 5: [REDACTED], do you as a standard practice file in your client's case file all corresponding letters, memos, emails, or written communications concerning discovery, exculpatory evidence, and/or Brady/Giglio material from the opposing party and/or forward to you by previous Counsel?

ANSWER TO NO. 5:

INTERROGATORY NO. 6: [REDACTED], were you in the courtroom when [REDACTED] stated on the record that he filed a "Notice of Alibi"?

ANSWER TO NO. 6:

INTERROGATORY NO. 7: [REDACTED], were you in the courtroom when [REDACTED] stated in the Court record that he advised his client, Mr. Riggs, to Plea Guilty?

ANSWER TO NO. 7:

INTERROGATORY NO. 8: [REDACTED], were you in the courtroom when [REDACTED] made reference to 10 witnesses that he was aware of?

ANSWER TO NO. 8:

INTERROGATORY NO. 9: [REDACTED], is it in conflict with a defendant's best interest to advise him to Plea Guilty knowing the he, the defendant, had an Alibi defense, exculpatory video footage, and 10 Alibi Witnesses?

ANSWER TO NO. 9:

INTERROGATORY NO. 10: [REDACTED], were you in the courtroom when Judge [REDACTED] stated that [REDACTED] did not issue subpoenas to an Alibi Witness who was called by the defense, for Trial preparation?

ANSWER TO NO. 10:

INTERROGATORY NO. 11: (REDACTED], were you in the court room when the Judge [REDACTED] made a personal attack against an Alibi Witnesses credibility?

ANSWER TO NO. 11:

INTERROGATORY NO. 12: [REDACTED], were you appointed, by the Court, to represent the interests of KELLY PATRICK RIGGS in his Appeal to the United States Court of Appeals?

ANSWER TO NO. 12:

INTERROGATORY NO. 13: [REACTED], did you present any of the foregoing matters, in this Interrogatory, or any other matters to the United States Court of Appeals as arguable issues in the appeal of KELLY PATRICK RIGGS?

ANSWER TO NO. 13:

INTERROGATORY NO. 14: [REDACTED], have you provided Mr. Riggs with his entire case/work file that you and other Court Appointed Attorneys generated during and pertinent to that client's defense?

ANSWER TO NO. 14:

INTERROGATORY NO. 15: [REDACTED], are you and/or have you purposely impeded the defense in the case of the United States of America v. Kelly Patrick Riggs in an effort to assist other Court Officers, known to you, to hamper and/or otherwise impede an investigation of [REDACTED] Murder, a Federal defendant in the [REDACTED] District of [REDACTED]?

ANSWER TO NO. 15:

Date:______________________________ /s/______________________________

[REDACTED]

UNITED STATES DISTRICT COURT

IN THE [REDACTED] DISTRICT of [REDACTED]

[REDACTED] DIVISION

UNITED STATES OF AMERICA, Respondent vs. KELLY PATRICK RIGGS Petitioner	CASE NO(S): [REDACTED]

FIRST SET OF INTERROGATORIES FOR [REDACTED]

COMES NOW the Petitioner, KELLY PATRICK RIGGS in *PRO SE*, in necessity, and hereby presents this first set of Interrogatories to [REDACTED], pursuant to *Federal Rules of Civil Procedure*, Rule 33, to be answered separately in writing and under oath within thirty (30) days. A place for your answer is provided below each Interrogatory, If additional space is needed for your answer use additional paper.

Each of the Interrogatories inclusive deemed to be a continuing Interrogatory pursuant to *Federal Rules of Civil Procedure*, Rule 26(e). The Petitioner, KELLY PATRICK RIGGS, requests that [REDACTED] amend or supplement answers to these Interrogatories promptly and fully if at a later: date,the Petitioner KELLY PATRICK RIGGS, obtains additional facts or obtains or make assumptions or reaches conclusions that are different from these set forth in the answer to these Interrogatories.

INTERROGATORY NO. 1: [REDACTED], did you represent the United States of America in United States v. Kelly Patrick Riggs, Criminal Case No.: [REDACTED], in the United States District Court for the [REDACTED] District of [REDACTED]?

ANSWER TO NO. 1:

INTERROGATORY NO. 2: Did you present the wording in the Indictment in this case to the Grand Jury as a reading of the Federal Statute 18 U.S.C. § 2422(b)?

ANSWER TO NO. 2:

INTERROGATORY NO. 3: Did the District Court issue a standing discovery order in this Criminal Case?

ANSWER TO NO. 3:

INTERROGATORY NO. 4: In the course of the United States Attorney's investigation of this case, did you or anyone in your office become privy to recorded telephone calls concerning this Criminal Case that were recovered from [REDACTED] Jail and/or [REDACTED] Jail.

ANSWER TO NO. 4:

INTERROGATORY NO. 5: Did you or your office provide to Court Appointed Counsel [REDACTED], the name of [REDACTED] after recovering his name from jailhouse phone recording?

ANSWER TO NO. 5:

INTERROGATORY NO. 6: Did you and/or your office, discover that there existed ALIBI WITNESSES and/or exculpatory video footage in this case?

ANSWER TO NO. 6:

INTERROGATORY NO. 7: Was this information presented to the Grand Jury?

ANSWER TO NO. 7:

INTERROGATORY NO. 8: Did you and your office provide ALL Brady/Giglio evidence to Court Appointed Counsel in this criminal Case?

ANSWER TO NO 8:

INTERROGATORY NO. 9: Did you provide the Security Video footage, recovered from the [REDACTED] and the [REDACTED], to Court Appointed Defense Counsel in this case?

ANSWER TO NO. 9:

INTERROGATORY NO. 10: Did you or your office Investigate the murder of [REDACTED] and/or the scheme to impede the investigation and/or cover up and prevent the discovery of the same?

ANSWER TO NO. 10:

INTERROGATORY NO. 11: Do you know [REDACTED]?

ANSWER TO NO. 11:

Date: ______________________________ /s/______________________________

[REDACTED]

UNITED STATES DISTRICT COURT

IN THE [REDACTED] DISTRICT of [REDACTED]

[REDACTED] DIVISION

UNITED STATES OF AMERICA, Respondent vs. KELLY PATRICK RIGGS Petitioner	CASE NO(S): [REDACTED]

FIRST SET OF INTERROGATORIES FOR [REDACTED]

COMES NOW the Petitioner, KELLY PATRICK RIGGS in *PRO SE*, in necessity, and hereby, presents this first set of Interrogatories to [REDACTED], pursuant to *Federal Rules of Civil Procedure*,

Rule 33, to be answered separately in writing and under Oath within Thirty (30) days. A place for your answer is provided below each Interrogatory. If additional space is needed for your answer use additional paper.

Each of the Interrogatories inclusive deemed to be a continuing Interrogatory pursuant to *Federal Rules of Civil Procedure*, Rule 26(e). The Petitioner, KELLY PATRICK RIGGS, requests that [REDACTED], amend or supplement answers to these Interrogatories promptly and fully if at a later date, KELLY PATRICK RIGGS, obtains additional facts or obtains or makes assumptions, reaches conclusions, and/or discovers that actual facts are different from those set forth in the answers to these Interrogatories.

INTERROGATORY NO. 1: [REDACTED], did you appear as the representative of the United States of America in UNITED STATES v. KELLY PATRICK RIGGS, Criminal No.: [REDACTED], on April 22, 2014, for the sentencing of Mr. Riggs, in the United States District Court for the [REDACTED] District of [REDACTED]?

ANSWER TO NO. 1:

INTERROGATORY NO. 2: Did you investigate the essential elements of the charged offense as they relate to fact and law prior to your seeking the finality of the case?

ANSWER TO NO. 2:

INTERROGATORY NO. 3: Did you hear Mr. Riggs' profession of INNOCENCE prior to the Court imposing sentence?

ANSWER TO NO. 3:

INTERROGATORY NO. 4: Did you hear Mr. Riggs' request that the Court and/or the Government provide proof that the pursuit of this Criminal Conviction was conducted with proper jurisdiction to do so?

ANSWER TO NO. 4:

INTERROGATORY NO. 5: Did you, as the representative of the United States, provide on the record, proof that the United States had subject-matter jurisdiction, over Rape; Second Degree Rape; Sodomy; and/or other alleged offenses that do not have as an essential element an economic nexus to Federal Law, to prosecute pursuant to the powers granted to the Government under the United States Constitution's Article I, Section 8, Clause 3, and/or the Interstate Commerce Clause?

ANSWER TO NO. 5:

INTERROGATORY NO. 6: Did you represent the United States of America in UNITED STATES v. [REDACTED]?

ANSWER TO NO. 6:

INTERROGATORY NO 7: Were you made aware by [REDACTED] that [REDACTED] had confessed to murdering his Co-Defendant [REDACTED]?

ANSWER TO NO. 7:

INTERROGATORY NO. 8: Were you made aware that [REDACTED]made Mr. Riggs give a statement to Deputy Marshal [REDACTED] concerning [REDACTED]?

ANSWER TO NO. 8:

INTERROGATORY NO. 9: Were you made aware that Mr. Riggs reported [REDACTED] confession to his Trial Judge, in letter in August 2, 2013?

ANSWER TO NO. 9:

INTERROGATORY NO. 10: Would you consider it a Conflict of interest of one client over another, if a client required that [REDACTED] reported to the Court that [REDACTED] confession to Mr. Riggs that he murdered [REDACTED] and that [REDACTED] would have to report that his client committed murder to gain protection for another client from the harm threatened by the first?

ANSWER TO NO. 10:

INTERROGATORY NO. 11: Did you move the Court for a downward departure for [REDACTED], A.K.A.[REDACTED], pursuant to Rule 35, for his substantial assistance regarding [REDACTED]?

ANSWER TO NO. 11:

INTERROGATORY NO. 12: Does a 5K.1 departure mention murder as a form of substantial assistance to the Government?

ANSWER TO NO. 12:

INTERROGATORY NO. 13: Was [REDACTED] chargeable for his active role in intimidating a witness in this case and/or guilty of hampering an investigation of the murder of a Federal Defendant?

ANSWER TO NO. 13:

INTERROGATORY NO. 14: Are you duty bound to report governmental misconduct to the appropriate professional ethics authority?

ANSWER TO NO. 14:

INTERROGATORY NO. 15: Who prosecuted felonies committed by Court Officers in the [REDACTED] District of [REDACTED]?

ANSWER TO NO. 15:

Date: ______________________________ /s/ ______________________________

[REDACTED]

KELLY PATRICK RIGGS

UNITED STATES DISTRICT COURT

IN THE [REDACTED] DISTRICT of [REDACTED]

[REDACTED] DIVISION

[YOUR NAME] vs. UNITED STATES OF AMERICA	CASE NO(S): [YOUR CIVIL CASE NO.] [YOUR CRIMINAL CASE NO.]

PETITIONER'S OBJECTION TO THE MAGISTRATE'S REPORT AND RECOMMENDATIONS

COMES NOW the Petitioner, [YOUR NAME] in *PRO SE*, in necessity, and hereby OBJECTS to the Magistrate's Report and recommendation (hereafter "R & R") that recommends that the Court deny Petitioner's 28 U.S.C. § 2255 motion without conducting an Evidentiary Hearing and/or opening discovery. The Petitioner avers that the Magistrate's R & R presents many EGREGIOUS ERRORS in an effort to forgo conducting an Evidentiary Hearing, open discovery, and/or resolve FACTUAL DISPUTES. The Petitioner particularizes the following OBJECTION with particularly, TO WIT:

[NOTE: here you MUST include FACTS particular to your personal case, you may use the following examples that apply.]

1) OBJECTION NO. 1: The Petitioner OBJECTS to the Magistrate Judge re-characterizing his Constitutional claims by rephrasing the claims and then addressing ONLY part of the claim and/or an entirely different claim then what was raised by the Petitioner, in his pleadings.

2) OBJECTION NO. 2: The Petitioner OBJECTS to the misstatements of the procedural history of the case as found in the Magistrate's "R & R." [follow here with particular misstatements in your R & R or omit this paragraph if none exists].

3) OBJECTION NO. 3: The Petitioner OBJECTS to the Magistrate's finding of fact based solely on the Presentence Report. The opinion of the Court of Appeals, and the Government's response to the Petitioner's § 2255. The Petitioner asserted FACTS throughout his § 2255 motion, which would have changed the outcome of the Petitioner's Criminal Case, and those FACTS warrant relief under 28

U.S.C. § 2255. [Note: Again, you MUST integrate facts from your case here or omit this objection. Remember, any unresolved claim is a "disputed factual issue."] The Magistrate's "R & R" fails to address the facts set forth in the Petitioner's filings, which if true, warrant relief under 28 U.S.C. § 2255 and requires this Court to conduct an EVIDENTIARY HEARING to resolve the FACTUAL DISPUTE. See *Holmes v. United States*, 876 F. 2d 1545, 1547 (11th Cir. 1989); *United States v. Millen* 760 F. 2d 1116 (11th Cir. 1985).

NOTE: Shepardize all citations and use cases from your Circuit if available.

4) OBJECTION NO. 4: The Petitioner OBJECTS to the Magistrate's addressing claims not raised in Petitioner's § 2255 motion. [NOTE: The Magistrate will often change your claim to avoid a meritorious claim such as exchanging your claimed failure to "investigate impeachment evidence" for "failure to present adequate defense." This changes the standard of review after which the Magistrate may apply the "presumption standard."] See Petitioner's filings in his § 2255 proceedings. The Magistrate's "R & R" DOES\ NOT address the claims raised by the Petitioner, which is a violation of *Clisby v. Jones*, 960 F. 2d 925, 935-936 (11th Cir. 1992)(en banc). Instead of addressing these claims the R & R states what occurred at Trial which DOES NOT address the claim and FACTS before the Court in the § 2255 pleadings.

NOTE: Objection #5 is ONLY used when the Government employs affidavits, provided by your Defense Counsel, in your § 2255 proceedings.

5) OBJECTION NO. 5: The Petitioner OBJECTS to the magistrate's findings of fact based solely on the affidavit provided by Defense Counsel. When the Court is faced with conflicting affidavits on material facts, contested factual issues MAY NOT be decided on the basis of affidavits alone, unless the affidavits are supported by other evidence in the record. See *United States v. Hughes*, 635 F. 2d 449, 451 (5th Cir. 1981). When facts are at issue in a § 2255 proceeding, a hearing is required if: (1) the record, as supplemented by the Trial Judge's personal knowledge or recollection, does not conclusively negate the facts alleged in support of the claim for § 2255 relief; and (2) the movant would be entitled to post-conviction relief as a legal matter if his factual allegations are true. See *Friedman v. United States*, 588 F. 2d 1010, 1015 (5th Cir. 1979); *United States v. Briggs*, 939 F. 2d 222, 228 (5th Cir. 1991). The Magistrate's "R & R" relies on Counsel's affidavit and fails to address the FACTS stated in the Petitioner's § 2255 pleadings.

NOTE: All the possible objections you may have cannot be listed here comprehensibly. Add all you find in subsequent objections here.

WHEREFORE NOW, above premises considered, the Petitioner hereby OBJECTS to the conclusions found in the Magistrate's "R & R." Based on these foregoing reasons stated herein, the Petitioner respectfully MOVES this Court to REJECT the Magistrate's "R & R," and its findings, and REMAND for an EVIDENTIARY HEARING before a NEW MAGISTRATE JUDGE.

Done This [DATE] Day of [MONTH], [YEAR]

Respectfully Submitted,

____

[YOUR NAME], *PRO SE*

[YOUR INMATE NUMBER]

[YOUR INSTITUTION]

[INSTITUTION ADDRESS]

UNITED STATES DISTRICT COURT

IN THE [REDACTED] DISTRICT of [REDACTED]

[REDACTED] DIVISION

KELLY PATRICK RIGGS,	
vs.	Civil Case No.: [REDACTED]
UNITED STATES OF AMERICA	Criminal Case No.: [REDACTED]

MOTION FOR AN EVIDENTIARY HEARING ON 28 U.S.C. § 2255 MOTION

COMES NOW the Petitioner, KELLY PATRICK RIGGS in *PRO SE*, in necessity, and hereby MOVES this Court to schedule and conduct an EVIDENTIARY HEARING in an EXPEDITIOUS MANNER as mandated by 28 U.S.C. § 2255 and Rules governing 28 U.S.C. § 2255, Rule 8(c). The Petitioner hereby avers that this Court's CONTINUAL DELAY of JUSTICE is in violation of his Constitutional/Civil Rights. Moreover, the mandatory language of Rule 8(c)'s prompt hearing requirement, the longstanding preference for promptly remedying unlawful incarceration, and the partial analogy to the Constitutional Right to a SPEEDY TRIAL afford incarcerated petitioners a basis for seeking to EXPEDITE HABEAS CORPUS PROCEEDINGS lest their right to prompt release from unlawful custody be mooted by unnecessary delay. The records in the Petitioner's case CLEARLY SHOW his INNOCENCE, even when reviewed by laymen at law, and that he is held HOSTAGE in VIOLATION of the CONSTITUTION and LAWS passed in pursuance thereof. Evidentiary Hearing is grossly overdue in this case, in support, the Petitioner shows the followings:

1) That the Petitioner has shown, to this court, that there exists an ALIBI DEFENSE in this case for over three (3) years.
2) That the Petitioner has shown, to this Court, that there existed a third-party confession recorded in a Jailhouse phone call by a Police Informant, in this case for over three (3) years.
3) That the Petitioner has requested that this Court make known to him ALL the ESSENTIAL ELEMENTS of the CHARGED OFFENSE as they relate to FACT as well as LAW for over 30 months, to NO avail.
4) That the Petitioner has and continues to request that this Court appoint adequate representation, to include competent Counsel and Investigators, for over three (3) years, to NO avail.

5) That Court appointed Counsel, [REDACTED], performed his duties under a CONFLICT of INTEREST as he was required to divide his loyalties between the Petitioner and [REDACTED]. A client who assisted [REDACTED] in COERCING the Petitioner to Plea Guilty under fear and duress that his wife and children would be killed also.

6) That the Petitioner filed his 28 U.S.C. § 2255 Motion with detailed FACTS concerning Defense Counsel's [REDACTED], inducement for Petitioner's Guilty Plea.

7) That the Petitioner attached to his 28 U.S.C. § 2255 Motion, several affidavits concerning Court Appointed Counsel's, [REDACTED], INEFFECTIVE ASSISTANCE OF COUNSEL to include but not limited to [REDACTED] inducement used to COERCE the Petitioner's Guilty Plea. Additionally, the Petitioner has made known to this Court previously and in his 28 U.S.C. § 2255 Motion, that there are three (3) witnesses who will ATTEST to Court Appointed Counsel's, [REDACTED], inducement.

8) The United States obtained NO affidavit from Court Appointed Defense Counsel [REDACTED] concerning his inducements to the petitioner and relies ONLY on the testimony of the District Judge [REDACTED], who is an obvious adverse party in this Proceeding.

9) This Court is faced with CONFLICTING SWORN STATEMENTS, based on DISPUTED FACTUAL ISSUES in this 28 U.S.C. § 2255 proceeding, and a BRAZEN BREACH of CONTRACT by the United States when, in its answer, it withdrew agreed upon considerations negotiated in the Plea agreement.

WHEREFORE NOW, above premises considered, the Petitioner MOVES this Court to, EXPEDITIOUSLY, Schedule and Conduct an EVIDENTIARY HEARING to resolve the DISPUTED FACTS ***POST HASTE***.

A Memorandum Brief is attached hereto and made part of this Motion by reference herein.

Done This [redacted] Day of [redacted], [redacted].

Respectfully Submitted,

[REDACTED]

Kelly Patrick Riggs, *PRO SE*
Reg # [redacted]

Federal Correctional Institution
Mailing Address
City, State and Zip Code

UNITED STATES DISTRICT COURT

IN THE [REDACTED] DISTRICT of [REDACTED]

[REDACTED] DIVISION

KELLY PATRICK RIGGS, Petitioner vs. UNITED STATES OF AMERICA Respondent	CASE NO(S). : [REDACTED]

MEMORANDUM BRIEF IN SUPPORT OF MOTION FOR AN EVIDENTIARY HEARING ON 28 U.S.C. § 2255 MOTION

COMES NOW the Petitioner, KELLY PATRICK RIGGS in *PRO SE*, in necessity, and files this Memorandum Brief in support of his motion for an EVIDENTIARY HEARING, pursuant to Rule 8, governing 28 U.S.C. § 2255 proceedings.

This Court is faced with what the Petitioner hopes is a unique situation. In this case, the Petitioner has, and continues to present, an AIR TIGHT ALIBI DEFENSE. Not one affidavit has been presented in contention to this FACT. Not one affidavit has been presented in contention to the Petitioner's claim of a CONFLICT OF INTEREST. Not one affidavit has been presented in contention to the Petitioner's claim that Court Officers in the [Redacted] District of [Redacted], have concealed the murder of [Redacted], or the FACT that his murder has adversely affected the Petitioner's Criminal Case and his Constitutionally PROTECTED CIVIL RIGHT to Counsel. The Government has ONLY presented the testimony of the District Judge to refute the veracity of the Petitioner's ALIBI DEFENSE in its Appendix. The Petitioner however, has presented SEVERAL AFFIDAVITS from himself, the ALIBI WITNESSES, and the transcripts in which [Redacted] testified that he "filed Notice of Alibi" and "issued subpoenas' for ten (10) witnesses," which would raise a reasonable doubt as to guilt in any "Honorable" Court seeking JUSTICE. The District Judge in this case has made herself AN ADVERSE PARTY as she is the ONLY party who has raised contention to the Alibi Defense asserted by the Petitioner and his Counsel. The District Judge ACTIVELY OBSTRUCTED the Petitioner's Rights by refusing to issue subpoenas to Alibi Witnesses and *BRAZENLY* confessing to this FACT in record.

This Court CLEARLY, has before it ***CONTESTED FACTUAL ISSUES***, concerning the Alibi Defense, and the effects of [Redacted's] murder. ***CONTESTED FACTUAL ISSUES*** may not be decided on the basis of AFFIDAVITS alone unless the affidavits are supported by other evidence in the record. *United States v. Hughes*, 635 F. 2d 449, 451 (5th Cir. 1981). When FACTS are at issue in a 28 U.S.C. § 2255 proceeding, a hearing is required if: (1) The record, as supplemented by the Trial Judge's personal knowledge or recollection, does not conclusively negate the FACTS alleged in support of the claim for 28 U.S.C. § 2255 relief; and (2) The Movant would be entitled to POST-CONVICTION RELIEF as a legal matter if his ***FACTUAL*** allegations are true. *Friedman v. United States*, 558 F. 2d 1010, 1015 (5th Cir. 1979); see *United States v. Briggs*, 939 F. 2d 222, 228 (5th Cir. 1991). It is CLEAR, by the Judge's failure to deny Petitioner's previous motion for a hearing, that Judge [Redacted] has no "knowledge or recollection" that ***CONCLUSIVELY*** negates the FACTS alleged.

Moreover, EVIDENTIARY HEARING is due based upon the Government's answer to Petitioner's 28 U.S.C. § 2255, which breached the Plea Agreement in the Petitioner's Criminal Case. The Plea Agreement contained a carefully considered right to appeal and/or COLLATERAL ATTACK, based upon INEFFECTIVE ASSISTANCE OF COUNSEL, inter alia, reserved to the Petitioner. In the Government's answer (Doc. 13, page 6 & 7), the United States Attorney, for the first time mentions "Pre-Plea Conduct" as a basis of WAIVER of APPEAL. The Petitioner has previously raised this issue in his TIMELY FILED REPLY to the Government's answer.

The determination of whether a party breached a Plea Agreement is governed by the Law of Contracts. *Puckett v. United States*, 173 556 U.S. 129, 137 (2009) (stating "plea bargains are essentially contracts"). However, concerns unique to the Criminal Justice system leads to greater scrutiny by Courts than would be afforded to general questions of Contract Law. Due Process requires that the agreement be interpreted in keeping with a defendant's reasonable understanding and that any ambiguity be construed against the Government. *United States v. Williams*, 444 F. 3d 1286, 1305 (11th Cir. 2006) (when ambiguity resolved in defendant's favor, written agreements omission of orally agreed-to terms did not preclude defendant's from benefiting from those terms.)

The Petitioner was denied his Right to appeal under the Plea Agreement when Ineffective Counsel filed *Ander's* Brief base upon alleged appeal waiver.

A defendant who alleges that the Government breached a Plea Agreement is entitled to an Evidentiary Hearing unless the allegations are incredible, frivolous, or false. *Blackledge v. Allison*, 431 U.S. 63, 76, 80-82 (1977)(allegations of breach entitles defendant to Evidentiary Hearing unless defendant's allegations are "palpably incredible" or "patently frivolous" or "false").

The Petitioner hereby avers that he has identified FACTUAL DISPUTES with respect to his INEFFECTIVE ASSISTANCE OF COUNSEL claims inter alia, that cannot be decided, in favor of the Government, on the basis of these affidavits alone. See *Hughes*, 635 F. 2d at 451. Therefore, the motions, files, and records in this case *DO NOT* show conclusively that the Petitioner, Kelly Patrick Riggs, is not entitled to any relief on his claims of INEFFECTIVE ASSISTANCE of Trial/Appellate Counsel. See 28 U.S.C. § 2255. See also *Fontaine v. United States*, 411, U.S. 213, 36 L. Ed. 2d 169, 93 S. Ct. 1461 (1973).

WHEREFORE NOW, based on the FACTS detailed in the 28 U.S.C. § 2255 and its supporting affidavits/attachments, the Petitioner, Kelly Patrick Riggs, MOVES this Court to EXPEDIENTLY SCHEDULE this case for an EVIDENTIARY HEARING to resolve the disputed facts.

Done This [redacted] Day of [redacted], 2016.

Respectfully Submitted,

[REDACTED]

Kelly Patrick Riggs, *PRO SE*
Reg # [redacted]

Federal Correctional Institution
Mailing Address
City, State and Zip Code

KELLY PATRICK RIGGS

UNITED STATES DISTRICT COURT

IN THE [REDACTED] DISTRICT of [REDACTED]

[REDACTED] DIVISION

[YOUR NAME] vs. UNITED STATES OF AMERICA	CASE NO(S): [YOUR CASE NO.]

PETITIONER'S MOTION TO COMPEL JUDGEMENT

PURSUANT TO FEDERAL RULE OF CIVIL PROCEDURE,

RULE 12(c).

COMES NOW the Petitioner, [YOUR NAME] IN *PRO SE*, in necessity, and hereby MOVES this Honorable Court to rule on his § 2255 motion. The Petitioner, herein, avers that all pleadings are closed- out and that this case is ripe for judgment in the Petitioner's favor. This Court has jurisdiction to rule upon the Petitioner's § 2255 motion pursuant to this, the Petitioner's request, and *Federal Rules of Civil Procedure*, Rule 12(c). In support, the Petitioner shows the Court the following:

1) On or about [Date of Filing], the Petitioner filed an instant 28 U.S.C. § 2255 motion to Vacate, Set Aside, or Correct.
2) On or about [Date of Gov. Response], the United States filed its response.
3) On or about [Date of Your Reply], the Petitioner filed his Reply.
4) Here now, the Petitioner MOVES this Court to render its ruling in GOOD FAITH.

WHEREFORE NOW, above premises considered, the Petitioner MOVES this Court to render judgment in his 28 U.S.C. § 2255 proceeding. The Petitioner respectfully MOVES this Court to enter judgment as required by Law, Liberty, and Justice.

Done This [DATE] of [Month], [YEAR].

Respectfully Submitted,

[Your Signature]
____

[YOUR NAME], *PRO SE*
[YOUR PRISON NUMBER]
[YOUR INSTITUTION]
[INSTITUTION ADDRESS]

KELLY PATRICK RIGGS

UNITED STATES DISTRICT COURT

IN THE [REDACTED] DISTRICT of [REDACTED]

[REDACTED] DIVISION

KELLY PATRICK RIGGS vs. UNITED STATES OF AMERICA	CASE NO(S): [REDACTED]

PETITIONER'S MOTION IN OPPOSITION TO THE COURT'S ORDER REGARDING SUMMARY DISPOSITION

COMES NOW the Petitioner, KELLY PATRICK RIGGS in *PRO SE*, in necessity, because the Court still refuses to appoint ADEQUATE REPRESENTATION, and hereby provides this Court with his written OPPOSITION in hopes of restoring enough INTEGRITY in the heart of the presiding Judge as to bring about a fair proceeding in favor of the Petitioner. A Petitioner, who, is an INNOCENT American father and husband. In support, the Petitioner shows this Court, and wishes to enter into record the following:

1) On or about 3/17/16, this Court filed into record its "ORDER Regarding Summary Disposition." The Petitioner hereby avers that this was an expected tactic to delay the EXPOSITION, or HIDE, JUDICIAL MISCONDUCT. In an attempt to shield the presiding Judge and other Court Officers from Prosecution for CORRUPTION, the United States District Court in the [REDACTED] District of [REDACTED], has concealed the MURDER of [REDACTED]; provided [REDACTED] (A.K.A. [REDACTED]) a downward departure for said MURDER; CONSPIRED to employ [REDACTED] to pose a threat of death against the Petitioners family to compel a Guilty Plea; REFUSED to issue Alibi Witness subpoenas; REFUSED to appoint adequate representation; and CONVICTED an INNOCENT American Citizen (The Petitioner) of a crime he DID NOT commit, notwithstanding an AIRTIGHT ALIBI DEFENSE known to the Court, and/or otherwise violated substantive DUE PROCESS in every conceivable way.

2) The Court is now attempting to once again violate DUE PROCESS based upon ASSERTED FACTS that the Court knows to be *FALSE*. The Petitioner has a *DUE PROCESS RIGHT* to present an Alibi Defense in support of his *ACTUAL INNOCENCE*. This was prevented by a presiding Judge who REFUSED, as reflected by the record, to sign subpoenas. (See Criminal Docket 114, Page 20, Line 10, [copy attached]). This DEFICIENCY committed by Federal Judge is one of many (See Civil Docket 1, in record), that causes us to examine what exactly DUE PROCESS means. In 1884, the Supreme Court defined DUE PROCESS as:

   "Any legal proceeding enforced by public authority, whether sanctioned by age and custom, or newly devised in the discretion of the legislative power, in furtherance of the public good,

> which regards and preserves these principles of liberty and justice, must be held to be due process of law."

Clearly there is in existence NO sound principle of "General Public Good" that authorizes this Court to prey on American Families for PROFIT. In the Petitioner's Criminal Case, this court has denied him DUE PROCESS and ULTIMATELY ***ORPHANED*** the children of and **INNOCENT American Citizen** for nearly four (4) years, while Alibi. Witnesses still yearn to be heard.

For these very reasons, in 1914, the United States Supreme Court gave a short and simple definition:

> "The fundamental requisite of due process of law is the opportunity to be heard." (This was not a dissent).

Because INNOCENT petitioners have a DUE PROCESS RIGHT to be heard and to present the testimony of Alibi Witnesses. The Public in the [REDACTED] District of [REDACTED] should have a vested interest in whether or not JUSTICE is served in this case. In support, the Petitioner shows the Court the following:

A. EVIDENTIARY HEARING

In the Court's ORDER it states that: "a hearing is not necessary in this action because no bona fide credibility issue exists." This statement, by the Court, is PALPABLY INCREDIBLE, basing its findings on *FRAUD*, TO WIT:

1) This Court supports its efforts by FALSIFYING a Supreme Court entry. In the Court's ORDER it combines the names of two (2) different cases into one that, in the opinion of this Petitioner, is to MISDIRECT a reviewing Court from the SECOND ***FALSE*** STATEMENT in support. The Court quotes a Supreme Court case, "*Schriro v. Loandrigan*," that does NOT EXIST. If you search by the digest location, the Court provided, you find the name "*Schriro v. Landrigan*." At first glance one may consider this to be a simple typographical error until you consider the FRAUDULENT quote the Court is attempting to hide.
2) In the Court's ORDER it quotes this HYBRID case as holding:

   "Such a hearing could enable an applicant to prove the *Petitioner's* factual allegations, which, if true, would entitle the applicant to habeas relief." (Emphasis added).

   In this statement the term,".. an applicant to prove the Petitioner's ...," shows the existence of "an applicant" - The Prisoner and "the Petitioner's" the prisoner's attorney. Which presents a situation completely discernible from the case at hand as the Court has CONTINUALLY DENIED this "Petitioner's factual allegation" is CLEARLY meaning the claims raised in any motion by the applicant's attorney once appointed. It DOES NOT refer to the claims in the *Petition* filed by the applicant as the Court is NOT BOUND by Rule or law to appoint Counsel until it has determined that."..an Evidentiary Hearing is warranted ... ." See Rules governing § 2255, Rule 8(c).

It is the opinion of the Petitioner that the court FALSIFIES this Supreme Court case to justify ONLY considering the FACTUAL ALLEGATIONS of the Petitioner's motions and NOT giving proper consideration to the petition itself along with its attachments, and/or reply to Government's response.

In the dogged efforts of this petitioner to seek JUSTICE and EQUITY in a *BIASED* Court, he discovered a similar Supreme Court case in 167 L. Ed. 2d 836, 550 U.S. 456 *Schriro v. Landrigan*, that contained a somewhat similar reading but a VERY DISPARATE meaning. In *Schriro v. Landrigan*, 550 U.S. 465, 474 (2007), the Court held that:

> "in deciding whether to grant an evidentiary hearing, a federal court must consider whether such a hearing could enable an applicant to prove the *Petition's* factual allegations, which, if true, would entitle the applicant to federal habeas relief." (Emphasis Added)

In this context the "Petition's factual allegations" CLEARLY means the claims raised by the applicant (prisoner) in his petition (filing). In this referenced case, the applicant, a state prisoner, is exercising his RIGHTS under habeas corpus pursuant to 28 U.S.C. § 2254. § 2254 is akin to an appellant proceeding in a Federal Court to evaluate the legality of a prisoner's restraint by a State Court. A.E.D.P.A. also requires Federal Habeas Courts to presume the correctness of State Courts factual findings unless applicants rebut this presumption with "clear and convincing evidence." § 2254(e)(1). Although, similar in many ways, a motion to vacate, set aside, or correct a sentence pursuant to § 2255 is DISTINCTLY DIFFERENT in at least two aspects: (a) it is not an appellate procedure, it is a step in a criminal proceeding (*Federal Habeas Corpus Practice and Procedure Manual*) and (b) § 2255 is brought before the Sentencing Court who has before it the ENTIRE RECORD, and therefore, may not presume the correctness of its own factual findings that are contrary to FACTS and EVIDENCE in the RECORD of the criminal case. In the criminal case, the record reflects that [REDACTED], appointed Defense Counsel, testified that he subpoenaed "at least ten (10) people in the case" who were called in support of an "AIRTIGHT" ALIBI DEFENSE. (See Criminal Docket 114, Page 55, Lines 19-20, [copy attached]). Defense Counsel further testified that "we actually filed a Notice of Alibi." (See Criminal Docket 114, Page 74, Line 19, [copy attached]). CLEARLY this testimony by a HIGHLY ESTEEMED Federal Public Defender, who the presiding Judge held above reproach, should be considered CREDIBLE by the Court and coupled with the Petitioner's PROFESSION of *INNOCENCE* on 10/5/13, which CANNOT be held as NEWLY PROFESSED, should, in any Honorable Court, serve as "Clear and convincing evidence" by which to rebut any possible presumption.

The Court has announced its intention to exercise an ARBITRARY approach to Justice by denying this Petitioner the DUE PROCESS RIGHT to present FACTS, EVIDENCE, and ALIBI WITNESSES that are indicative to his *FACTUAL INNOCENCE*. The Petitioner is of the opinion that the Court's actions may be due to its IGNORANCE of LAW. The Petitioner respectfully suggest that the Court review the *Federal Habeas Corpus Practice and Procedure Manual*.

As found in the *Federal Habeas Corpus Practice and Procedure Manual*, Chapter § 20.1 et al (b) Evolution of Fact-Developed Standards, you will find in the seventh paragraph the following:

> "federal habeas corpus hearings are required if three conditions are met. (l) The petition alleges facts that if proved, entitle the petitioner to relief; (2) The fact based claims survive summary dismissal because their factual allegations are not palpably incredible or patently frivolous or false. The standard for summary dismissal in habeas corpus proceedings; and (3) For reasons beyond the control of the Petitioner and his/her lawyer (assuming the lawyer rendered constitutionally satisfactory assistance), the factual claims were not previously the subject of a full and fair hearing ..."

In the very paragraph of the Court's ORDER that "denies Mr. Riggs' motion for an Evidentiary Hearing," the Court takes Judicial Notice of the testimony and findings of that hearing, "the Court finds no need for additional testimony to resolve credibility issues relating to the effectiveness of his Counsel or any other ground in his habeas motion."

"In a previous hearing on 12/20/13, this Court determined that Court appointed Counsel, [REDACTED] did provide effective assistance of counsel and took notice of his credibility. At that hearing, [REDACTED] testified that he did give Notice of an Alibi. Defense and subpoenaed 10 witnesses. An Alibi. Defense complete with 10 witnesses would support the Petitioner's claim of ***ACTUAL INNOCENCE***. The testimony of the subpoenaed witnesses currently stands OUTSIDE of the RECORD. It is CLEAR by this, that if the

Court is correct and [REDACTED] was effective and credible in his testimony, then the Court is DUTY BOUND to hold an EVIDENTIARY HEARING and open DISCOVERY to ascertain the veracity of [REDACTED] subpoenaed Alibi. Witnesses. If this Court has determined that [REDACTED] was INEFFECTIVE for supplying FALSE TESTIMONY to this Court concerning Alibi Witnesses, and perhaps the Petitioner just missed it, then the Petitioner and the Government/Court are in dispute concerning a CONTESTED FACTUAL ISSUE. In both possibilities, the Court is DUTY BOUND to hold an EVIDENTIARY HEARING and open DISCOVERY to determine the value of the Alibi Defense, Witness testimony, and the Petitioner's claim of ACTUAL INNOCENCE Along with if, this Court holds *ACTUAL INNOCENCE* as grounds to entitle a Petitioner to Post-Conviction Relief as a legal matter in this Court. Please see the Petitioner's motion and brief "For an Evidentiary Hearing on 28 U.S.C. § 2255 motion," filed in this Court on the 24th of February 2016.

In the case at hand, the Court has taken Judicial Notice of the Petitioner's Alibi Defense and Supporting Witnesses as asserted by the testimony of [REDACTED]. The Alibi Defense CLEARLY supports the Petitioner's claim of "*ACTUAL INNOCENCE*." "*ACTUAL INNOCENCE*" is one of approximately 30 claims raised in the Petitioner's § 2255 many of which are DISPUTED FACTUAL ISSUES. It is CLEAR that an Evidentiary Hearing would be required in any Honorable Court. The Petitioner would guide this Court, however, to consider the holding of *Haines V. Kerner*, 404 U.S. 519. which stated in its summary that:

> "On Certiorari, the United States Supreme Court reversed, in a per curiam opinion, expressing the unanimous views of the Court, it was held that since it did not appear beyond doubt that the inmate could prove no set of facts in support of his claim which would entitle him to relief, he was entitled to an opportunity to offer proof."

See also; 404 U.S. 519, 520-521 which states in pertinent part that:

> "We cannot say with assurance that under the allegations of the *pro se* complaint, which we hold to less stringent standards than formal pleading drafted by lawyers, it appears 'beyond doubt that the plaintiff can prove no set of facts in support of his claim which would entitle him to relief.' Conley v. Gibson, 355 U.S. 41, (1957), See *Dioguardi. v. Durning*, 139 F.2d 774 (CA2 1944).
>
> Accordingly, although we intimate no view whatever on the merits of Petitioner's allegations, we conclude that he is entitled to an opportunity to offer proof." (This unanimous decision by the Supreme Court is not a dissent).

B. APPOINTMENT OF COUNSEL

The Petitioner hereby avers that the District Court abused its discretion by denying an EVIDENTIARY HEARING in this case. (The subject of an ensuing INTERLOCUTORY APPEAL). In the Court's ORDER it states that, ."..this Court has found that no hearing is necessary, it also finds that Mr. Riggs is not entitled to appointment of Counsel in this case and DENIES his motion. "Here in this issue, and all that follows, the Court stacks ABUSE upon ABUSE to exact its personal agenda. As in the execution of the Petitioner's Criminal case, the cause of this action, the Court did and continues to deny ADEQUATE REPRESENTATION. Throughout the Petitioner's criminal case, he repeatedly requested from the Court, Investigators, Witness Subpoenas, Forensic Evaluations, *Brady* information, Particularized Grand Jury charges, Video Evidence, Witness Affidavits ... etc. The Court repeatedly DENIED all including the RIGHT to develop his ALIBI DEFENSE.

When the Court dismissed appointed Counsel [REDACTED], in its efforts to AVOID A CONFLICT OF INTEREST claim, the Court appointed [REDACTED]. [REDACTED], upon appointment, failed to prepare himself to represent the Petitioner at a hearing to withdraw his Guilty Plea held on 12/20/13. [REDACTED] provided Constitutionally INEFFECTIVE ASSISTANCE of COUNSEL in that proceeding by failing to

1) Call the Witnesses subpoenaed by [REDACTED];
2) Assert the Petitioner's claim of ACTUAL INNOCENCE;
3) To argue the CONFLICT OF INTEREST between [REDACTED] representation of [REDACTED] when [REDACTED] proffered the testimony of one against the other;
4) Investigate the case in any way; or
5) To revise the Petitioner's *pro se* motion to withdraw his Guilty Plea to clarify the Petitioner's claims to the Court.

During a well-rehearsed proceeding called "Motion Hearing" staged on December 20, 2013, in a substandard Court, [REDACTED] was so apathetic that the Court had to prompt him to recite his lines stating, "I do not know, your Honor, frankly if it is, we would object to it being read subject to the Court's ruling." (See Criminal Docket #114, Page 47, Lines 7-9).

At sentencing, notwithstanding the Petitioner's protest for sentencing an *INNOCENT* man based upon Plea Agreement, the Court states that.".. any problems that may have existed with prior Counsel and your disagreement with them have been cured by [REDACTED] representation of you." (See Criminal Docket #116, Page 18, Lines 17-20). This is CLEARLY a Fraudulent statement as up to that point, [REDACTED] was NOT appointed to represent the Petitioner's interests in his criminal case. But ONLY to represent the Petitioner in .".. litigating his *pro se* motion to set aside his Guilty Plea."

You will find absolutely NO mention of [REDACTED] and/or his INEFFECTIVENESS in the court's ORDER that is the subject of this motion because of the Court's apparent FRAUD. The Claim of [REDACTED] 's INEFFECTIVENESS is particularized to the best of the Petitioner's ability, as a layman at law, in the Petitioner's initial § 2255 motion. This Court however, has made a MOCKERY of the United States Supreme Court opinion in *Schriro v. Landrigan*, 505 U.S. 465, by changing the word "PETITION," meaning the applicant's filing, to the word "PETITIONER'S" meaning the person making the filings, in an effort to consider ONLY the claims in this Petitioner's subsequent motions, rather than the "PETITIONER'S" claims found in his *ORIGINAL* "PETITION," where he PLAINLY PARTICULARIZES his claim of *INEFFECTIVE ASSISTANCE of COUNSEL* against [REDACTED].

The Petitioner has just recently received a letter from [REDACTED] addressed to the Alabama State BAR, that he sent a year ago on January 29, 2015. The Petitioner hereby presents to this Court as *NEW EVIDENCE*. [REDACTED]'s letter that sets out his understanding of his *pro se* motion ..." and his understanding that there existed" ... a waiver in his [Petitioner's] Plea Agreement that he was to forfeit any right to appeal ..." NOTWITHSTANDING the FACT that the Plea Agreement contains a carefully considered provision for the Petitioner to appeal. (See attached [REDACTED].

This is CLEARLY a CONTESTED FACTUAL ISSUE concerning EFFECTIVE ASSISTANCE of COUNSEL. Once again, the Petitioner refers this Court to the *Federal Habeas Corpus Practice and Procedure Manual* that in Chapter 12.3, the Statutory Right to Counsel, that states:

> "In non-capital habeas corpus cases, Rule 8(c) of Habeas Rules makes clear that district Judges have the discretion to order 'the appointment of Counsel under the Criminal Justice Act at any stage of the proceedings ... ' The appointment of Counsel becomes mandatory for indigent non-capital petitioners, namely, (a) when Counsel is 'necessary for effective use of the discovery' procedures that Habeas Rule 6(a) authorizes district courts to authorize 'for good cause' ..."

The DENIAL of Counsel in the Petitioner's case is an ABUSE of DISCRETION perpetrated by this Court to hide "BONA FIDE credibility issues" from an Honorable Reviewing Court.

C. DISCOVERY AND APPOINTMENT OF EXPERTS AND INVESTIGATORS

Once again, the Court makes a FALSE STATEMENT in its ORDER. The opinion of the Petitioner is that this is meant to MISLEAD a reviewing Court. Perhaps it would be prudent for the Petitioner to remind this Court that his current situation is dire and he should not be expected, nor required, to check references, however, in the Interest of Justice - he will.

In this ORDER, the Court repeatedly states that, "Mr. Riggs has shown no good cause ..." when to the contrary, the Petitioner (Mr. Riggs) has repeatedly shown, over nearly four(4)years of litigation, that an ALIBI DEFENSE exists to support the claim of *ACTUAL INNOCENCE*. This Claim and its supporting Witnesses would show "GOOD CAUSE" in any HONORABLE Court.

The Claim of an ALIBI is one of a possible 30 claims in the Petitioner's § 2255. The Petitioner realizes that nothing he presents to the Court will be FRUITFUL due to the presiding Judge's PREJUDICE. Therefore, the Petitioner will ONLY discuss the ALIBI DEFENSE here and refer this Court to his § 2255 in its ENTIRETY as an OBJECTION to preserve the other 29 issues for appeal.

The Petitioner hereby avers that this Court has recognized in its ORDER that the Petitioner claims his *ACTUAL INNOCENCE*.

The Court has in its ORDER stated that it finds the question of [REDACTED]'s credibility answered and the Court "Taking Judicial Notice" of the Court's findings on 12/20/13 hearing testify that there existed a reason to give Notice of ALIBI and subpoena 10 Witnesses.

Either [REDACTED]'s testimony is credible as noticed by this Court and THERE EXISTS an *ALIBI DEFENSE* to support *ACTUAL INNOCENCE*, or [REDACTED] lied to this Court and the Court JUDICIALLY NOTICED his fraud making him incredible in his testimony.

Either of these conditions would show GOOD CAUSE. As the Court will find, the Petitioner filed "Petitioner's Motion for Discovery and Production of Documents pursuant to Rule 6 Governing 28 U.S.C. § 2255 Proceedings" on the 25th of November 2015. In that motion at 11 A(3) states "seeks the appointment of an investigator to take statements from ALIBI WITNESSES."

In the Memorandum Brief attached to the motion for Discovery, page 2 II 2 contains a very specific allegation concerning the ALIBI DEFENSE.

This Court will also discover that three out of the six Interrogatories filed in this case raise questions and concerns about the obtaining of ALIBI testimony and/or memorializing testimony in Witness affidavits.

Therefore, there exists a "specific allegation" concerning a failure to raise an ALIBI DEFENSE, "The Petitioner demonstrates that fully developing the record" with the supporting ALIBI testimony and/or proof that it had been neglected "would establish his detention as ILLEGAL and deserving of relief" because the Petitioner is *ACTUALLY INNOCENT* and appointed counsel failed to present these *FACTS* to the Trial Court, thereby imprisoning an *INNOCENT* American Citizen that in any other HONORABLE Court would be considered an EGREGIOUS VIOLATION of the Constitution of the United States and the FUNDAMENTAL RIGHTS it PROTECTS from PREDATORY COURTS such as this one.

In the Court's ORDER, it claims that: "Good cause exists when, through specific allegations, the Petitioner demonstrates that fully developing the record would establish his detention is ILLEGAL and deserving of relief." The Court here lists *Harris v. Nelson*, in support of this statement even though the Court wisely

NEGLECTS to use quotation marks, because this statement is NOT FOUND in the listed Supreme Court case.

The Supreme Court case referenced in this Court's ORDER *Harris v. Nelson*, 394 U.S. 286, 300 CLEARLY states in pertinent part that:

> .".. where specific allegations before the court show reason to believe that the petitioner may, if the facts are fully developed, be able to demonstrate that he is confined illegally and is therefore, entitled to relief, *it is the duty of the court* to provide the necessary facilities and procedures for an adequate inquiry. Obviously, in exercising this power, the court may utilize familiar procedures, as appropriate, whether these are found in civil or criminal rules or elsewhere in the 'usages and principles of law'.." See also *Teleguz v.Zoole*, 806 F.3d 803 (4th Cir. 2015); quoting *Quesinberry v, Taylor*, 162 F.3d at 279 (4th Cir. 2009).

Even though this Petitioner has EFFECTIVELY ESTABLISHED that he has shown "GOOD CAUSE" by this Court's more stringent standard, he was ONLY bound to show "GOOD CAUSE" according to the standards set out by the Supreme Court of the United States in *Harris v. Nelson*.

D. PLEA AGREEMENT

In the Court's ORDER, it attempts to finally resolve the entire issue, concerning the Petitioner's "*ACTUAL INNOCENCE*," based upon a COERCED PLEA AGREEMENT.

The Court's assertion in its final resolution is that, "Mr. Riggs forgets one important detail - he plead guilty and the Court has already held a hearing and found that plea to be voluntary." This short statement defines an OBVIOUS CONTRADICTION in the Court's ORDER.

The Trial Court did in FACT hold a hearing on December 20, 2013, at which testimony was received from Defense Counsel [REDACTED]. (Criminal Docket [REDACTED]). At that hearing, the presiding Judge found [REDACTED]'s testimony to be CREDIBLE. In that hearing, [REDACTED] testified he gave ALIBI Notice and subpoenaed Ten (10) Witnesses. The Court's ORDER, that is issue of this "Motion in. Opposition," is a reflection of this Court's "taking Judicial Notice of the testimony and findings at that hearing ... ."

The Petitioner hereby continues his DECLARATION that the VALIDITY of the Plea Agreement is a "CONTESTED FACTUAL ISSUE." On December 22, 2015, the Petitioner filed a detailed "Reply To United States' Answer to Movant's 28 U.S.C. § 2255 Motion to Vacate, Set Aside, or Correct Sentence." (Civil Docket [REDACTED]. The Petitioner hereby avers that the Court's contradiction in its ORDER, provides that the validity and/or circumstances concerning the Plea Agreement are STILL a "CONTESTED FACTUAL ISSUE." The Petitioner therefore, realleged and incorporates by reference the Petitioner's "Reply ..." (Civil Docket [REDACTED] and ALL contentions and claims contained therein, in this his ."..Motion in Opposition to the Court's Order Regarding Summary Disposition." (attached hereto [REDACTED]). The Petitioner hereby reminds the Court of the following:

1) On or about May 26, 2012, this Petitioner was attempting to purchase insurance for a used motorcycle he had just agreed to purchase. While waiting at the Insurance Office, the Petitioner was attacked by 6-8 HEAVILY ARMED MEN.
2) The Petitioner vehemently declared his INNOCENCE from 5/26/12 to 9/6/13. In the process of his defense, the Petitioner asserted an ALIBI DEFENSE in the first week. Due to the failures by Court appointed Lawyers, the Petitioner moved the Trial Court on many occasions to provide: Counsel, Investigators, Evidence, Hearings, Fair Trial, Expert Witnesses, Subpoenas, orders for *Brady/Giglio*

materials, and a copy of the obviously ALTERED Video Confession, ALL of which were denied by the Trial Court. (See Criminal Dockets [REDACTED]).

3) On September 5, 2013, the Petitioner had been called to a hearing before Magistrate Judge [REDACTED] to hear the Petitioner's contentions concerning a CONFLICT of INTEREST. The conflict affected two of [REDACTED]'s clients, one who had reported the other for murder and threat to commit murder. This was also reported to the Trial Judge in a letter on or about 8/6/13.

4) On September 5, 2013, Court appointed Counsel, [REDACTED] compelled this Petitioner, to provide statements to Deputy U.S. Marshal [REDACTED] concerning [REDACTED]'s confession of murdering [REDACTED] and his threat to murder [REDACTED] and his family. This act created a Conflict of Interest because [REDACTED] involved the Petitioner in another threatening situation that had nothing to do with the Petitioner's defense. By this, [REDACTED] compelled the testimony from one of his clients against another one of his clients CLEARLY dividing his loyalties.

5) Later on the 5th of September 2013, [REDACTED] learned of the Petitioner's statement to the Marshals and threatened to KILL the Petitioner's WIFE and CHILDREN.

6) [REDACTED], CLEARLY suffering from a CONFLICT OF INTEREST, counseled this Petitioner concerning U.S.S.G. 5K.1 and Rule 35 motions, and advised the Petitioner to Plea Guilty notwithstanding the Notice of ALIBI DEFENSE and 10 subpoenas issued days before.

7) "INEFFECTIVE ASSISTANCE of COUNSEL may result from an Attorney's CONFLICT OF INTEREST. In *Cuylet v. Sullivan*, the Supreme Court ruled that a defendant can demonstrate a Sixth Amendment violation by showing that (l) Counsel was ACTIVELY REPRESENTING conflicting interests; and (2) The conflict had an adverse effect on specific aspects of Counsel's performance. When the defendant alleges that a guilty plea resulted from Counsel's Conflict of Interest, the defendant MUST show that, but for the conflicts effects on Counsel's advice, a reasonable probability existed that he or she would have insisted on a trial." See 42 GEO. L.J. ANN. REB. CRIM. PROC. 564 (2013). [REDACTED] advised this Petitioner to plead guilty as a means to gain protection for his family from the threats of [REDACTED] The threat of harm was propagated by a circumstance outside of the Petitioner's case, therefore, he was not threatened into pleading guilty, he was advised by Counsel to accept guilt as a *VEHICLE FOR PROTECTION*. This Court will find that the hearing on the 5th of September 2013, was to determine if [REDACTED] could continue to TRIAL as Petitioner's Counsel. It is CLEAR that short of this advice, the Petitioner would have proceeded to trial to present his ALIBI DEFENSE and proven his *ACTUAL INNOCENCE*.

8) In proceedings at which the Sixth Amendment Right to Counsel applies, Judges have an "INDEPENDENT DUTY" to safeguard a criminal defendant's rights to CONFLICT-FREE COUNSEL in order to ensure that the defendant receives a trial that is FAIR and does NOT contravene the Sixth Amendment. *Wheat v. United States*, 486 U.S.153, 161-162 (1982). If a Judge is "alerted to a possible Conflict of Interest and fails to take adequate steps to ascertain whether the conflict warrants separate Counsel (id at 160), the Judge has unconstitutionally forced the defendant to choose between proceeding with a Lawyer who has an apparent conflict or giving up the right to be represented by Counsel. It's CLEARLY established in the record that this happened to this Petitioner who is DUE RELIEF. See also *Smith v. Lockhart*, 923 F.2d 1314 (8th Cir. 1991); *Coleman v. Thompson*, 501 U.S. 754; *Gray v. Pearson*, 526 Fed. Appx. 331, 332-34 (4th Cir. 2013); Boykin v. Webb, 541 F.3d 638 (6th Cir. 2008); *Houston v. Lockhart*, 982 F.2d 1246, 1250-53 (8th Cir. 1993); *Burden v. Zant*, 871 F.2d 956, 957 (11th Cir. 1989); *Stricklan v. Washington*, 466 U.S. 668, 80 L. Ed. 2d 674 (1984).

9) In the Court's ORDER, the issue of this motion, "Judicial Notice" is taken concerning credibility.

The Petitioner assumes this Court finds the testimony of the Trial Judge credible as a matter of record. On December 20, 2013, the Trial Judge testified that, .".. [REDACTED] had found that the same conflict did not preclude [REDACTED] from representing you at the Plea hearing or at trial." The Trial Judge makes CLEAR by this that a CONFLICT EXISTS. The Petitioner is DUE RELIEF. (Criminal Docket [REDACTED]).

10) The Court record, in [REDACTED], reflects that this Petitioner was "RUSHED TO JUDGMENT" just 18 hours after he was COERCED into signing a Plea Agreement at 8:00 P.M. the night before. The Petitioner was set for a Change of Plea Hearing on 9/6/13.

11) In the Change of Plea Hearing on 9/6/13, the presiding Judge failed to make known, to the Petitioner, the ESSENTIAL ELEMENTS of the charged offense. The Judge failed to even give an accurate reading of the charging statute.

12) In the Change of Plea Hearing, the Petitioner DID NOT utter a single word concerning the charged offense or the alleged conduct. The Trial Court determined the Petitioner's guilt based upon rehearsed responses that included 34 yeses, 11: noes and 3 guilties.

13) The Trial Judge accepted the Plea of guilty just days after Court appointed Counsel gave Notice of ALIBI and subpoenaed 10 Witnesses in support as Judicially Noticed by this Court. This is CLEARLY in CONFLICT of a Plea of Guilty. The Guilty Plea was accepted in PLAIN ERROR because it failed to reach the mandated requirements of Federal Rules of Criminal Procedure, Rule 11.

14) ABA Standard 1.6 declares that, notwithstanding the acceptance of a Guilty Plea, the Court should NOT enter a judgment upon such a plea without making inquiry as may satisfy it that there is a FACTUAL BASIS for the plea. The NAC position is that the Trial Judge should refuse to accept a plea from a defendant who asserts FACTS inconsistent with guilt or is "unable or unwilling to recount facts establishing guilt," even though there may be "FACTUAL BASIS" for the plea as required by the ABA Standard. Thus, the NAC position is stronger than the ABA's in requiring that, not only MUST there be a FACTUAL BASIS for the plea, but the defendant MUST also admit FACTS consistent with guilt of the offense to which he pleads.

15) In the Petitioner's Plea Hearing he DID NOT admit to a single element of the charged offense. See *United States v. Sylvester*, 583, F.3d 285, 288 (5th Cir. 2009). "When determining whether the factual basis for a guilty plea is sufficient, the district court must compare the conduct which defendant admits and the elements of the offense."; *United States v. Hildenbrand*, 527 F.3d 466, 475 (5th Cir. 2008)' cf. *United States v. Marek*, 238, F.3d 310, 315 (5th Cir. 2001) (en banc). "The acceptance of a guilty plea is a factual finding reviewed for clear error." The Petitioner's Guilty Plea is obviously INVALID and a DISPUTED FACTUAL ISSUE.

16) In the Petitioner's case a Plea Agreement was executed as a vehicle to gain protection, for the Petitioner's family, from an unrelated THREAT. The Plea Agreement was withdrawn 29 days later after the Petitioner learned of the participation of the Federal Public Defender's Office in propagating the THREAT against the Petitioner's family. The Petitioner asserted his ACTUAL INNOCENCE and ALIBI DEFENSE to the best of his ability. The motion to withdraw was NOT refined by Counsel. The Petitioner DID NOT have close assistance of Counsel at this stage in the proceedings.

17) The petitioner's *pro se* motion to withdraw was the subject of the hearing conducted on 12/20/13. Upon hearing the evidence and testimony available to the Court, Judicial Notice was taken. The Trial Court Noticed that [REDACTED]'s testimony was true and accurate. [REDACTED]'s testimony included the FACT that he, in GOOD FAITH, found ample reason to file a meritorious "NOTICE

OF ALIBI" on behalf of the Petitioner. Moreover, [REDACTED] testified that he issued subpoenas for 10 people on behalf of the Petitioner's ALIBI DEFENSE. By taking JUDICIAL NOTICE, the Trial Court CERTIFIED the Petitioner's claim of ACTUAL INNOCENCE asserted on 10/5/13.

18) The Trial Court in this case was DUTY BOUND to allow the Petitioner to withdraw his Guilty Plea. The Trial Judge went on to say that if she had any doubts as to guilt, she would not hesitate to withdraw the Plea. The Trial Judge had 10 doubts, the ALIBI WITNESSES subpoenaed by [REDACTED], according to his testimony.

19) Its been long held that after a District Court has accepted a Plea and before Sentencing, a defendant may withdraw a Guilty Plea if he can demonstrate "a fair and just reason for requesting the withdraw." Federal Rules of Criminal Procedure, Rule 11(d)(2)(B). See e.g. *United States v. Buckles*, 843 F.2d 469, 471-72 (11th Cir. 1988); *United States v. Fairchild*, 803 F.2d 1121, 1123 (11th Cir. 1986). *United States v. Mosely*, 173 F.3d 1318, 1322 (11th Cir. 1999). There is no doubt that the District Court ABUSED its discretion by FAILING to allow the Petitioner to withdraw his Plea.

20) At the Time the Petitioner signed his Plea Agreement (8:00 P.M. on 9/5/13), he fully intended on filing for appeal once the threat of harm to his family had been averted. This was fully discussed with Counsel on 9/5/13 as indicated in the transcripts at the Change of Plea Hearing. The Petitioner carefully considered the right to appeal in the Plea Agreement. The Petitioner gave Notice of Appeal at the Sentencing Hearing and specifically objected to the validity of the Plea Agreement. On appeal, Court appointed Counsel filed an Ander's Brief stating that the Petitioner waived the right to appeal. Being present as Counsel at the 12/20/13 hearing and raising NO OBJECTION to the presiding Judge's ABUSE OF DISCRETION rendered Court appointed Counsel's [REDACTED], assistance CONSTITUTIONALLY INEFFECTIVE, the subject of the Petitioner's § 2255. As [REDACTED] continued as Appellate Counsel, he was DUTY BOUND to raise his own INEFFECTIVENESS at Appeal. His, the second, CONFLICT OF INTEREST prevented him from performing his duty, under the Constitution, to provide Effective Assistance of Counsel at Appeal.

21) Currently the Petitioner has in litigation his claims, in a § 2255 proceeding, that 1) [REDACTED] provided Constitutionally Ineffective Assistance of Counsel and 2) That his Plea Agreement is *INVALID*. Among other things, these are contested FACTUAL ISSUES. To date, there has NOT been an Evidentiary Hearing, nor has the Court opened Discovery for FACT DEVELOPMENT. Still remaining outside the record are the availability of unexplored ALIBI STATEMENTS and *FACTS* surrounding [REDACTED]'s murder.

22) The Court, as of March 17, 2016, announced its intention to grant SUMMARY JUDGMENT in favor of the Government notwithstanding the FACTS in this case. The Petitioner is of the opinion that this is an effort to continue to conceal the involvement of court Officers in [REDACTED]'s murder and the effects it had on the Petitioner's criminal case. [REDACTED]'s murder and the concealment of it is subject of the Petitioner's INTERROGATORIES.

23) In the Court's ORDER, it declares that "the court finds that a hearing is not necessary in this action because no bona fide credibility issue exists." and "The Court finds no need for additional testimony to resolve credibility issues relating to the Effectiveness of his Counsel or any other ground in his Habeas Motion." In this, the Court ABUSES its DISCRETION in an effort to hide that an ALIBI DEFENSE was available and went unexplored and the unsolved murder of [REDACTED]. The Court NOTICES its intent to issue SUMMARY DISPOSITION. However, this Court "forgets an important detail" - This action has long since passed Rule 4 scrutiny. Rules governing § 2255, Rule 4(b) states that:

"The Judge who receives the motion must promptly examine it. If it plainly appears from

> the motion, any attached exhibits, and the record of prior proceedings that the moving party is not entitled to relief, the Judge must dismiss the motion and direct the Clerk to notify the moving party. If the motion is not dismissed, the Judge must order the United States Attorney to file an answer, motion, or other response within a fixed time, or take other action the Judge may order."

This Court found NO grounds to dismiss and issued a SHOW CAUSE ORDER. Rule 4 scrutiny is the *ONLY* time for the District Court to dispose of the case if the Petitioner's criminal case was resolved by a valid Plea Agreement. Therefore, this Court resorts to the holdings of *McBride v. Sharpe*, 25 F.3d 962 (11th Cir. 1994) upon which to determine this Habeas action "ripe for Summary Disposition." As a CLEAR matter of *LAW* and *COURT RULE*, this Court's finding is MISPLACED and yet another ABUSE OF DISCRETION. The simplest of minds would find *McBride* discernible from the Petitioner's case.

24) This Court references the case of Emory Jackson McBride, who was indicted for rape and aggravated sodomy of a 14-year-old girl. In addition, the indictment charged McBride with recidivism based upon a previous conviction of rape and aggravated assault.

The Georgia Court held a fair trial for Mr. McBride who was found guilty by a Jury by clear and convincing physical evidence and witness testimony. Mr. McBride petitioned the Court for a new trial and was denied.

Mr. McBride exercised his right to a Direct Appeal at which he was appointed new Counsel. McBride raised two issues, one of which was that he "was deprived of the right of effective representation and confrontation ..." Mr. McBride's conviction was reversed. "The Supreme Court of Georgia, however, reversed ..."

Mr. McBride filed for Collateral Review in the State by filing an application for WRIT of *habeas corpus* in the Superior Court of Dodge County, Georgia, for which McBride received a hearing.

Mr. McBride followed by filing in *pro se* for Federal habeas relief. The Federal Court did not grant a hearing and denied McBride's motion.

McBride appealed the District Court's judgment to dismiss his petition. The Court of Appeals appointed Counsel who filed a meaningful brief to supplement Mr. McBride's *pro se* brief and appeared at Oral Argument. The Court of Appeals affirmed the District Court's judgment.

In this case, Mr. McBride, did "not contend that anything in the record excerpts was inaccurate, incomplete, or misleading," as this Petitioner has and continues to claim in his.

25) The case of Mr. McBride and the Petitioner's case in issue are HIGHLY DISCERNIBLE on many points.

1) In *McBride* physical evidence, supporting his guilt, was presented at a fair trial with Counsel present to represent him. In this Petitioner's case, he was deprived of trial by threat of harm to his family first, and then again when the Trial Judge abused her discretion notwithstanding a Noticed Alibi Defense.

2) In *McBride* the State Appeals Court, the Supreme Court, the Federal Court of Appeals, reviewed his case, appointing Counsel more than once and holding hearings; the Petitioner was deprived of Direct Appeal because

3) of Breach of Plea Agreement and Ineffective Assistance of Appellate Counsel, and here now this Court has deprived this Petitioner of Counsel, Discovery, and a

4) Hearing, in his first Collateral Motion, leaving the INEFFECTIVENESS of [REDACTED], Court appointed Counsel unresolved.

Mr. McBride raised no issue that there existed evidence outside the record nor did he assert actual innocence. The Petitioner, however, has a Judicially Noticed ALIBI DEFENSE that supports his claim of ACTUAL INNOCENCE, has shown in the Court record that evidence that proves his INNOCENCE stands outside the record, and that the Court's concealment of an unsolved murder has unduly aggravated this Petitioner's defense.

The last of the many disparities the Petitioner will show, though not all, is that Mr. McBride did not raise any claim in any proceeding that the Court violated substantive DUE PROCESS; In the Petitioner's cases over the last four (4) years, DUE PROCESS has been violated so much that the Petitioner is of the opinion that the Court may not know what DUE PROCESS *IS*, but does know how to increase the unlawful incarceration of an INNOCENT Petitioner in an effort to MOOT the *habeas corpus* proceedings through *UNNECESSARY DELAY* (ref Rule 8(c)).

Again, the Petitioner avers that the Court ABUSES its DISCRETION by *DENYING* the Petitioner's request for Counsel, Discovery, Evidentiary Hearing.

In a more recent case, the Court of Appeals for the Eleventh Circuit, in *Rodriguez v. Florida Dept., of Corrections*, 748 F.3d 1073 (11th Cir. 2014), held:

> "We review a District Court's order denying a motion for reconsideration for abuse of discretion. *Richard v. Johnson*, 598 F.3d 734, 740 (11th Cir. 2010). A District Court abuses its discretion when it 'applies the wrong law, follows the wrong procedure, bases its decision on clearly erroneous facts, or admits a clear error in judgment.' *United States v. Brown*, 415 F.3d 1257, 1266 (11th Cir. 2005). A District Court's misinterpretation or misapplication of a procedural rule constitutes an abuse of discretion. See *Richards*, 598 F.3d at 788-4Q; *Conner v. Hall*, 645 F.3d 1277, 1289-92 (11th Cir. 2011)(disagreeing with and reversing the District Court's determination that Mr. Conner's claim was procedurally defaulted *Lonchar v. Thomas*, 517 U.S. 314, 324, 116 S. Ct. 1293, 1299, 134 L. Ed. 2d 440 (1996)("Dismissal of a first habeas petition is a particularly serious matter, for that dismissal denies the petitioner the protections of the Great Writ entirely, risking injury to an important interest in human liberty.")" None of these opinions are found in a dissent.

26) This Court, having taken JUDICIAL NOTICE of [REDACTED]'s credibility and OVERALL EFFECTIVENESS, may not dispute the Petitioner's claim of ACTUAL INNOCENCE that is based on [REDACTED]'s assertion of an ALIBI defense and then (10) Witnesses, as a matter of law. Federal Rules of Evidence, Rule 201(f), states:

> "In a Civil case, the court must instruct the Jury to accept the noticed fact as conclusive."

For these reasons, the expeditious issuance of the Writ is paramount as to fulfill this Petitioner's RIGHT to prompt release from his UNLAWFUL custody. Further delay would deny DUE PROCESS, mooting the right to *habeas corpus* through unnecessary delay.

Therefore, this Court has no authority to dispute the Petitioner's claim of "ACTUAL INNOCENCE," in a subsequent action, and/or otherwise summarily dispose of the Petition and/or its MERITORIOUS CLAIMS. The Petitioner hereby avers that this Court is DUTY BOUND to "ORDER the IMMEDIATE issuance of the WRIT OF HABEAS CORPUS," ordering the Warden, [REDACTED] to remove the Petitioner from Federal Bureau of Prisons properly instanter, TO WIT:

IMMEDIATELY and/or within 72 hours of ORDER eject the Petitioner from Federal

Correctional Institution Oakdale, Louisiana property with sufficient funds and public transportation to the Northern District of Alabama, POST HASTE.

The Petitioner MOVES this Court to GRANT this motion and issuance of the above-mentioned Writ.

The court's Judicial authority to summarily dispose of the Petitioner's claims has been foreclosed by the JUDICIAL NOTICE.

27) Finally, and even though a motion that could encompass all the Court's deficiencies would rival the King James Version of the Holy Bible in length. The Petitioner ends his opposition to "SUMMARY DISPOSITION" by *OBJECTING* to this Court's EX PARTE communication with an adverse party, [REDACTED] " without NOTICE of SERVICE to the Petitioner, to resolve a DISPUTED *FACTUAL* ISSUE that was raised in the Petitioner's § 2255 Motion. Once again, the Petitioner is PREJUDICED by the Court's deviation from *DUE PROCESS.*

WHEREFORE NOW, above premises considered, the Petitioner hereby gives NOTICE of INTERLOCUTORY APPEAL from this Court's ABUSE of DISCRETION and *PLAIN ERROR* in its 3/17/2016 ORDER denying; the Petitioner's Evidentiary Hearing, Discovery, and Appointment of Counsel motions. Moreover, the Petitioner hereby *OBJECTS* to and OPPOSES this Court's intention to dispose of the Petitioner's § 2255 motion summarily. It's Clear that RULE, LAW, and Court PRECEDENT requires further proceedings and that summary disposition would be an ABUSE OF DISCRETION committed in PLAIN ERROR. The Petitioner hereby MOVES this Court to forward his NOTICE OF INTERLOCUTORY APPEAL to the Eleventh Circuit Court of Appeals and/or process the same in accordance with LAW, and provide ALL other RELIEF REQUIRED by LAW, LIBERTY, AND JUSTICE.

Done This [DATE] Day of [MONTH], [YEAR]

Respectfully Submitted,

____

[NAME], *PRO SE*
Reg # [NUMBER]

Federal Correctional Institution
Mailing Address
City, State and Zip Code

FILING AN APPEAL

Well here we are, you have discovered that your district, like mine, is simply satisfying its judicial quota to bolster its district's budget.

You will find that once your district court has grown tired of wasting your time and resources it will deny your § 2255 proceeding. Please also consider that this statement covers most district courts in the United States. However, I also want you to know that there are some truly honorable courts out there. They are few in number, but there are a few.

That said, you will discover that the final decision in your *habeas* case ***is not*** appealable. See 28 U.S.C. § 2253(3)(1)(B):

> "Unless a Circuit Justice or Judge issues a Certificate of Appealability, an appeal may not be taken to the Court of Appeals from - (b) the final order in a proceeding under section 2255."

As you can see, an appeal is not acceptable without a "Certificate of Appealability," that's why your district court will try to fool you by issuing its orders in a pair. Yes, you are going to, or already have, received two orders: One denying your § 2255 for some half-baked procedural error; and another order denying you a Certificate of Appealability. The second order is your key to appeal.

On the page that follows, you will find a Notice of Appeal of the district court's order denying a Certificate of Appealability. Once you file this in the district court, it's off to appeal! If this is denied, appeal that denial.

If you need my book on appeals from § 2255 denials, you can purchase *Post-Conviction Relief – The Appeal* from Freebird Publishers at the address in the front of this book.

UNITED STATES DISTRICT COURT

IN THE [Your DISTRICT] DISTRICT of [Your STATE]

[Your DIVISION] DIVISION

[YOUR NAME]	CASE NO.:
vs.	[YOUR § 2255 CASE NO.]
UNITED STATES OF AMERICA	

NOTICE OF APPEAL

COMES NOW the Petitioner, [YOUR NAME] in *PRO SE*, in necessity, and hereby gives NOTICE OF APPEAL from this Court's ORDER that DENIED the issuance of a Certificate of Appealability. The Petitioner avers that this Court's ORDER issued on [DATE OF THE ORDER] was issued in error. The Petitioner appeals to the United States Court of Appeals for the [YOUR CIRCUIT] Circuit from this Court's judgment, entered for record in the above styled action on the [DATE OF YOUR APPEAL] Day of [MONTH OF YOUR APPEAL], [YEAR OF YOUR APPEAL].

Respectfully Submitted,

[YOUR SIGNATURE]

[YOUR NAME], *PRO SE*

Reg # [YOUR REG NO.]

[YOUR FACILITY]

[YOUR FACILITY'S ADDRESS]

CERTIFICATE OF SERVICE

I, the undersigned, do hereby certify that I have served a copy of the foregoing instrument on all parties, TO WIT: The Clerk of this Court and Assistant United States Attorney, [NAME AND ADDRESS OF YOUR PROSECUTOR].

This service has been made via United States mail, properly addressed, first class postage prepaid affixed thereto, and placed in the internal mailing system of [YOUR FACILITY], as made available to inmates for legal mail.

Done This [DATE] Day of [MONTH], [YEAR].
Respectfully Submitted,

[YOUR SIGNATURE]

____

[YOUR NAME], *PRO SE*
Reg # [YOUR REG. NO.]
[YOUR FACILITY]
[YOUR FACILITY'S ADDRESS]

GLOSSARY

A FORTIORI (a for-she-o'-rye). With stronger reason; all the more.

A PAIS (ah pay). At issue.

A POSTERIORI (a pos-te-re-o'-rye). From a later point of view. From the effect to the cause.

A PRIORI (a pre-o'-rye). From what has gone before. From the cause to the effect.

A QUO (a kwo). From which.

AB (ab). From, by, of.

AB ANTE (ab an'-te). In advance; before.

AB ANTECEDENTE (ab an-te-see-dent'-te). Beforehand.

AB INITIO (ab in-nish'-i-o). From the beginning. Entirely.

ABANDON (a-ban'-don). To give up fully a right or interest.

ABANDONMENT (a-ban'-don-ment). The relinquishment of property or rights.

ABATE (a-bate'). To beat down, destroy, put an end to.

ABDICATION (ab-di-kay'shun). The giving up or renunciation of an office, power, or right.

ABDUCTION (ab-duck'-shun). The taking or carrying away of a person by force or through fraud. Originally, the person was either a man's wife, child, or ward.

ABET (a-bet'). To command, incite, or aide another to commit an offense.

ABEYANCE (a-bay'-ans). In expectation; The condition of property or rights when held in a state of suspension or in expectancy.

ABIDE (a-bide'). To obey, wait for, or conform to.

ADJUDICATE (ab-jude'-i-kate). To take away or consider wrong by judgment of a court.

ABRIDGE (a-brij'). To shorten, cut down, or reduce.

ABRIDGEMENT (a-brij'-ment). A shortened version of a larger work. A condensation.

ABROGATION (ab-ro-gay'-shon). The repeal of a former law. Annulment.

ABSCOND (ab-skond'). To withdraw from one's usual haunts to avoid legal proceedings.

ABSQUE (abz'-kwee). Without.

ABSQUE HOC (abz'-kwee hoke). Without this.

ABSTRACT (ab'-strakt). An abridgment. A brief history of proceedings or of some record.

ACCESSORY (ak-sess'-o-ree). A person who while not actually present contributes to or aids in the commission of a crime: (1) by inciting, encouraging or commanding another to commit it (accessory before the fact); (2) by standing by and not giving such aid as is in his power to prevent the crime (accessory during the fact); or (3) by aiding and concealing the offender with knowledge that a crime has been committed (accessory after the fact).

ACCOMPLICE (ak-kom'-pliss). One who unites with other in the commission of a crime.

ACCORD (a-kord'). An agreement to accept something different from or less than that which was originally bargained for. When the agreement has been executed and the obligation extinguished, it is known as accord and satisfaction.

ACCUMULATIVE JUDGMENT (a-ku'-mulay-tiv juj'-ment). A second or additional judgment or sentence passed upon one who has already been convicted, to go into effect after expiration of the first.

ACCUSATION (ak-u-zay'-shon). A formal declaration that another is guilty of an offense or misconduct.

ACKNOWLEDGMENT (ak-noll'-ej'-ment). An avowal or admission of the truth of certain facts.

ACQUIESCENCE (ak-wee-ess'-ens). Passive compliance or conduct from which consent may be implied.

ACQUITTAL (a-kwitt'-al). A release, discharge, or deliverance from some engagement or charge of guilt.

ACT (akt). That which is done, established or performed. A statute or law passed by some legislative body.

ACT IN PAIS (akt in pay). Not a matter of record; a judicial act performed out of court.

ACTA PUBLICA (ak'ta poob'-li-ka). Things of general knowledge and concern.

ACTIO (ak'-she-o). An action or cause of action.

ACTION (ak'-shun). An act or series of acts; the proceedings in court to enforce a right or to punish a wrong.

ACTION EX CONTRACTU (ak'-shun eks kontrak-tu'). An action for breach of a duty or obligation based on an expressed or implied contract.

ACTION EX DELICTO (ak'-shun eks de-lik'-to). An action arising from breach of a duty not based on contract.

ACTIONABLE (ak'-shun-a-ble). For which an action lies or remedy exists.

AD HOC (ad hoke). For this; for this special purpose.

AD INTERIM (ad in'-te-rim). In the meantime.

AD LITEM (ad lye'-tern). For the suit.

AD RESPONDENDUM (ad re-spon-den'-dum). To make answer.

AD SATISFACIENDUM (ad sa-tis-fa-she-en'-dum). To satisfy.

ADJECTIVE LAW (aj'-ek-tiv law). That part of the body of law which provides the method for enforcing rights or of redressing injuries. The rules of procedure by which substantive law is given effect.

ADJOURNMENT (a-jurn'-ment). The dismissal of a hearing or assembly either finally (adjournment sine dies) or to some other appointed time (temporary adjournment).

ADJUDGE (a-juj'). To decide judicially.

ADJUDICATION (a-ju-di-kay'-shun). A judgment; the pronouncing of the judgment in a case.

ADMISSIBLE (ad-miss'-i-bl). Capable of being admitted, conceded, or allowed.

ADMISSION (ad-mish'-on). An acknowledgment of the existence or truth of certain facts; acts by which one may become a member of a company, society, or profession.

ADVOCATE (ad'-vo-kate). An adviser; one who pleads for another in court.

AFFIANT (a-f ye '-ant). One who makes an affidavit.

AFFIDAVIT (af'-i-day'-vit). A statement or declaration reduced to writing and sworn to before an officer authorized to administer an oath.

AFFIRM (a-firm'). To make firm, ratify, or confirm the judgment of a lower court; to ratify or confirm a voidable contract.

AFFIRMATION (af-er-may'-shun). A solemn declaration of the truth of some fact, to take the place of an oath.

AFORESAID (a-four'-sed). Previously described or spoken; before mentioned.

AFORETHOUGHT (a-four [1]thawt). Premeditated; thought of beforehand.

AGENDA (a-jen'-da). An outline of things to be done; a program of matters to be attended to.

AGGRAVATION (ag-ra-vay'-shun). That which increases the seriousness of a crime or tortuous act, or is reason for enhancing damages for an injury.

ALIAS (ay'-lee-us). Otherwise; otherwise known as. May also refer to a second or similar writ as one issued before in the same.

ALIBI (al'-i-bye). Elsewhere; evidence to prove that one charged with a crime was in a different place at the time an offense was committed.

ALIEN (ale'-yen). A foreigner. A person holding allegiance to a foreign government.

ALITER (al'-i-ter). Otherwise.

ALIUS (ay'-li-us). Other; another thing or person.

ALLEGATION (al-ee-gay'-shun). An assertion; the statement of a party as to what he can prove.

ALLOCUTION (al-o-kue'-shun). The formality of asking a prisoner, adjudged guilty, why sentence should not be pronounced.

AMBIGUITY (am-bi-gue'-i-ti). Uncertainty of meaning in some expression of a written instrument. Latent ambiguity arises where the instrument itself seems clear but some matter aside from the instrument gives doubt to its meaning. Patent ambiguity is that which is apparent from study of the instrument itself.

AMENABLE (a-meen[1]-a-bl). Tractable; easily influenced or governed. Liable to punishment; responsible.

AMENDMENT (a-mend'-ment). The correction, by court permission, of an error committed in the progress of a cause. An addition to or modification of an existing law.

AMICUS CURIAE (a'mye'-kus ku'-ri-ee). A friend of the court. Any person who with no interest in the cause may be permitted to interpose and inform the court as to the law or on some matter of which the court may be in doubt.

ANCILLARY (an[1]-si-lare-ee). Auxiliary; subordinate but aiding another proceeding.

ANIMO (a'-ni-mo). With intent.

ANIMO FELONICO (a'-ni-mo fe-lo'-ni-ko). With felonious intent.

ANIMUS (an'-i-mus). Mind. The intention with which an act is

ANIMUS CANCELLANDI (an'-i-mus kan-selan'-dye). An intention to destroy or cancel.

ANIMUS CAPIENDI (an'-i-mus kap-i-en'-dye). The intention to take.

ANIMUS FURANDI (an'-i-mus fu-ran'-dye). The intention to steal.

ANIMUS MANENDI (an'-i-mus ma-nen'-dye). The intention of remaining.

ANIMUS RECIPIENDI (an'-i-mus re-sip-i-en'-dye). The intention of receiving.

ANNOTATION (an-no-tay'-shun). A footnote in a book to add to the meaning of some statement.

ANNUL (a-null'). To make void; to nullify or abolish.

ANTE (an'-te). Before. Often used in a book to refer the reader to a previous section.

ANTE-DATE (an'-tee-date). To date an instrument with a time that occurred prior to its execution.

ANTE-LITAM (an'-tee lye'-tam). Before suit.

APPEAL (a-peel'). The resort to a higher court to correct the mistake of an inferior one.

APPEAR (a-peer'). To be properly before a court. When relating to facts or evidence, it means clear to the understanding.

APPEARANCE (a-peer'-ans). The submission of a party to the jurisdiction of the court.

APPELLANT (a-pel'-ant). The one who makes appeal from one court to another.

APPELLATE COURT (a-pel'-ate kort). A reviewing court, to which causes may be taken by appeal, certiorari, or writ of error.

APPELLEE (ap-e-lee'). The party against whom an appeal is taken, may also be known as respondent.

APPREHEND (ap-re-hend'). To understand; to be conscious or sensible of. To seize a person or arrest.

ARCHIVES (ar'-kyvez). A place where ancient records or documents are kept. The records or writings themselves, which are preserved for posterity.

ARRAIGNMENT (a-rain'-ment). The formality by which a defendant in a criminal case is called before the bar of a court so that he may be informed of the offense with which he is charged and asked whether he is guilty or not guilty.

ARREST (a-rest'). To deprive a person of his liberty by authority of law.

ARREST OF JUDGMENT (a-rest' of juj'-ment). Refusal of a court, after verdict, to render judgment in a case, because on the face of the record the verdict appears to be wrong.

ASSAULT (a-salt'). A threat or intentional attempt to do physical injury to another. An assault coupled with intent to commit some additional crime, such as rape or robbery, is considered aggravated assault.

ASSUMPSIT (a-sump'-sit). (Lat. He has undertaken) The name of an action to recover damages for breach of an oral or simple contract. If the promise or contract is expressed, special assumpsit is the action; if implied by law, general assumpsit is proper.

AT LARGE (at larj). Free; unrestrained; open to controversy. Fully; in detail.

ATTEST (a-test'). To witness or testify. To affirm to be true. To witness the execution of an instrument and to subscribe one's name in testimony thereof.

ATTESTATION (at-es-tay'-shun). The act of witnessing the execution of an instrument and subscribing to it as a witness. The sentence or clause indicating such subscription and manner thereof, is called the attestation clause.

ATTORNEY (a-ter'-nee). One who acts for another under appointment by the latter. An attorney appointed for one particular purpose. Except a proceeding at law, when he is called an attorney at law, is known as an attorney in fact.

AUTREFOIS ACQUIT (owe-tre-fwa' a-kee'). A plea made by the defendant in a criminal action that he was previously tried for the same offense and acquitted.

AUTREFOIS CONVICT (owe-tre-fwa' konvikt'). The same plea as autrefois acquit except that the defendant was convicted.

AVER (a-ver'). To assert; to verify; to make or prove true.

AVERMENT (a-ver'-ment). A positive statement of facts, as opposed to an uncertain one.

BAIL (bale). The release of a person from legal custody on his own assurance or that of others that he will appear at the appointed time to answer the charge against him. The person or persons act as sureties for the appearance of the one released.

BAIL BOND (bale bond). The bond or obligation signed by the defendant with sureties, conditioned on the appearance of defendant or performance by him of such acts as he is required to perform.

BAN (ban). A proclamation or public notice; announcement of an intended marriage. A sentence of excommunication.

BANC (bank) or BANCUS (ban'-kus). A bench; the seat or bench of justice.

BAR (bar). The railing in a courtroom to separate the public from the officers of the court. The members of the legal profession. A legal obstacle or barrier. A plea, constituting an answer to an action of law, defeating the action altogether.

BATTERY (bat'-er-ee). The willful and unlawful use of force or violence upon the person of another, or even the mere unlawful touching of the person of another by an aggressor or by any object put in motion by him.

BENCH (bench). The seat occupied by judges in courts; the court itself; or the judges as a whole, as distinguished from counselors, who are known as the bar.

BEQUEST (be-kwest'). A gift of personal property by will.

BILATERAL CONTRACT (by-lat'-er-al kon'-trakt). A contract containing mutual promises between the parties, as in a sale, where one becomes bound to deliver the thing sold and the other to pay the price for it.

BILL (bill). The complaint in a suit of equity; a written statement of one's claim or account against another; the draft of a new law to be presented to a legislature for enactment.

BILL OF INDICTMENT (bill of in-dite'-ment). A written document presented to a grand jury accusing a person or persons of a crime or misdemeanor.

BILL OF INFORMATION (bill of in-for-may'-shun). A bill in equity instituted by the attorney general or other proper officer in behalf of the state.

BILL OF PARTICULARS (bill of par-tick'-ulars). A detailed statement of a party's cause of action or setoff, in order to acquaint opposing party of all matters about which he should have information.

BLACKMAIL (black'-male). Extortion; the exaction of money by threats of violence or exposure of weaknesses or crimes of the victim.

BONA FIDE (boe'-na fyed'-d). In good faith; honestly; without fraud or deceit. Real; genuine.

BONDAGE (bon'-daje). A form of restraint; captivity; involuntary servitude; slavery.

BREACH (breech). The violation of a right, duty, or law.

BREACH OF TRUST (breach of trust). A violation by a trustee of any duty which he owes to the beneficiary of the trust.

BRIEF (breef). A summary, abstract, or condensed statement. A document prepared by a counsel to acquaint an appellate court with the essential facts of his client's case, the questions of laws involved, and the principles which should apply.

BURDEN OF PROOF (her'-den of proof). The necessity imposed on one party to prove facts in dispute on an issue raised between parties in a suit.

CANON (kan'-on). A church officers. A law, rule, or doctrine.

CAPTION (kap'-shun). An arrest or seizure. The heading of a legal instrument.

CARTE BLANCHE (kart blonsh). A white sheet of paper; an instrument signed in blank, that is, with the terms to be filled in by the one to whom it is delivered. Thus, the words "carte blanche" have come to mean "unlimited authority."

CASE (kase). An action, cause, suite, or controversy either at law or in equity. An abbreviated name for "action on the case" or "trespass on the case."

CASE LAW (kase law). Principles and rules of law developed by judicial decisions, as distinguished from those created by statues.

CAUSE (kawz). The reason, motive, or justification of an act. A suit, action, or any question contested before a court of justice.

CAUSE OF ACTION (kawz of ak'-shun). Ground on which or matter for which an action may be brought.

CERTIFICATE (ser-tiff'-i-kate). A signed statement by one in some official capacity authenticating the facts related therein.

CERTIORARI (ser-she-o-ray'-rye). A writ directed against an inferior court to bring the record of a cause into a superior court for reexamination and review.

CHARGE (charj). A duty or obligation or duty to impose such obligation. To accuse; to instruct a jury on matters of law.

CIRCUIT (ser'-kit). The district in which a judge may hold court in several places.

CIRCUMSTANTIAL EVIDENCE (ser-kumstan'-shal ev'-i-dense). Evidence that proves facts indirectly or by inference.

CITATION (sy-tay'-shun). A reference to legal authorities or precedents to prove the existence of some proposition. A writ or summons issued by a court ordering the one named therein to appear on a certain day and do what is mentioned therein.

CITE (site). To quote; to refer to legal authorities in support of an argument. To summon or order the appearance of a person in court.

CIVIL RIGHTS (siv'-il rites). Rights to which any person, as a citizen, is entitled.

CLAIM (klame). A demand; the assertion of a right. The assertion in a patent application as to precisely what the patent is. The tract of wild or mineral land staked out by a settler or miner for acquisition from the government.

CODE (kode). A complete and systematic body of law enacted by the legislature of a state, arranging and classifying existing laws into a logic system.

COERCION (ko-er'-shun). Compulsion; force; compelling a person whether by physical force or by reason of superior authority to do an act against his will.

COGNIZABLE (kog-ni'-ze-bel). Capable of being known or recognized. Capable of being judicially tried or examined before a designated tribunal; within the Court's jurisdiction.

COGNOVIT (kog-no'-vit). Defendant's admission that he has no defense and consent to have judgment entered against him. (Also known as cognovits actionem.)

COLLATERAL (ko-lat'-e-ral). Indirect; additional or auxiliary; related to.

COLLUSION (ko-lue'-zhon). An agreement between persons to defraud another of his rights or obtain an object forbidden by law, as in the case of divorce where husband and wife connive to procure a divorce on trumped-up grounds.

COLOR (kull'-or). A deceptive appearance of right or title; a prima facie or apparent right.

COMITY (kom'-i-tee). Courtesy; respect; willingness to abide by the law of another county, state,. Or nation although not required to do so.

COMMITMENT (ka-mitt'-ment). The process by which a person is confined by order of court.

COMMON LAW (kom'-on law). That system of jurisprudence developed in England that is the basis of the law in United States and other English-speaking countries. Those principles and rules that rest upon custom and usage or upon the judgments of the courts rather than upon the enactments of legislative bodies.

COMPETENCY (kom[1]-pe-ten-see). The quality of legal fitness or admissibility that renders the testimony of a witness or the introduction of other evidence acceptable.

COMPLAINANT (kom-play'-nant). The one who makes a complaint. The plaintiff in an equity processing.

COMPLAINT (kom-plaint'). The formal charge made before the proper officer that some person has committed a designated offense. The initial pleading, stating plaintiff's case and corresponding to the declaration under common law practice.

COMPULSION (kom-pul'-shun). Force exerted upon a person to make him do what he otherwise would not.

CONCEALMENT (kon'-seel'-ment). The improper suppression of any fact or circumstance, which in justice ought to be known by one party to a contract from the other.

CONCLUSIVE (kon-klue'-siv). That which is final or decisive.

CONCURRENT (kon-kur'-ent). Contemporaneous; having the same authority; contributing to the same event.

CONFESSION (kon-fesh'-on). The admission by a person that he committed the crime with which he is charged.

CONFLICT OF LAWS (kon'-flikt of laws). A division of the subject of intentional law, also known as private international law, that determines the rights of parties who may by certain acts be liable to conflicting laws of different states or countries.

CONFRONTATION (kon-frun-tay'-shun). The act of bringing a witness face to face with the accused in court, so that the prisoner may object to him or cross-examine, and so that the witness may identify the accused and maintain the truth of his testimony in his presence.

CONJECTURE (kon-jek'-chur). An idea, notion, or guess founded upon slight evidence or none at all.

CONSENT (kon-sent'). Agreement; to be of one mind.

CONSIDERATION (kon-sid-e-ray'-shun). One of the essentials of a valid contract, and consisting of either a benefit to the promisor or a loss or detriment to the promisee.

CONSPIRACY (kon-spir'-a-see). An agreement or combination of two or more persons to do an unlawful act or to do an act that may be lawful if done by one person but becomes unlawful if done in concert with others.

CONSTITUTION (kon-sti-tu'-shun). The basic and underlying system of laws and principles by which a state, corporation, or other group governed.

CONSTRUCTION (kon-struck'-shun). The interpretation or determination of the meaning and application, in some particular instance, of the provisions or terms of a constitution, statute, will, other instrument, or oral agreement.

CONSTRUCTIVE (kon-struct'-tiv). Inferred; implied; that which is considered by the law to be an act although the act is not actually performed.

CONTEMPT (kon-tempt'). A willful disregard, disobedience, or des- obedience, or despising of a public authority.

CONTINGENCY (kon-tin'-jen-see). The possibility of happening; an event that may occur without design, foresight, or expectation.

CONTINGENT (kon-tin'-jent). Doubtful or uncertain, depending upon a future event that is itself uncertain.

CONTINUANCE (kon-tin'-u-ans). The postponement or adjournment of the trial of a cause.

CONTRABAND (kon'-tra-band). Articles that are against the law to import or export.

CONTRACT (kon'-trakt). An agreement between two or more parties to do or not to do a particular thing.

CONVICT (kon-vikt'). To find guilty of a crime or misdemeanor.

CONVICT (kon'-vikt). The person condemned or found guilty of a crime.

CONVICTION (kon-vikt'-shun). The judgment in a criminal trial of the guilt of the accused.

CORAM (ko'-ram). Before; in presence of.

CORAM NOBIS (ko'-ram no'-bis). Before us.

CORAM VOBIS (ko'-ram vo'-bis). Before you; in your presence.

CORPUS (kor'-pus). A body. The substance. The capital of a fund or estate as distinguished from the income.

CORPUS DELICTI (kor'-pus de-lik'-ty). The body of the offense; the essence of the crime; the substantial fact that a crime has been committed, necessary to be established before there can be a conviction.

CORROBORATING EVIDENCE (ko-rob'-orate-ing ev'-i-dense). Additional evidence to that already given to confirm and strengthen it.

CORRUPTION (ko-rup'-shun). Something against or forbidden by law. Any special influence on or delinquency in the administration of a public office.

COUNSEL (koun'-sel). One or more attorneys representing parties in an action. Knowledge. Advice.

COUNT (kount). The plaintiff's statement of his cause of action, or the different parts of a declaration, each of which alone might suffice as a ground for action.

COUNTER-PLEA (koun'-ter-plee). A plea made in reply to another plea.

COURT (kort). A place where justice is judicially administered. The judge or judges themselves, when duly convened.

CRIME (kryme). A wrong that the government considers as injurious to the public and therefore punishes in a criminal proceeding in its own name.

CRIMINAL INTENT (krim'-men-l in'-tent[1]). The intent to commit a crime; the evil state of mind accompanying a criminal act.

CROSS-EXAMINATION (kraws-ek-zam-inay[1]-shun). The examination of a witness by the party opposing the party who called him.

CULPABLE (kul'-pa-bl). Deserving of moral blame rather than of criminal liability; censurable; blamable.

CULPRIT (kul'-prit). A person who is guilty or who may be found guilty of a crime.

CUMULATIVE (kue'-mue-lay-tiv). Additional; by way of increase.

CURIA (kue'-ri-a). A court of justice.

CUSTODIA LEGIS (kus-toe'-di-a lee'-jis). In the custody of the law.

CUSTODY (kus'-toe-di). The care and control of anything without necessarily divesting another of its possession. Imprisonment; physical detention.

CUSTOM (kus'-turn). Anything that has become established as law through long usage.

DAMAGE (dam'-aj). The loss or injury caused by one person to another, or to his property, either through accident, negligence, or actual design.

DE FACTO (dee fak'-toe). Actually; in fact; in deed; a thing actually done although the legality of it may be questioned.

DE NOVO (dee noe'-voe). Anew; afresh; a second time.

DECEDENT (de-see'-dent). A deceased person.

DECEIT (de-seet'). Any false representation or impression, knowingly made with intent to deceive, and resulting in damage to the one imposed upon.

DECISION (de-sizh'-on). A judgment given by a person or by a tribunal.

DECLARANT (de-klare'-ant). One who makes a declaration.

DECLARATION (dek-la-ray'-shun). The pleading by which a plaintiff sets out his cause of action. A statement made by one of the parties to a transaction, sometimes admissible as evidence, as in the case of a dying declaration.

DECLARATORY (de-klare'-a-tor-ee). Something that explains or ascertains what before was uncertain or doubtful, as a declaratory judgment, that gives the court's opinion on a question of law without ordering anything to be done, or a declaratory statute, that merely declares or explains the law as it stood previous to the statute, in order to put an end to any doubt as to what the law is.

DECREE (de-kree'). The judicial decision or order of a court of equity, corresponding to the judgment of a court of law.

DEFAMATION (def-a-may'-shun). The offense of injuring a person's character or reputation by false and malicious statements, either written or spoken.

DEFAULT (de-fawlt'). The failure to perform a duty or obligation. Failure of any party to take a step required of him in the progress of a cause.

DEFAULT JUDGMENT (de-fawlt' juj'-ment), Judgment given to plaintiff by reason of failure of defendant to appear and make defense,

DEFECT (de-fekt'). The lack of something required by law.

DEFENDANT (de-fen'-dent). The party who is summoned to answer a charge or complaint in any type of action, civil or criminal, at law or in equity,

DEFENSE (de-fense'). The answer of defendant to the plaintiff's action. The conduct of a trial on behalf of the defendant. The means of resistance against an attack.

DEFINITIVE (de-fin'-i-tiv). Conclusive; final; that which terminates a suit.

DEFRAUD (de-frawd[1]). To cheat; to wrong another by fraud.

DELICT or **DELICTUM** (de-likt') or (de-lik'- turn). A wrong or injury a tort; an offense.

DELINQUENCY (de-ling'-kwen-see). Misconduct; failure or violation of one's duty.

DELINQUENT (de-ling'-kwent). One who is guilty of an offense or failure of duty. Due and unpaid (as regards a debt). Negligent, dishonest, or unworthy of credit (as regards a person).

DEMURRER (de-mer'-er). An objection, made by one party to his opponent's pleading because of some defect in law in the pleading, and alleging that even though the facts of the pleading may be true, they are insufficient in law to compel the objecting party to proceed further.

DEPONENT (de-poe'-nent). One who gives information, under oath, respecting some facts known to him; a person making a deposition.

DEPORTATION (de-por-tay'-shun). The removal out of the country of an alien deemed dangerous to the public welfare.

DEPOSE (de-poze'). To give testimony under oath. To remove one from public employment or office.

DEPOSITION (dep-o-zish'-on). The testimony of a witness, taken elsewhere than in court, properly authenticated, and to be used subsequently on the trial of some question of fact in a court.

DERELICT (der'-e-likt). Abandoned; forsaken; deserted.

DETAINER or **DETENTION** (de-tay'-ner) or (de-ten'-shun). Holding a person against his will or withholding the possession of personal or real property from the owner.

DETRIMENT (det'-ri-ment). A loss or damage suffered in person or property.

DEVEST (de-vest'). To deprive; to take away.

DICTUM (dick'-turn). An observation or opinion, such as one expressed by a court on a matter not necessarily involved in a case and therefore lacking the authority of a judicial decision.

DIGEST (dy'-jest). A book or set of books, containing the important substance of other books, court decisions, or statutes, and prepared in an orderly manner of individual topics arranged alphabetically

DILATORY PLEA (dil'-la-tor-ee plee). One that does not answer to the true merits of the case but that nevertheless may defeat or at least delay the action, such as a plea to the jurisdiction or a plea in abatement.

DILIGENCE (dil'-i-jens). That particular care or attention expected of a person in any particular situation or activity; the opposite of negligence.

DIMINUTION OF THE RECORD (dim-i-nu'- shun of the rek'-ord). A term signifying that the record sent on appeal from an inferior court to a higher court is deficient in some respect, which deficiency may be rectified by certiorari.

DIRECT EVIDENCE (di-rekt' ev'-i-dens). Proof by witness who testify as to their own knowledge of the principal facts to be proven.

DIRECT EXAMINATION (dir-rekt' eg-zam-inay'-shun). The first examination of a witness by the party who calls him.

DIRECTED VERDICT (di-rek'-ted ver'-dikt). A verdict returned by a jury without deliberation and according to the result specified or directed by the court.

DIRECTORY (di-rek'-to-re). Suggestive or advisory, rather than imperative or mandatory, such as suggestive provisions in a statute as opposed to mandatory ones.

DISBAR (dis-bar'). To take away from a person the right to practice as an attorney at law.

DISCHARGE (dis-charj'). To release or set free. To cancel or extinguish an obligation. The release or dismissal from employment or service. The unloading of a cargo.

DISCOVERY (dis-kuv'-er-ee). The finding, ascertaining, or acquiring knowledge of something that previously was unknown or hidden. An equitable remedy to secure evidence resting entirely within an adversary's knowledge or control.

DISCREPANCY (dis-krep'-an-see). A variance; a difference between two things that should be the same.

DISCRETION (dis-kresh'-on). The ability to distinguish between good and evil and to know what is lawful or unlawful. The right or power of a judge or other official under certain circumstances, where there may be a choice of action, to act according to his own best judgment.

DISCRIMINATION (dis-krim-i-nay'-shun). Favoritism. Failure in one or more respects to treat all alike.

DISJUNCTIVE ALLEGATION (dis-jungk'-tiv al-e-gay'-shun). A statement in a pleading that is expressed in an alternative form, that is, by implying one of two or more alternatives, such as that he murdered or caused to be murdered.

DISMISSAL (dis-miss[1]-al). Termination or discontinuance of an action without an actual trial on it merits. A discharge from employment.

DISPOSITIVE (dis-poz-e-tiv). Being a deciding factor; bringing about a final determination. Of, relating to, or effecting the disposition of property by will or deed.

DISSOLUTION (dis-o-lu'-shun). Termination; abrogation; disintegration; the extinction of the binding force holding something together.

DISTRICT (dis'-trikt). A certain portion of a state or country, separated from the rest for some special purpose, such as judicial.

DISTRICT ATTORNEY (dis'-trikt a-ter'-nee). The officer appointed or elected to represent the state or federal government in a specified judicial district.

DOCKET (dock'-et). A formal record of the proceedings of a court.

DOCTRINE (dok'-trin). A principle, theory or rule of law, as doctrine of last clear chance.

DOCUMENT (dok[1]-u-ment). A record of some matter, written, printed, drawn, photographed, or expressed in some manner so as to constitute it a record of the matter in question.

DOCUMENTARY EVIDENCE (dok-u-men'-taree ev'-i-dense). Evidence supplied by writing and documents of all kinds.

DUE (due). Just and proper, as due care, due process of law. Owning or owed; that which legally should be paid or done.

DULY (due'-lee). Properly; regularly; according to law.

DUPLICITY (du-plis'-i-tee). A violation of the common law rule that pleadings must not be double, by writing two or more offenses in the same count of an indictment, two or more causes of action in the same count of a declaration, two or more grounds of defense in one plea, etc.

DURESS (du-ress'). Such unlawful restraint, imprisonment, physical violence, or threats of either, as to cause a person to act contrary to his will.

DUTY (due'-tee). Not only a legal obligation but a moral obligation or responsibility as well. A tax on the importation or exportation of goods.

DYING DECLARATION (dye'-ing dek-la-ray'-shun). A statement made by a person in the honest belief that his death is certain and very close.

EDICT (ee'-dikt). A law proclaimed and established by a sovereign.

EN AUTRE DOIT (en awe'-tre droyt). In the right of another.

EN FAIT (en fay). In fact; actually.

EN MASSE (en mass). In a mass; in an entire body or group.

ENACT (e-nackt'). To decree; to establish by law.

ENJOIN (en-join'). To command; to order or direct; to forbid or restrain.

ENTIRETY (en-tire'-tee). An undivided whole of anything, rather than part of it.

EQUITABLE (ek-wi-ta-bl). Just; according to equity; cognizable in equity.

EQUITY (ek'-wi-tee). Natural, moral and ethical right or justice. The system of jurisprudence administered by courts of chancery, to give the relief that law courts are incompetent to give.

ERROR (err'-or). Mistaken judgment as to facts or as to application of the law. The writ to review the judgment of an inferior court by a superior court for errors appearing on the face of the record.

ESTOPPEL (es-top[1]-el). A bar or impediment, preventing the denial of a certain set of facts as a result of previous conduct or admission or because of a final adjudication of the matter in a court of law.

ESTOPPEL IN PAIS (es-top'-el in pay). An equitable estoppel – one that is occasioned other than by deed or record.

ET (ett). And.

ET AL. (et al.). An abbreviation for et alii, meaning and others, or et alias, in the singular, meaning and another.

ET CETERA (ett set'-er-a). And other things; and so forth.

ET NON (ett non). And not.

ET SEQUITOR (ett sek'-wi-ter). And as follows.

ET SIC (ett sick). And so.

EVIDENCE (ev'-i-dense). All kinds of proof by which any alleged matter of fact, the truth of which is subject to investigation, is established or disproved.

EX DELICTO (eks de-lik'-to). Actions that result from a crime or tort.

EX DOLO MALO (eks doe'-lo ma'-lo). Out of fraud or deceit.

EX MALEFICIO (eks ma-le-fi[1]-she-o). On account of an illegal act or misconduct.

EX PARTE (eks par'-te). Of the one part; by or in behalf of one party only.

EX POST FACTO (eks post fak'-to). From or by an after act; by subsequent matter, as an ex post facto law, which is enabled after the offense has been committed.

EXECUTE (ek'-se-kute). To complete; to do; to perform; to make.

EXECUTE (ek[1]-se-ku-ted). Performed; done; completed; effectuated.

EXECUTION (ek-se-ku'-shun). Accomplishment or fulfillment of an undertaking. Putting a convict to death in fulfillment of a sentence. The writ or process by which a court's judgement is enforced.

EXEMPLARY DAMAGES (ek-zem'-pla-ree dam'-ajs). Damages in excess of ordinary damages to compensate for particular wrongful acts.

EXHIBIT (eg-zib'-it). To show or display; to produce or present in public. A paper, document or other thing produced during a hearing as evidence of facts connected with the case.

EXONERATION (eg-zon-e-ray'-shun). The removal or release of a charge or obligation, especially in the administration of an estate, to relieve the real estate of a mortgage contracted by the testator, by placing the charge against the personal estate. The right of indemnity, which a person has, who has been forced to pay what another should have paid in full.

EXPRESS (eks-press'). Clear; implicit; plain; definitely stated; that which is made known and not left to implication; the opposite of implied.

EXTORTION (eks-tor'-shun). In a strict sense, the unlawful taking by an officer, by authority of his office, of any money or other thing of value that is not due him. More commonly now, any unlawful taking or oppression under color of right.

EXTRA-JUDICIAL (eks-tra-ju-dish'-al). That which is done outside of or beyond the regular course of legal procedure.

EXTRA-TERRITORIAL (eks-tra-tare-i-tor'-ial). Beyond the boundaries of a state or country.

EXTRINSIC (eks-trin'-sik). Foreign; outside; coming from without.

EXTRINSIC EVIDENCE (eks-trin'-sik ev'-idense). Evidence from some outside source to explain the meaning of a document or agreement.

EYEWITNESS (eye-wit'-ness). One who actually saw the act or transaction to which he testifies.

FABRICATE (fab'-ri-kate). To devise falsely; to falsify; to counterfeit.

FACE (fase). Whatever appears on a written or printed instrument or document, without reference to any outside source; the outward appearance or normal aspect of a thing.

FACIAS (fay'-she-as). That you cause. (Scire facias--that you cause to know). (Fieri facias - that cause to be made).

FACT (fakt). An act; a thing done; an event or circumstance; that which is true.

FACTO (fak'-toe). In fact; indeed; by the act or fact.

FACTUM (fak'-tum). An act or deed; the doing or making.

FALSE PRETENSE (fawls pre-tense'). Any false representation or statement made with fraudulent design to obtain property, and with intent to cheat.

FALSE REPRESENTATION (fawls rep-re-sentay'-shun). A deceitful representation, known to be untrue and made with the intent to damage another.

FAULT (fawlt). Negligence; any shortcoming or neglect of care; an improper act or omission, arising from ignorance or carelessness rather than from intentional error.

FAVOR (fay'-vor). Bias; prejudice; partiality.

FEASIBLE (fee'-si-bl). Capable of being done or accomplished.

FEDERAL (fed'-e-ral). A league or union of two or more states. Pertaining to or organized under the laws of the United States, which is a union of several states.

FELON (fell'-on). A person convicted of a felony.

FELONIOUS (fe-lo'-ni-us). Malicious; done with intent to commit a crime.

FELONY (fell'-on-ee). A crime more serious in nature that a misdemeanor and punishable by death or imprisonment in a penitentiary.

FICTION (fick'-shun). A legal assumption that something is true even though it may be false.

FICTITIOUS (fick-tish'-us). Feigned; imaginary; pretended; having the character of a fiction.

FICTITIOUS PARTY (fick-tish'-us par'-tee). A party in whose name an action may be brought but who is ignorant of it or has not authorized it.

FIDUCIARY (fi-du[1]-shi-ar-re). Relating to or founded upon a trust or confidence. A trustee or one who holds a thing in trust for another.

FINAL (fy'-nal). Last; conclusive; decisive; with respect to suits and judgments, it is contrasted with interlocutory.

FINDING (fine'-ding). The conclusion arrived at by a court or jury as to a matter before it.

FORENSIC or **FORENSIS** (fo-ren'-sick) or (foren'-sis). Belonging to or relating to courts of law.

FORFEITURE (for'-fi-chure). A penalty or fine; a loss of a right in consequence of the non-performance of some obligation or condition.

FORGERY (for'-jer-ee). The fraudulent making and alteration of a writing to the prejudice of another person's rights. The fraudulent alteration of evidence to create an erroneous impression.

FORM (form). The technique, manner, or order of a legal proceeding or instrument, as distinguished from the substance of it. A model or bare outline of a legal instrument to be completed or followed in describing the substance or details of a specific matter.

FORSWEAR (for-sware'). To swear falsely; to commit perjury.

FORTUITOUS (for-two'-i-tus). Depending on or happening by chance; Accidental; casual.

FORUM (for'-urn). A court or place of justice; a place; jurisdiction.

FRAUD (frawd). Bad faith, dishonesty, infidelity, unfairness. Any form of misrepresentation, trickery, concealment, or: cunning by which a person may intend and does obtain an advantage over another.

FUNDAMENTAL (fun[1]-dament'-1). Of or being a base or foundation; essential; primary.

GENERAL ISSUE (jen'-er-al ish'-oo). A plea by the defendant amounting to an absolute denial of the entire indictment or declaration, thus reaching an issue at once.

GENUINE (jen'-u-in). True; real; not false, spurious, simulated, or counterfeit.

GOOD CAUSE (good kaws). Such reasonable grounds or justification as to afford a legal excuse.

GOOD FAITH (good fayth). Sincerity; innocence; honesty of intent ion; absence of bad faith or malice.

GRAND JURY (grand joor'-ee). A body of men, consisting at common law of not less than twelve nor more than twenty-three, and organized for the purpose of inquiring into the commission of crimes within the county from which its members are drawn and to find indictments against such as are supposed to be offenders.

GRAND LARCENY (grand lar'-sen-ee). Larceny wherein the value of the property stolen exceeds a certain amount - twelve pence, under the common law, but usually much higher where the distinction between grand and petty larceny is still maintained.

GROSS NEGLIGENCE (gross neg'-li-jens). Such want of care and regard for the rights of others as implies a disregard of consequences or willingness to inflict injury.

GROUND OF ACTION (grownd of ak'-shun). The basis of a suit; the foundation or circumstances upon which a cause of action rests.

GUARDIAN AD LITEM (gar'-di-an ad ly'-tem). A guardian appointed by a court to represent a ward of the court in some action pending before it to which the ward is a party.

GUILD (gild). An association of people following the same trade, art profession or business, organized to regulate and promote their common interests.

GUILT (gilt). That which renders an act or motive wrongful or criminal; a disposition to violate the law; the opposite of innocence.

GUILTY (gill'-tee). The state or condition of one who has committed an offense or crime. The plea by which a defendant in a criminal prosecution admits the crime with which he is charged.

HABEAS CORPUS (hay'-be-as kor'-pus). (Lat. That you have the body.) The popular writ to preserve personal freedom, directed to the person in whose custody a person is kept, ordering the body of the person so kept being brought before the court issuing the writ, so that judicial inquiry may be made into the legality of the restraint or imprisonment and appropriate judgment rendered thereon.

HABEAS CORPUS AD DELIBERANDUM ET RECIPIENDUM (hay'-be-as kor'-pus ad de-lib-er-an'-dum et re-si-pi-en'-dum). The habeas corpus writ for removal of a prisoner to the jurisdiction where the offense was committed.

HABEAS CORPUS AD PROSEQUENDUM (hay'-be-as kor'-pus ad pro-se-quen'- dum). The habeas corpus writ to remove a prisoner in order to prosecute in the proper jurisdiction wherein the fact was committed.

HABEAS CORPUS AD RESPONDENDUM (hay'-be-as kor'-pus ad res-pon-den'- dum). The habeas corpus writ issued when one who is in custody under process of an inferior court is removed to a higher court so that the claim may be pressed against him there.

HABEAS CORPUS AD SATISFACIENDUM (hay'-be-as kor'-pus ad sa-tis-fa- she-en'-dum). The habeas corpus writ designed to bring a prisoner from an inferior court where he has had judgment against him to a superior court for execution of the judgment.

HABEAS CORPUS AD SUBJICEDDUM (hay'-be-as kor'-pus ad sub-ji-she-en'- dum). The habeas corpus writ for deliverance from illegal confinement, directed to the person detaining another and commanding him to produce the body of the prisoner and to submit to the court's order.

HABEAS CORPUS AD TESTIFICANDUM (hay'-be-as kor'-pus ad tes-ti-fi- kan'-dum). The habeas corpus used to produce a prisoner so that he might testify or give evidence to the court.

HEARING (here'-ing). A trial; any formal or informal proceeding or examination of some matter before a tribunal or person authorized to pass judgment on the matter.

HEARSAY EVIDENCE (here'-say ev'-i-dense). Such evidence as is derived from what others have said or written rather than from what a person has actually experienced himself.

HOMICIDE (horn'-i-side). The killing of a human being, accidental or otherwise, by the act or fault of another.

HYPOTHETICAL QUESTION (hy-po-thet'-ikal kwes'-chun). An assumed or actual situation or state of facts, presented to an expert for his opinion, so that such opinion may be used as evidence on similar or identical facts in the trial of a case.

IBIDEM (i-by'-dem). (abbreviated as ibid., ib., or id.) The same; in the same place; in the same book or on the same page.

ID EST (id est). That is.

ILLEGAL (i-lee[1]-gal). Unlawful; contrary to law.

ILLEGITIMATE (ill-e-jit'-i-mate). Not authorized by law; a bastard, or child born out of wedlock.

ILLICIT (i-liss[1]-it). Unlawful; unauthorized; not permitted.

IMMATERIAL (im-a-tere'-i-al). Of no consequence or significance; not important, essential or necessary.

IMMEMORIAL (im-e-more'-i-al). Beyond human memory; time out of mind.

IMMIGRATION (im-i-gray'-shun). The migrating or coming of foreigners into a country for permanent residence.

IMMORAL (im-more'-al). Contrary to good morals; dissolute; unprincipled.

IMMUNITY (im-mue'-ni-tee). A privilege; a right conferred to one or more contrary to the general rule; exemption from some duty or penalty.

IMPAIR (im-pare'). To weaken; to affect in an injurious manner.

IMPANEL (im-pan'-el). To select a jury to try a case.

IMPARTIAL (im-par'-shal). Disinterested; unbiased; equitable.

IMPEACH (im-peech'). To accuse; to challenge; to question; to discredit.

IMPEACHMENT (im-peech'-ment). A proceeding to remove a public officer from office for misconduct, neglect of duty or commission of a crime.

IMPEDIMENT (im-ped'-i-ment). A restriction or disability; legal hindrance, preventing one from performing an act or contracting

IMPLEAD (im-pleed'). To sue or prosecute by due course of law; to make other persons parties to a suit.

IMPLIED (im-plide'). Manifested by implication or deduction from circumstances and conduct rather than by express words. The opposite of express.

IMPRISONMENT (im-priz'-on-ment). Confinement in a prison; any physical restraint or deprivation of a person's freedom of movement.

IMPUTED (im-pew'-ted). Attributable to one because of a peculiar association or relationship to another.

IN (in). (Lat.) In; into; upon; against; within.

IN AUTRE DROIT (een owe'-tre draw). In another's right.

IN CHIEF (in cheef). Principal; primarily; directly obtained.

IN CUSTODIA LEGIS (in kus-toe'-di-a lee'-jis). In custody of the law.

IN DELICTO (in de-lik'-toe). In fault.

IN ESSE (in ess'-e). In being; in existence.

IN FUTURO (in fu-tu'-ro). At a future time.

IN GENERE (in jen'-e-ree). In kind; of the same kind.

IN HOC (in hok). In this; in respect to this.

IN INFINITUM (in in-fi-ny'- turn). Indefinitely; forever.

IN INITIO (in in-nish'-i-oh). In or at the beginning.

IN JURE (in joo'-ree). In law; in the right.

IN LIMINE (in lim'-i-nee). In or at the beginning.

IN PARI DELICTO (in pa'-rye de-lik'-toe). In equal fault; equal in guilt.

IN PRAESENTI (in pre-zen'-tye). At the present time.

IN PRINCIPIO (in prin-sip'-e-oh). At the beginning; in the inception.

IN PROPRIA PERSONA (in pro'-pri-a per-so'-na). Himself; in his own person.

IN RE (in ree). Relating to; in the matter of.

IN STATU QUO (in stay'-to kwo). In the same situation or condition.

INADEQUATE (in-ad'-e-kwat). Insufficient; failing to meet standards or requirements.

INADMISSIBLE (in-ad-miss'-i-bl). Unacceptable; not permitted by law to be received as evidence.

INCAPACITY (in-ka-pass'-i-ti). Lack of power or legal ability to act or do something that others normally can do.

INCARCERATION (in-kar-se-ray'-shun). Imprisonment; confinement in jail.

INCEPTION (in-sep[l]-shun). The beginning or commencement.

INCHOATE (in-kho'-ate). That which is not yet completed or finished; imperfect; partial.

INCIDENT (in'-si-dent). An event or happening. Something that appertains, depends on, or follows another thing that is more fundamental, as a contract may have certain incidents that are a part of it and that are not necessary to specifically reserve.

INCUMBENT (in-kum'-bent). The person who is in possession of an office.

INCUR (in-ker'). To have liabilities placed upon one by operation of law or the result of acts not primarily designed to bring them about.

INDEBITATUS ASSUMPSIT (in-deb-bi-tay[l] -tus as-sump[l]-sit). (Lat. Being indebted, he promised.) The action of assumpsit used to recover damages for breach of simple contract, express or implied.

INDEMNIFY (in-dem'-ni-fye). To make good; to secure a person against loss or damage; to reimburse.

INDEPENDENT (in-de-pen'-dent). Not subject to the control, advice or restrictions of a superior authority.

INDETERMINATE (in-de-ter'-mi-nate). Uncertain; undersigned; not fixed; unascertained.

INDICIA (in-dish'-i-a). Signs; marks; indication; symbols; circumstances that lead to a certain belief.

INDICT (in-dite'). To accuse by the finding or presentment of a grand jury.

INDICTABLE (in-dye'-ta-bl). Liable to be indicted; subject to indictment.

INDICTED (in-dye'-ted). Charged formally with the commission of a crime.

INDICTEE (in-dye-tee'). The person who is indicted.

INDICTMENT (in-dite'-ment). A written accusation of a crime presented upon oath by the grand jury.

INDIRECT EVIDENCE (in-di-rekt' ev'-idense). Circumstantial evidence; evidence to prove some fact, not by testimony of a witness to such fact, but by collateral circumstances ascertained by competent means.

INDIVISIBLE (in-di-viz'-i-bl). Not susceptible to division; entire; that which cannot be separated.

INDUCEMENT (in-duse'-ment). The motive or reason for doing a thing. A portion of a declaration or plea, introductory to and necessary to explain the principal portion of the plea.

INFAMOUS CRIME (in'-fa-mus krime). A crime punishable by imprisonment in a penitentiary.

INFAMY (in'-fa-me). Loss of reputation, credit, and formerly of legal status through conviction of a crime; disgrace; disqualification of acting as witness or juror.

INFERENCE (in'-fer-ense). The reasoning by which a fact is proved as a logical consequence of other facts known to be true or already admitted.

INFERIOR COURT (in-fere'-i-or kort). A court of special or limited jurisdiction or one from which an appeal lies to an appellate court.

INFORMATION (in-for-may'-shun). An accusation, in the form of an indictment, presented by a prosecuting attorney or other competent officer instead of by a grand jury.

INFRA (in'-fra). Below, under, underneath, beneath; within.

INFRINGEMENT (in-frinj'-ment). A trespass or violation of a law or right; invasion of rights secured to another by patent, copyright, or trademark.

INHERENT (in-here[1]-ent). Intrinsic; belonging to or resulting from the nature of a thing; characteristic of anything itself.

INHERENTLY (inher'-ant-lee). Existing in something as an essential or permanent attribute.

INJUNCTION (in-jungk'-shun). A prohibitory writ, issued by a court of equity, forbidding a person from doing some act that is deemed inequitable as far as the rights of another may be concerned.

INJURIA (in-jure'-i-a). (Lat.) A wrong; injury; violation of right.

INJURY (in'-jure-re). A tort; any wrong done another.

INNUENDO (in-u-en'-doe). To hint at; meaning. An averment or clause in a declaration, indictment, or pleading explaining some previous statement, such as the meaning of libelous words.

INQUEST (in'-kwest). The proceeding or injury made by a coroner to determine the reason a person may have died suddenly or violently.

INQUISITION (in-kwi-zish'-on). An inquest; any judicial inquiry.

INSTANTER (in-stan[1] -ter). Immediately; without delay; forthwith.

INSTIGATE (in'-sti-gate). To incite one to action; to abet; to aid or encourage in the commission of an offense.

INSTITUTE (in'-sti-tute). To begin or commence; to originate; to constitute or appoint.

INSTITUTES (in'-sti-tutes). Textbooks containing an orderly arrangement of fundamental legal principles.

INSUFFICIENCY (in-su-fish'-en-see). Weakness in form and substance of a pleading; lack of fullness or completeness.

INTENT (in-tent[1]). The meaning, purpose, and significance of a person's words or acts; the design, purpose, and determination to use certain means to affect a desired result.

INTER (in'-ter). (Lat.) Between; I among.

INTER ALIA (in'-ter ay'-li-a). Among other things.

INTER ALIOS (in'-ter a'-li-ose). Between other persons - strangers to the suit in question.

INTER SE (in'-ter see) or INTER SESE (in'-ter see'-see). Among themselves.

INTTER VIVOS (in'-ter vy'-vos). Between living persons.

INTEREST (in'-ter-est). The right of property that a person has in anything. The relation or concern that one may have in another or in some matter. The compensation allowed by law or fixed by the parties to a contract for the use or forbearance or detention of money.

INTERFERENCE (in-ter-fere'-ense). The conflict or proceeding in the patent office to determine the priority of two inventions that make the same claims.

INTERIM (in'-ter-im). In the meantime; meanwhile.

INTERIM ORDER (in'-ter-im or'-der). A preliminary order or injunction; one made by a court pending the outcome of the suit.

INTERLOCUTORY (in-ter-lok'-u-tor-re). Provisional; temporary; intervening; something done between commencement and end of suit, deciding some point in relation to the suit only temporarily.

INTERPRETATION (in-ter-pre-tay'-shun). The determining of the intent or meaning of words, signs, or any symbol of expression that may not at first glance be evident.

INTERROGATORIES (in-ter-rog'-a-tor-eez). Questions, usually in writing, designed to elicit from witnesses the facts in some matter.

INTERSTATE COMMERCE (in'-ter-state kom'-erse). Intercourse, trading, or transportation of persons or property from one state to another.

INTERVENTION (in-ter-ven'-shun). The proceeding by which a person, not a party to some pending suit, is permitted to make himself a party to such suit to protect a right or interest of his which might be affected by it.

INTRA (in'-tra). (Lat.) In; within; within the bounds of.

INTRA VIRES (in'-tra vy'-reez). Within the powers; within the authority given by law; the opposite of ultra vires.

INTRINSIC (in-trin'-sik). The true, basic, essential and inherent character or value of a thing.

INURE (in-ure'). To result; to accrue to the benefit of a person.

INVOLUNTARY (in-vol'-un-tare-re). Unintentional; without will or power of choice.

IPSO FACTO (ip'-so fak'-toe). (Lat. By the fact itself.) By the very act.

IRRELEVANT (ir-rel'-e-vant). Not pertinent; not related to the matter at issue.

ISSUE (ish'-oo). All descendants of a common ancestor. A question of right to be determined between parties, with one party claiming a certain right or truth of some matter and the other party denying it. To go or send forth; to promulgate; to put into circulation.

JACTITATION (jak-ti-tay[1]-shun). A false claim or boast.

JEOPARDY (jep'-ar-dee). Hazard, peril, danger; the peril faced by a prisoner when he is charged with a crime before a tribunal competent to try him.

JOINDER (join'-der). Union; concurrence; uniting two or more parts in one or joining two or more persons in one action.

JOINT (joint). Undivided; united; coupled together in interest or liability.

JOINT ACTION (joint ak'-shun). An action prosecuted or defended by two or more persons together.

JOINT AND SEVERAL (joint and sev'-er-al). The option of suing one or more persons separately or all together.

JUDGE (juj). A public officer properly appointed or elected to preside and administer the law in a court of justice.

JUDGMENT (juj'-ment). The final determination of a court upon some proceeding before it. The knowledge or experience upon which competent action or proper understanding is made. An opinion.

JUDICIAL (joo-dish[1]-al). Belonging to or related to a judge of the administration of justice.

JUDICIAL NOTICE (joo-dish'-al no'-tis). The doctrine of acceptance of certain facts without proof, the truth of such facts being commonly known and not questioned.

JUDICIARY (joo-dish'-i-ar-re). Pertaining to the courts or the administration of justice. The system of courts or the branch of government that administers the law.

JURAT (jur'-rat). The certification or statement at the bottom of an affidavit indicating when and before whom such affidavit was sworn.

JURISDICTION (jur-ris-dik'-shun). The power of a court to take cognizance of, hear, and determine a cause, as well as the power to render and enforce judgment in such cause.

JURISPRUDENCE (jur-ris-proo'-dense). The body of law considered as a science, that is, one made up of a systematic collection of rules and principles, which form the basis upon which all legal questions are settled.

JURIST (jur'-rist). A person skilled or versed in the science of the law.

JUROR (jur'-or). A person who serves on a jury.

JURY (jur'-re). A specified group or number of persons chosen to hear the evidence or facts in a judicial proceeding and to ascertain the truth on questions of fact in such proceeding.

JUS (jus). Right; law; equity.

JUSTICE (jus'-tis). A judge. The objective or end to which the administration of law is directed.

JUSTIFIABLE (jus-ti-fy'-a-bl). Rightful; warranted or sanctioned by law.

JUSTIFICATION (jus-ti-fi-kay'-shun). Just cause or excuse; a valid defense to an action.

KIDNAPPING (kid'-nap-ing). A form of false imprisonment aggravated by removal of the person to some other place and holding for some unlawful purpose.

LACHES (lach'-ez). Such unreasonable delay or lack of diligence, especially in regard to prosecuting a claim, that injustice would result if such negligence were overlooked.

LAPSE (laps). To pass slowly or by degrees; to fall or fail. The end of a right or privilege through failure to exercise such right or because of the happening of a contingency preventing its enforcement.

LARCENY (lar'-sen-nee). The taking and carrying away of the property of another against his will and without his consent, with the intent to deprive the owner permanently of it or to convert it to the use of the taker.

LASCIVIOUS (la-siv'-i-us). Indecent, obscene, lewd, depravity of morals.

LATENT DEFECT (lay'-tent de-fekt'). A defect in some object of sale, known to the seller but not apparent to the buyer and not discoverable by mere observation.

LAW (law). Something established or ordained. The rules by which any society regulates or controls the actions of its members.

LAWFUL (1 aw'-ful). Legal; that which is sanctioned or authorized by law.

LAWSUIT (law'-sute). Litigation; any action or cause instituted in a court of law.

LAWYER (law'-yer). A person skilled in the law. One licensed to practice law.

LEADING QUESTION (leed'-ing kwes'-chun). A question so worded as to suggest the answer to be given by the one to whom the question is put.

LEAVE OF COURT (leeve of kort). Permission granted by a court to do something which, without such permission, would not be proper.

LEGAL (lee'-gal). Proper; lawful; according to or allowed by law. Pertaining to a court of law, rather than to equity.

LEGAL NOTICE (lee'-gal no'-tis). Such notice as is required by law to be given in some particular situation.

LEGISLATION (lej-is-lay'-shun). The preparation and enactment of laws by a competent body.

LEGITIMATE (le-jit'-i-mate). Legal; recognized by law. To make lawful.

LIABILITY (ly-a-bil'-i-tee). Any kind of debt, obligation, or responsibility; the state or condition of one who is bound or obligated in law or justice.

LIBEL (ly'-bel). Anything, written or printed, reflecting on the character or reputation of another, published without justification or excuse and exposing him thus to ridicule, hatred, or contempt. The written statement by the plaintiff in an admiralty suit of his cause of action; the pleading in an admiralty suit serving the same purpose as the declaration in a common law action.

LIBERTY (lib'-er-tee). Freedom from restraint; the right and power of deciding and doing what one decides without restriction from an outside source.

LOCUS CRIMINIS (lo'-kus crim'-i-nis). The place of the crime.

LOCUS DELICTI (lo'-kus de-lik'-ty). The place where the tort or injury has been committed.

MAGISTRATE (maj'-is-trate). An inferior judicial officer. Any public officer invested with some judicial power.

MAGNA CARTA (mag'-na kar'-ta). The great charter - more specifically, the one obtained from King John of England on June 19, 1215, by his barons, reconfirming the fundamental laws of England and establishing the principal grounds of liberty that are recognized today as protective of the individual.

MAL (mal). A prefix meaning bad, wrong, or fraudulent.

MALA (mal'-a). Bad.

MALA IN SE (mal'-a in see). Acts or things wrong in themselves, that is, morally wrong, rather than such as may be mala prohibita (forbidden by law).

MALA PROHIBITA (mal-a pro-hib'-i-ta). Those acts of things that are specifically prohibited by law.

MALADMINISTRATION (mal-ad-min-is-tray'-shun). Bad or wrongful administration.

MALEFACTOR (mal'-e-fak-tor). One who has committed a crime.

MALFEASANCE (mal-fee'-zanse). Ill conduct; the unjust performance of an act that a person has no right to do.

MALICE (mal'-is). Ill-will; an evil intent or condition of the mind as is associated with the doing of a wrongful act without excuse or justification.

MALICE AFORETHOUGHT (mal'-is a-fore'-thawt). A technical phrase used in conjunction with murder to indicate that the killing was intentional rather than the result of chance.

MALICIOUS (ma-lish'-us). Characterized by malice; wrongful; without just cause.

MALICIOUS PROSECUTION (ma-lish'-us pross-e-ku'-shun). The institution of criminal or civil action against another without probable cause and with malice.

MALO ANIMO (may'-lo an'-i-mo). With malice; with bad intent.

MALPRACTICE (mal-prak'-tis). Failure to perform professional duties such as those of a doctor, with the skill, learning, and care reasonably expected of one in like circumstances.

MALUM (may'-lum). Bad; evil; wicked.

MALUM IN SE (may'-lum in see). A crime or offense that is wrong in itself, that is, because of its inherent nature rather than because it is declared unlawful.

MALUM PROHIBITUM (may'-lum pro-hib ' - i.tum). A wrong prohibited by law.

MANDAMUS (man-day'-mus). (Lat. We command.) One of the extraordinary legal remedies, used when ordinary modes of proceeding are ineffectual. It is an order from a superior court commanding, in the name of the state or sovereign, an inferior court, corporation, or natural person to do some particular thing that he or it has the power to perform.

MANDATE (man'-date). A direction or request. A judicial command or an authoritative order. A gratuitous bailment, involving work or service on the property rather than safe-keeping of it.

MANDATORY (man'-di-tor-re). Peremptory; imperative; essential; compelling.

MANIFEST (man'-i-fest). Plain; evident; visible. A written document giving an account of a ship's ownership, destination, cargo passengers and baggage.

MANIFESTO (man-i-fes'-toe). A solemn declaration by the constituted authority of one nation, justifying the declaration of war or the taking of other nation.

MANSLAUGHTER (man'-slaw-ter). The unlawful killing of another, either voluntary or involuntary, but without malice.

MATERIAL (ma-tere'-i-al). Important; substantial; going to the essence of a thing or the merits of a proposition.

MATERIAL ALLEGATION (ma-tere'-i-al al-egay'-shun). An allegation essential or necessary to a claim or defense - one that could not be omitted without leaving the claim or defense insufficient

MATERIAL EVIDENCE (ma-tere'-i-al ev'-idense). Evidence that is relevant and goes to the essence of the matter in dispute.

MATTER (mat'-er). A fact or facts constituting a ground of action or defense. Any substantial or perceptible thing.

MATTER IN ISSUE (mat'-er in ish'-oo). A disputed point or question. A point affirmed on one side and denied on the other.

MATTER OF FACT (mat'-er of fakt). A truth that can be proved by one of the senses or the testimony of witnesses.

MATTER OF LAW (mat'-er of law). Matters of truth and fact in which is determined by rules of law or reasoning based on legal principles.

MATTER OF RECORD (mat'er of rek'-ord). A fact that can be proved by the production of a record.

MAXIM (mak'-sim). A generally accepted rule, law, or principle; a principle of law universally admitted as sound and reasonable

MEMORANDUM (mem-o-ran'-dum). A simple and informal writing or record of some fact or agreement; any writing that may assist the memory.

MENACE (men'-us). A threat; an evident disposition to inflict an injury upon another.

MENS REA (menz re'-a). A guilty mind; a criminal intent.

MERITS (mare'-its). Actual legal rights as opposed to matters of form; the justice of a cause rather than technicalities.

MINORITY (mi-nor'-i-te). Infancy; the state of being a minor. The smaller number of votes or persons, as opposed to the majority.

MISDEMEANOR (mis-de-me'-nor). Any crime or offense inferior to a felony.

MISFEASANCE (mis-fee'-zance). A wrong or trespass; the doing of a lawful act in an unlawful or wrongful manner.

MISPRISION (mis-prizh'on). A misdemeanor that has no particular name or the offense of obstructing justice or concealing a crime.

MISREPRESENTATION (mis-rep-re-zen-tay'-shun). An untrue statement of fact; any manifestation leading another to believe a condition or state of facts that does not exist.

MITIGATION (mit-i-gay'-shun). Lessening the amount of a penalty or punishment due to extenuating circumstances.

MITTIMUS (mit'-i-mus). The final process in a criminal case, ordering the sheriff or other officer to convey the offender to prison.

MODUS (mo'-dus). Mode; manner; means; form.

MOOT (moot). Unsettled; undecided. The practice of arguing hypothetical cases.

MOOT QUESTION (moot kwes'-chon). An unsettled point of law.

MORAL TURPITUDE (mor'-al ter[1]-pi-tude). Conduct of a person characterized by disregard of the rights ordinarily accorded another person.

MOTION (mo'-shun). An application to a court by a party to a suit, requesting a rule or order by the court in his behalf. The method by which a proposal is submitted to a formal meeting for consideration.

MOTIVE (mo'-tiv). The cause or reason that leads one to do an act.

MOVE (moov). To make a motion.

MULTIPLICITY OF ACTIONS or SUITS (mul-ti-plis'-i-te of ak'-shuns or suits). Numerous different suits of actions unnecessarily brought upon the same issue against one defendant.

MURDER (mer'-der). The willful killing of a human being by another in accordance with a deliberate purpose or design.

NATIVE (nay'tiv). A citizen by birth.

NATURALIZATION (nach-u-ral-i-zay'-shun). The process by which an alien is made a citizen of a state or nation.

NEGLIGENCE (neg'-li-jense). The omission of such care, diligence, or skill as the ordinary person would employ under like circumstances.

NEW TRIAL (noo try'-al). A rehearing of a case tried once before. It is within the discretion of a court to grant a new trial as a matter of practical justice.

NEXT FRIEND (nekst frend). The person acting on behalf of an infant or other person unable to act for himself.

NIHIL PiCIT (nye'-hil dye'-sit). (Lat. He says nothing.) The name of the judgment rendered against a defendant who fails to plead or answer plaintiff's declaration.

NISI (nye'-sye). Unless; except.

NISPI PRIUM (nye'-sye pry'-urn). Unless before. A trial by jury of issues of fact before a single judge.

NOLLE PROSEQUI (nol'-e pros'-e-kwy). The declaration made on the record by plaintiff or prosecutor that he will proceed no further.

NOLO CONTENDERE (no'-lo kon-ten'-der-re). (Lat. I do not desire to contend.) The plea of defendant in a criminal action, not wishing to contest, the prosecution. It has the same effect as a plea of guilty, although it may be considered in mitigation of the punishment.

NON COMPOS MENTIS (non kom'-pos men'-tis). Not of sound mind. A term used to denote any form of mental derangement.

NON DISPOSITVE (non dis-poz-e'-tiv). Not being a deciding factor; not bringing about a final determination.

NON FEASANCE (non fee'-zanse). The failure to perform an act required of one.

NON OBSTANTE (non ob-stan'te). Notwithstanding.

NON OBSTANTE VEREDICTO (non ob-stan'-te ve-re-dik'-to). Notwithstanding the verdict of the jury.

NOT GUILTY (not gil'-te). A plea of the general issue in criminal prosecutions and some civil actions. The verdict in favor of the defendant in a criminal action.

NOTARY PUBLIC (no'-ta-re pub'-lik). An officer authorized by a state to attest the genuineness of written instruments and to authenticate the facts contained in them.

NOTICE (no'-tis). Knowledge; the communication of information, advice, or a warning, given by one person to another concerning some matter.

NOTORIOUS (no-tor'-i-us). Open, known, or manifest to all persons. Of questionable reputation.

NULL (nul). That which does not exist or is of no validity or effect.

NULL AND VOID (nul and void). The same as null, as the words "null" and "void" mean the same thing.

NULLITY (nul'-i-te). An act or proceeding that is of no effect whatsoever.

NUNC PRO TUNC (nunk pro tunk). Now for then. A term used to indicate that a thing is done now that ought to have been done before.

NUNQUAM (nun'-kwam). Never; nowhere.

OATH (othe). A solemn affirmation of the truth of a statement.

OBJECTION (ob-jek'-shun). A formal remonstrance by a party to the legality of something said or done during the course of a trial, the object being to obtain the court's ruling thereon and to make exception thereto if the ruling is unfavorable.

OBLIGATION (ob-li-gay'-shun). Any duty imposed by law, contract, family relationship, or society in general.

OBLOQUY (ob'-lo-kwe). Blame; censure; reproach.

OBSCENE (ob-seen[1]). Indecent; offensive to chastity and modesty; tending to excite sexual desires.

OBSTANTE (ob-stan'-te). Withstanding; hindering.

OFFENSE (o-fense'). Any breach of penal or criminal laws; a crime or misdemeanor.

OFFER (off'-er). A proposal of terms and conditions upon which one is willing to enter into contractual relationship with another in respect to a certain matter.

OFFICER DE JURE (off'-i-ser de joo'-re). The one lawfully entitled to an office but not performing the duties of such office.

OFFICIAL (o-fish'-al). Pertaining to a public office. an officer or one invested with a public office.

OPEN COURT (o'-pen kort). A court that has formally convened and in which its judicial functions are performed in public as opposed to judge's chambers privately.

OPINION (o-pin'-yon). An inference or conclusion drawn by a person upon facts observed or presented to him. The reasons given by a judge for his decision in a particular matter.

ORAL (or'-al). Expressed in words by the mouth; verbal; spoken words as opposed to written ones.

ORAL DEFAMATION (or'-al def-a-may'-shun). Slander, that is, defamation by spoken words.

ORDINANCE (or'-di-nanse). A law passed by the legislative body of a municipal corporation. Any law or statute.

ORDINARY (or'-di-nare-re). Usual; common; customary; according to standard of the average person.

ORE TENUS (o'-re tee'-nus). By word of mouth; orally; verbally.

ORGANIC LAW (or-gan'-ik law). A fundamental law, such as is established by a constitution.

ORIGINAL (or-ij'-i-nal). First in order; depending on no outside authority or influence; a document or instrument from which copies are made.

ORIGINAL PROCESS (or-ij'-i-nal pro'-sess). The process or means by which a suit is commenced, and summons served to obtain the appearance of defendant.

ORIGINAL WRIT (or-ij'-i-nal ritt). A writ or order, emanating from the king and directed to the sheriff of the county where the injury incurred, requiring him to obtain the presence of the wrongdoer in court, which writ formerly was required to give the court jurisdiction of the matter.

OVERT (o'-vert). Open; manifest.

OVERT ACT (o'-vert akt). An actual physical act, indicating the design or intent of the doer.

PANEL (pan'-el). A list of jurors returned by a sheriff, to serve at a particular court or for the trial of some particular action

PARAMOUNT (par'-a-mount). That which is superior; of higher rank.

PARDON (par'-don). Freeing one from the punishment prescribed for an offense, either before or after conviction.

PARENS PATRIAE (pay'-renz pay'-tri-ee). Father or parent of the country. The state which, as sovereign, has power of guardianship over persons under disabilities.

PARI DELICTO (pa'-rye de-lik'- toe). Equally at fault.

PARI PASSU (pa'-rye pas'-u). In equal degree.

PARTICEPS CRIMINIS (par'-ti-seps krim'-inis). A party to the crime an accomplice.

PARTIES (par'-teez). All persons who take part in any act or are directly interested in the prosecution or defense of any legal proceedings.

PARTY (par'-tee). Any person concerned or interested in an affair, transaction, or proceeding.

PASSIVE (pass'-iv). Inactive; submissive; permissive.

PAUPER (paw'-per). A public charge; one so poor and destitute as to require public aid to exist.

PECUNIARY (pe-ku'-ni-ar-re). Pertaining to money; consisting of money or that which can be valued in terms of money.

PENAL (pee'-nal). Punishable; denoting punishment imposed by a state for a crime.

PENAL ACTION (pee'-nal ak'-shun). An action, either civil or criminal, to enforce a penalty or punishment imposed by law.

PENAL CLAUSE (pee'-nal klawse). A clause in a statute or contract declaring the penalty for violation of proceeding clauses.

PENAL STATUTE (pee'-nal stat'-ute). One imposing a penalty or punishment for violation thereof.

PENALTY (pen'-al-tee). A deprivation of property or right or the exaction of money as punishment for the non-performance of a promised act or performance of an unlawful act.

PENDENTE LITE (pen-den'-te lye'-tee). During the pendency of a suit or action.

PENDING (pen'-ding). Undetermined; in process of settlement.

PER (per). By; through; by means of.

PER ANNUM (per an'-num). By the year.

PER AUTRE VIE (per o'-tre vee). For another's life; for such period of time as another person may live.

PER CAPITA (per ka'-pi-ta). By the heads; equally, share and share alike; the opposite of per stirpes.

PER CURIAM (per ku'-ri-am). By the court, as a whole, rather than a single judge.

PER SE (per see). By himself or itself; in itself; taken alone.

PEREMPTORY (per-emp'-tor-re). Final; absolute; conclusive; demanding immediate consideration.

PEREMPTORY CHALLENGE (per-emp'-tor-re chal'enj). The absolute right to exclude a juror for no particular reason, which right is given to the defense in a criminal case for a restricted number of times.

PERFORM (per-form'). To complete or discharge one's obligation.

PERFORMANCE (per-form'-anse). The act of doing something; the fulfillment of one's promise or obligation.

PERJURY (per'-joo-re). The willful stating, under oath, of matter that is untrue.

PERMISSION (per-mish'-on). Leave, license, or authority to do a thing.

PERMISSIVE (per-miss'-iv). Allowable; that which is permitted to be done.

PERMIT (per-mit'). To allow, consent, suffer, tolerate, or authorize.

PERMIT (per'-mit). A license or written instrument authorizing an act ordinarily forbidden.

PERPETRATOR (per'-pe-tray-tor). The one who actually commits a crime or tort; a principal in the first degree, as distinguished from an accessory.

PERPETUAL (per-pet'-u-al). Eternal; lasting forever; continuous; without interruption.

PERPETUATING TESTIMONY (per-pet'-uate-ing tes'-ti-mo-ne). A right afforded by statute to reduce to a written record the testimony of witnesses who may not be available later to testify in person, so that their testimony may be used in a subsequent proceeding.

PERSON (per'-son). A natural being, as a man, or an artificial being, as a corporation.

PERSONAL (per'-son-al). Relating to or belonging to an individual.

PERSONAL ADVICE (per'-son-al adviz'). Recommendation on how to act.

PETIT (pet'-e). Small; little; petty; of minor importance.

PETIT JURY (pet'-e joo'-re). A trial jury as distinguished from the grand (large) jury.

PETIT LARCENY (pet'-e lar'-sen-ne). (Also known as petty larceny.) Larceny in which the value of the property taken is only nominal. If over a certain amount, it is considered grand larceny.

PETITION (pe-tish'-on). A written application to one in authority for the grant of a favor or privilege. The initial pleading, as a declaration, in a court action.

PIRACY (pye'-ra-see). The offense of robbery committed on the high seas. Plagiarism or the infringement of a copyright.

PLAINTIFF (plane'-tiff). The person who brings an action; the one who makes complaint.

PLEA (plee). A pleading; any one of the series of pleadings; the defendant's answer to the plaintiff's declaration, setting up matters of fact rather than of law.

PLEADING (plee'-ding). The stating in legal form and in proper order the facts that make up the plaintiff's cause of action or defendant's ground of defense.

PLENARY (plee'-na-re). Full; complete; formal.

POLICE POWER (po-leese' pou'-er). The right existing in a state to restrict persons or the use of property in any way to promote the comfort, health, welfare, and safety of the people generally.

POLICY (pol'-i-see). The fundamental purpose or principle by which a government, organization, or person is guided in his or its relations with others. The instrument expressing the contract of insurance entered into against some risk, peril, or contingency.

POSITIVE EVIDENCE (poz'-i-tiv ev'-i-dense). Direct proof of a matter at issue, as testimony of an eyewitness, for example, as opposed to circumstantial evidence.

POSITIVE FRAUD (poz'-i-tiv frawd). Actual fraud, namely intentional deception, rather than constructive fraud.

POSITIVE LAW (poz'-i-tiv law). Law actually enacted or recognized as a controlling force rather than a natural law, which comprises such forces of justice and right as are universally recognized by all.

POSSESSION (po-zesh'-on). The dominion, control, and custody of anything that may be the subject of property by one for his own use and enjoyment.

POSSIBILITY (pos-i-bil'-i-te). An uncertainty. A contingent interest, in the nature of an expectancy, in real or personal estate.

POST DIEM (poste dye'-em). After the day.

POST LITEM MOTAM (poste dye'-em). After the day.

POST LITEM MOTAM (poste lye'-tern moe'-tam). After the commencement of the suit.

POSTEA (post'-te-a). Afterwards; a record of the proceedings in a case after it is ready for trial.

POSTERITY (pos-ter'-i-te). All the descendants of a person in a direct line to the remotest generation.

POWER OF ATTORNEY (pou'-er of a-ter'-nee). An instrument giving one the right to act as agent or attorney for another.

PRACTICE (prak'-tis). The manner and method by which suits are conducted and tried in a court.

PREAMBLE (pre'-am-bl). A statement at the beginning of a constitution or statute explaining the reason for enacting it and the purposes for which it is adopted.

PRECEDENT (pres'-e-dent). Any legal instrument or decision that that serves as a pattern for subsequent rulings or instruments of the same nature.

PREJUDICE (prej'-oo-dis). Partiality; bias; preconceived opinion; a leaning toward one side of a cause for personal reasons rather than for honest belief.

PRELIMINARY (pre-lim'-inare-re). Coming before and leading up to the main part of something happening before something that is more important, often in preparation for it.

PRELIMINARY INJUNCTION (pre-lim'-inare-re in-jungk'-shun). An injunction or order issued at any time before or during trial of a cause but before a final adjudication.

PREMEDITATION (pre-med-i-tay'- shun). The thinking of beforehand; the design formed to do some act, such as a crime.

PREMISES (prem'-i-ses). Facts or statements previously recited. The narrative part of a bill in equity, setting forth the essential grounds of complaint. A piece of land, building, or real estate.

PREPONDERANCE OF EVIDENCE (prepon'-der-anse of ev'-i-dense). Evidence of greater weight or more readily believed.

PREROGATIVE (pre-rog'-a-tiv). A power or will which is unfettered, that is, uncontrolled by any other will, such as that of a sovereign.

PREROGATIVE WRITS (pre-rog'-a-tiv ritts). Writs resulting from an exercise of the extraordinary power of the state and affecting the sovereignty of the state; its rights, or the liberties of its people.

PRESENTMENT (pre-zent'-ment). An accusation of crime made by a grand jury from their own knowledge or from evidence furnished them by witnesses. The production of a bill of exchange to the party on whom it is drawn, or of a note to the person liable thereon, with the request that it be accepted or paid.

PRESUMPTION (pre-zump'-shun). That which may be taken for granted, as a result of reason or experience, without further proof.

PRESUMPTIVE EVIDENCE (pre-zump'-tiv ev'-i-dense). Evidence of a fact from which the existence of another fact may be inferred.

PRIMA FACIE (prye'-ma fay'-shi-e). At first sight; a fact presumed to be true until disproved.

PRIMA FACIE CASE (pry'-ma fay'-shi-e kase). One that is established by sufficient evidence, which can be overcome only by rebutting evidence produced by other party.

PRIMA FACIE EVIDENCE (pry'-ma fay'-shi-e ev'-i-dense). Evidence sufficient to establish a fact unless rebutted by contrary evidence.

PRIMARY EVIDENCE (pry'-mare-re ev'-i-dense). The evidence which, under the circumstances, best proves the matter in question.

PRINCIPLE (prin'-si-pl). A fundamental rule or doctrine, from which other rules may be developed.

PRIORITY (pry-or'-i-te). Precedence; the quality of being first in point of time.

PRISON (prizz'-n). A place or building used for the confinement of persons, either for punishment of a crime or for some other reason in the administration of justice.

PRISONER (prizz'-ner). A person deprived of his liberty and confined against his will.

PRIVY (priv'-ee). One who has an interest in an action, matter, or thing.

PRO (pro). For; in consideration of; on behalf of; before.

PRO CONFESSO (pro kon-fess'-o). As confessed. A degree in equity based upon failure of defendant to appear or answer the complaint.

PRO FORMA (pro for'-ma). As a matter of form.

PRO INDIVISO (pro in-di-vy'-so). For an undivided part. The joint occupation and possession of lands as a whole.

PRO RATA (pro ray'-ta). According to a certain rate, percentage or proportion; proportionately.

PRO SE (*pro se*e). For one self; in one's own behalf.

PRO TANTO (pro tan'-toe). For so much; for as far as it goes.

PRO TEMPORE (pro tern'-po-re). For the time being; temporary.

PROBABILITY (prob-a-bil'-i-te). Likelihood; reasonable ground for belief.

PROBABLE (prob'-a-bl). Having the appearance of truth; apparently true but open to doubt.

PROBABLE CAUSE (prob'-a-bl kawz). A reasonable and sincere belief in the existence of facts that warrant a cause of action or legal proceedings.

PROBATE (pro'-bate). Relating to proof; relating to proof of wills, as the word has commonly come to be known now. Any matter coming within the jurisdiction of a probate court.

PROBATIVE FACT (pro'-ba-tiv fakt). An evidentiary fact that actually does prove an ultimate fact or the fact sought.

PROCEDURE (pro-see'-dyur). That part of law that deals with the method or mechanism by which the legal system is conducted, such subjects as pleading, practice, and evidence relate to the method of conducting litigation.

PROCEEDING (pro-seed'-ing). The manner of carrying on a legal suit.

PROCESS (pros'-es). The writ by which a person is brought into court or compelled to obey its order. The method of operation or procedure by which a result or effect is produced.

PROHIBITION (pro-hi-bish'-on). Order of restraint; interdiction; the name of a writ designed to restrain a court from proceeding in a matter over which it does not have jurisdiction.

PROLIXITY (pro-lik'-si-te). The injection of superfluous and unnecessary facts in a pleading.

PROLONGATION (pro-long-gay'-shun). A lengthening, usually referring to the time in which something is to be done.

PROMULGATION (pro-mul-gay'-shun). Making something known; notification to the public of the passage and execution of a law.

PROOF (proof). The demonstration by proper evidence of a matter that previously was doubtful.

PROPOSAL (pro-poe'-zal). An offer. The thing or proposition offered.

PROPTER (prop'-ter). On account of; by reason of; because of.

PROROGATION (pro-ro-gay'-shun). Prolongation; putting off to another time.

PROSECUTE (pross'-e-kute). To follow up by appropriate means to a conclusion; to proceed against a person by judicial action.

PROSECUTION (pross-e-ku'-shun). A criminal proceeding or the means by which an offender is brought to justice. The government, state, or person conducting a criminal trial. It may also refer to the course of a civil action.

PROSEQUI (pro'-se-kwy). To follow up; to prosecute.

PROTEST (pro'-test). A formal notice of nonpayment or non-acceptance of a note or bill of exchange. A declaration of non-assent or disapproval of some act required of one or of action taken by others.

PROTESTATION (prot-es-tay'-shun). A manner of pleading by which a fact is neither affirmed nor denied.

PROVE (proov). To make certain; to establish by evidence.

PROXIMITY (prok-sim'-i-tee). Nearness; relationship; kinship.

PUBLIC (pub'-lik). The people as a whole of a state or of a smaller community. Pertaining to the people as a whole. Open to all; notorious.

PUBLIC CHARITY (pub'-lik chare[1]-i-tee). A gift or charity so indefinite in its object or for the benefit of so large a class as to be deemed for the benefit of the public generally.

PUBLIC WRONGS (pub'-lik rawngs). Violations of rights and duties affecting the entire community;

crimes and misdemeanors.

PUBLICATION (pub-li-kay'-shun). The act by which a thing is published or made known to the public.

PUBLISH (pub'-lish). To make known to the public generally; to issue; to put into circulation.

PUIS (pwis). Afterwards; since.

PUNISHMENT (pun'-ish-ment). The penalty inflicted by authority for the transgression of the law.

PUNITIVE (pu'-ni-tiv). Relating to punishment; having the effect of inflicting a penalty or punishment; vindictive.

PURGATION (per-gay'-shun). The clearing oneself of a criminal charge by denial under oath or the testimony of others who swear to his innocence.

PURVIEW (per'-vu). The design, purpose, and actual scope of a statute; that part of a statute commencing with "Be it enacted" and continuing to the repealing clause.

QUAERE (kwe'-re). Query; doubt; question.

QUAESTIO (kwest'-she-o). An inquest or the tribunal empowered to investigate a crime.

QUALIFIED (kwol'-i-fide). Fitting; competent; capable. Limited, restricted; imperfect.

QUARE (kway'-re). Wherefore; why; for what reason; because.

QUASH (kwosh). To make void; to annul; to dismiss.

QUASI (kway'-sy). Analogous to; as if; almost; relating to or having resemblance of.

QUASI-CONTRACT (kway'-sy kon'-trakt). A contract implied in law, that is, one in which the obligation arises as a result of legal implications from the facts or circumstances rather than as a result of an agreement or the intention of the parties.

QUASI-CRIME (kway'-sy krime). A wrong done to the public that may not be quite an indictable offense.

QUA SUPRA (kway su'-pra). As appears above.

QUESTION (kwes'-chon). A problem or a matter subject to debate or controversy. An interrogation put to a witness as to the truth or falsity of a matter.

QUID PRO QUO (kwid pro kwo). What for what. The consideration of a contract.

QUOAD HOC (kwo[1]-ad hok). As to this; with respect to this; as for as this matter is concerned.

QUORUM (kwo'-rum). A majority of an entire body. Such a number of the members of a body as is competent to transact the business of the body in the absence of the other members.

RAPE (rape). The ravishing of a woman married or not, against her will, both before and after.

RATIFICATION (rat-i-fi-kay[1]-shun). The adoption of the act of another or the confirmation of a previous act of the party himself, the latter thereby receiving the benefits or obligations of the original act.

RATIO LEGIS (ray'-she-o lee'-jis). The reason for a law; the occasion of making law.

RE (ree). In regard to; in the matter of; in the case of.

REAL EVIDENCE (ree'-l ev'-i-dense). Evidence consisting of things themselves, available for inspection, as distinguished from the testimony of witnesses.

REASONABLE (re'-zon-l-bl). Rational; proper; consistent with reason or good sense.

REBUT (re-but'). To deny; to contradict; to overcome by weight of evidence.

RECALL OF WITNESS (re-kawl' of wit'-ness). The recalling back of a witness who has completed his testimony for further examination.

RECEIVING STOLEN GOODS (re-see[1]-ving sto'-len goodz). The offense of receiving or accepting from another property with the knowledge that it has been stolen, embezzled, extorted, or otherwise feloniously obtained.

RECESS (re-sess'). A time in which a court is not actually engaged in business. An interruption, not amounting to an adjournment, of a meeting.

RECIPROCAL (re-sip'-ro-kal). Mutual.

RECOGNIZANCE (re-kog'-ni-zanse). An obligation, in the nature of a bond, entered into before some court, to assure the court of performance of some specified condition.

RECOGNIZE (rek'-og-nize). To ratify. To examine or look into the truth of a matter. To become bound by a recognizance.

REDRESS (re-dress'). Indemnity; satisfaction for a loss or injury sustained.

REDUCTIO AD ABSURDUM (re-duk'-she-o ad ab-ser'-dum). Proving an argument false by showing it leads to an absurdity.

RE-EXAMINATION (re-ek-zam-i-nay'-shun). A second or new examination of a thing. The examination of a witness, after cross-examination.

REGULATE (reg'-u-late). The subject to control by superior authority; to direct by rule or restriction.

REGULATION (reg-u-lay'-shun). The act of regulating. A rule or order by which a superior authority directs the action of those under its control.

REHEARING (re-here'-ing). A new or second hearing and consideration by a court of a case already heard by it, in order to correct a possible oversight or error in the first one.

RELEASE (re-leese'). The giving up or relinquishment of a right or claim to one against whom it exists or may be enforced.

RELEVANCY (rel'-e-van-se). The legal relationship between evidence and the issue that the evidence is supposed to prove.

REMAND (re-mand'). To return or send back; to order a prisoner returned to custody; to send a cause back to the court from which it came for further proceedings.

REMEDIAL (re-mee'-di-al). Pertaining to redress or remedy; affording a remedy.

REMEDY (rem'-e-de). The means used to enforce a right or redress an injury.

REMIT (re-mit'). To pardon; to annul a fine or forfeiture. To transmit or send money, check, or other thing in payment.

REMOVAL OF CAUSE (re-moo'-val of kawze). Change of venue; the transfer of a cause from one court to another, more commonly from a state court to a United States court.

RENUNCIATION (re-nun-si-ay '-shun). The abandonment of a right.

REPLY (re-ply'). The plaintiff's answer to the defendant's defense.

REPORT (re-port'). A formal account or statement of facts upon some matter that the person making the report was required to investigate or administer. The word also refers to the printed account of a court case with the facts, decision, and opinion of the court given in considerable detail, the reports of all cases, mostly of higher court, being gathered together in volumes, known as reports, and made available for reference use.

REPRESENTATION (rep-re-zen-tay'-shun). A statement of a fact, or actions, implying the existence of such fact, made by one relative to the subject matter of a contract to induce another to enter into the contract. The method by which a person is put in the place of another and succeeds to the same rights and liabilities as the person represented.

REPRIEVE (re-preve'). The withdrawing of a sentence or a judgment of a court for a period of time, thus staying or postponing the execution of the sentence.

REPUGNANCY (re-pug'-nan-see). An inconsistency or opposition between statements in a pleading, contract, deed, or any instrument.

RES (reez[1]). The thing; the object or property involved in a suit; a matter.

RES IPSA LOQUITUR (reez ip'-sa lo'-kwi-ter). The thing speaks for itself. A doctrine by which certain things are presumed to be true unless rebutted.

RES JUDICATA (reez ju-di-kay'-ta). A thing or matter that has been definitely and finally decided by a court of competent jurisdiction.

RES NOVA (reez no'-va). A new matter; a question not previously decided.

RETAINER (re-tane'-er). The employment of counsel or an attorney by a client. The preliminary fee that the client pays the attorney to secure the right to his services.

RETROACTIVE (re-tro-ak'-tiv). Retrospective; applying to things past.

RETROSPECTIVE (ret-ro-spek'-tiv). Looking backward; having reference to events in the past.

RETROSPECTIVE LAW (ret-ro-spek'-tiv law). A law that affects acts or rights that accrued before the law came into existence; a law impairing vested rights or attaching new rights or obligations to transactions already past.

RETURN (re-tern'). An official statement in writing by an officer as to how he has executed a writ, process, or other command from a superior authority.

RETURN DAY (re-tern' day). The day stated in a writ or process when the officer is required to return it and when the defendant must make an appearance.

REVERSAL (re-ver'-sal). The decision of a superior court by which the judgment of an inferior court is annulled.

REVERT (re-vert'). To return to; to go back.

REVIEW (re-vu[1]). A new trial or re-examination of the issues, especially by an appellate court.

RIGHT (rite). A power, privilege, or legal claim. The correlative or obligation, as every right in one person produces a corresponding obligation on another.

RIGHT OF ACTION (rite of ak'-shun). A legal right to bring suit to enforce a debt or obligation.

ROBBERY (rob'-er-re). The taking of goods or money from the person of another or in his presence by actual or constructive force without his consent and with the intent to steal.

RUDIMENTARY (roo'-de-men'-tere). Elements or first principles of a subject. Imperfect or undeveloped beginning of something.

RULE (rool). To command; to decide a question of law. A principle, standard, or guide for a regulation of conduct. An order or court. A law.

RULE ABSOLUTE (rool ab'-so-lute). A final or imperative rule; a final rule of court upon some matter on which it may have ruled tentatively previously.

RULE NISI (rool ny'-sy). A rule that is to become final unless (nisi) the party against whom the order is directed shows cause why it should not be enforced.

RULES OF COURT (rools of kort). The rules by which the practice of the court is governed.

SANCTION (sangk'-shun). To ratify, confirm or assent. The penalty or punishment by which a law is enforced.

SAVING CLAUSE (save'-ing klawz). That part of a legal instrument or statute exempting something from the normal operation of the instrument or statute.

SCIENTER (sy-en'-ter). Knowingly. That allegation in a pleading indicating in a defendant the knowledge of wrong with which a crime or tort was committed.

SECONDARY EVIDENCE (sek'-un-dare-re ev'-i-dense). Such evidence as is acceptable after satisfactory proof is made that an original document or primary evidence is lost or inaccessible.

SEDUCTION (se-duk'-shun). The wrongful act of a man, by means of persuasion or guile rather than force, in inducing a previously chaste female to have sexual intercourse with him.

SELF-INCRIMINATION (self-in-krim-i-nay'-shun). Acknowledgment of one's guilt in a crime. Acting as a witness against oneself.

SENTENCE (sen'-tense). The judgment of the court upon conviction in a criminal case, announcing the punishment imposed.

SET ASIDE (set a-side'). To annul; to make void.

SIC (sik). So; thus; in the manner.

SLANDER (slan'-der). The speaking of false, defamatory words, which are injurious to another's reputation.

SOLICITATION (so-lis-i-tay'-shun). The offense of inducing another to commit a crime.

SPECIFIC PERFORMANCE (spe-sif'-ik perfor'-manse). The actual carrying out or fulfilling of an obligation by the party bound to do so. The name of the equitable remedy by which a party is compelled to fulfill his contract as originally intended.

STARE DECISIS (stay'-re de-sy'-sis). To abide by former decisions. The maxim or principle followed by courts, that when a point has been settled by decision, it forms a precedent which is to be followed when the same point arises again in litigation.

STATUTE (stat'-ute). A law enacted and established by the legislative department of the government.

STAY (stay). To stop temporarily further proceedings. An order of court, stopping or arresting judicial proceedings.

STIPULATION (stip-u-lay'-shun). A matter agreed upon. An agreement between opposing attorneys on some matter before a court. An understanding in the nature of a bond, filed in an admiralty proceeding, to secure the release of a ship.

STRIKING A JURY (strike'-ing a joo'-re). The selecting of a jury or twelve people, usually called a special jury, by striking off names on a specially prepared list until it has been reduced to twelve.

SUB (sub). Under; subordinate to; upon.

SUBJECT-MATTER (sub'-jikt-mat'-er). The issue presented for consideration; the thing in which a right or duty has been asserted; the thing in dispute.

SUBORNATION OF PERJURY (sub-or-nay'-shun of per'-joo-re). The crime of inducing or inciting another to commit perjury.

SUBPOENA (sub-pee'-na). The process to cause a person by reason of possible penalty, to appear in court and give testimony in a cause.

SUBPOENA DUCES TECUM (sub-pee[1]-na du'-seez tee'-kum). The same process as the usual subpoena with the additional order upon the witness to bring the books, papers, documents, etc. mentioned in the subpoena.

SUBSTANTIVE LAW (sub'-stan-tiv law). Those rules of law that define general rights and duties that make up all law except those rules that prescribe a remedy or method of redress, which latter are called remedial or adjective law.

SUI GENERIS (su'-i jen'-er-is). Of its own kind; peculiar to itself.

SUI JURIS (su'-i joo'-ris). In his own right; capable of contracting and acting for himself.

SUMMARY (sum'-ar-re). Short; immediate; peremptory; without a jury.

SUMMONS (sum'-onz). A writ or process to secure the appearance of a defendant in court to answer a civil suit against him.

SUO NOMINE (su'-o no'-mi-nee). In his own name.

SUPERIOR COURT (su-pere'-i-or kort). A court not limited in its jurisdiction as in the case of an inferior court.

SUPPLEMENTAL (sup-le-men'-tal). Something added to another thing in order to make it more complete or to correct a defect.

SUPRA (su'-pra). Above; upon; previously mentioned.

SUPREME COURT (su-preme' kort). The court of last resort in most of the states, as well as in the government of the United States.

SURPLUSAGE (ser'-plus-aj). Any matter in a pleading that is not required or is unnecessary.

SURREBUTTER (ser-re-but'-er). The pleading of the plaintiff serving as a reply to defendant's rebutter.

SWEAR (sware). To declare under oath, duly administered, the truth of some matter. To become bound by an oath; to administer an oath to another.

SWORN (sworn). Verified; given or executed under oath.

SYLLABUS (sil'-a-bus). An abstract; a condensation; a brief statement as to the content, meaning and import of a longer writing; the headnote proceeding a reported case and stating the rule of law that the case sets forth.

TACIT (tas'-it). Implied; unspoken assent; understood because of the nature of the thing or because of lack of open dissent.

TANGIBLE (tan'-jebel). Having or possessing physical form. Capable of being touched and seen; perceptible to the touch; capable of being possessed or realized. Capable of being understood by the mind.

TERM (term). An extent of time for which an estate is granted, as well as the manner by which the estate is held. The duration of time that a court is in session or that a person holds an office. A word, phrase, or expression that has come to have a recognized technical meaning.

TESTIFY (tes'-ti-fy). To give evidence as a witness.

TESTIMONY (tes'-ti-mo-nee). Oral evidence; statements made by a witness under oath.

TORTIOUS (tor'-shus). Wrongful; having the qualities of a tort.

TRAVERSE (trav'-ers). To put off, delay, or deny. A pleading that denies the allegations of the pleading of the opposite party.

TRIAL (try'-al). Any proceeding before a competent tribunal to determine the rights of parties or the issues placed before it.

TRUE BILL (troo bill). A bill of indictment indorsed with the words "Billa vera" (true bill), indicating that a grand jury has found sufficient cause for the trial of the accused, from which words the indictment is called a true bill.

UNA VOCE (u'-na vo'-se). With one voice; unanimously.

UNDUE INFLUENCE (un-doo' in'-floo-ense). Such influence as compels one to act against his will because of fear, desire for peace, misplaced confidence, or any feeling that may be imposed upon.

UNILATERAL CONTRACT (u-ni-lat' -er-al kon'-trakt). A contract in which one party makes a promise or engages to perform without receiving a similar promise in return from the other, or one in which one party has performed already.

UNILATERAL MISTAKE (u-ni-lat[1]-er-al mi-stayk'). A mistake on the part of only one of two parties to a contract.

USE (use). To employ. Act of employing something. The purpose that anything may have. The predecessor of the present-day trust, by which land was placed in the hands of one with the intention that it be utilized and disposed of for the benefit of another, called the cestui que use.

USQUE (us'-kwee). Until; up to; as far as.

VACATE (vay'-kate). To move or leave unoccupied. To annul; to make void.

VALID (val'-id). Legal; effective; binding; not void.

VENIRE (ve-ny'-re). To come. Technically, the writ by which a jury is summoned, although it is sometimes used as meaning the entire body of names so summoned.

VENIREMAN (ve-ny[1]-re-man). A person summoned for service on a jury.

VENUE (ven'-u). The county in which a case rightfully can be tried and from which the jurors are to come.

VERDICT (vir'-dikt). The decision of the jury reported to the court on the matters of fact submitted to the jury for trial.

VERIFICATION (ver-i-fi-kay'-shun). Confirmation of the truth of a statement or writing by affidavit or oath or by the offering of proof.

VERSUS (vir'-sus). Usually abbreviated v. or vs. in the title of a cause, it means against.

VEST (vest). To take effect; to give an immediate, fixed interest in property or a fixed right to future enjoyment of the property.

VIDELICET (vi-del'-i-set). Namely; that is to say; to-wit. Usually abbreviated as "viz."

VOID (void). Empty; null; of no legal force or effect.

VOIDABLE (voi'-da-bl). That which may be declared void; of full force and effect until or unless a party has the right to consider it ineffectual and does so.

VOLUNTARY MANSLAUGHTER (vol'-untare-re man'-slaw-ter). A somewhat less heinous offense than murder, in that the killing, while intentional, is without malice or premeditation and the result of reasonable provocation.

WAIVE (wave). To abandon or give up a right; to throw away; to forsake; to relinquish.

WAIVER (way'-ver). A voluntary relinquishment or denial of a known right.

WANTON (wan'-ton). Willful; done with reckless disregard to consequences.

WARDEN (war'-dn). A keeper; a guardian; the superintendent of a prison.

WARRANT (war'-ant). To assure the truth of a matter. A writ issued by competent authority directing the arrest of a person named therein. An acknowledgment of debt by a municipality or town and order to pay such debt when funds are available for the purpose.

WITHOUT PREJUDICE (with-out' prej'-oodis). Without the loss of any right or privilege except what is actually conceded.

WITHOUT RECOURSE (with-out' re-korse'). Without liability to person signing thusly.

WITNESS (wit'-ness). A spectator or listener. One who because of first-hand knowledge or experience is able to testify as to some fact or matter. To subscribe one's name to a document for the purpose of proving its execution if the authenticity of the document should subsequently be questioned.

WRIT (rit). An order in writing, issued by a court or other competent jurisdiction in the name of the state or sovereign, directed to the sheriff or other proper officer to execute the same, and directing the defendant or party mentioned therein to do what the order calls for.

WRIT OF ERROR (rit of er'-or). A writ directed to a court of record by a higher court so that the appellate court may review errors claimed to have been made and possibly correct them.

WRIT OR ERROR CORAM NOBIS (OR VOBIS) [rit of er'-or kor'-am no'-bis (or vo'-bis)]. A writ sued out by a party to correct an error of fact and directed to the same court in which judgment was rendered in order to correct the error.

WRITTEN LAW (rit'-en law). Statute law; law established by legislative enactments, as distinguished from unwritten law or the law developed by the courts.

WRONG (rawng). A tort; the invasion of some legal right.

ABOUT THE AUTHOR

Throughout the years, Kelly P. Riggs has led a relatively unremarkable life. He was quite content being a loving father and guide to his children, until his course was redirected by a rogue court operating under the guise of dispensing justice in Birmingham Alabama. His life has always been the product of choices, both good and bad, all of which he applied over the years to achieve the best possible outcome available. One of those choices included providing information to the F.B.I. In 2011, Mr. Riggs was forced to report the activities of a D.E.A. agent to the F.B.I., the rogue agent was trafficking large quantities of drugs into the Birmingham Alabama area. This one choice started an investigation into Mr. Riggs' life, once arrested he was held for a crime the Chief district judge freely admits that he didn't commit. After Mr. Riggs' refusal to change his testimony the district judge, at sentencing, stated that it was about time he learned to tell the truth, as she said it would be.

His growing up in the home of an abusive alcoholic father, who consequently died in a car accident in 1981, gave way to extreme culture shock for the remaining family members as they moved from Hinkley California to Blountsville Alabama in 1983. In 1985 Mr. Riggs dropped out of high school and signed to join the United States Army. In the Army, he finished his studies at Aberdeen Proving Grounds Maryland, which were subsequently accepted by J.B. Pennington high school in Blountsville Alabama. With high school behind him, Mr. Riggs began his study of military law with aspirations of becoming a J.A.G. lawyer. After over two years of intense correspondence study and hours under the scrutiny of various proctors, Mr. Riggs discovered that the prospective oath required to become a J.A.G. lawyer was in conflict with his military oath, "to defend the constitution" and his own personal strict moral code. This prompted an unprecedented career change. Mr. Riggs used the skills he learned in the Army to become a valuable asset in the electrical trade as a leader, problem solver, and teacher.

Over the next two decades Mr. Riggs quietly continued his studies to satisfy his own desire to possess an intimate knowledge of the law and provided only limited assistance to those in the practice thereof. In the course of his assistance Mr. Riggs found himself ethically bound to report the corruption of public officials and federal agents, some of which are, now under indictment. By May of 2012 he was charged with a crime he didn't commit by the same Federal district he made his report in. Mr. Riggs entered a guilty plea as a vehicle to gain protection from a death threat against his family that was later discovered to have been propagated by the Federal public defender's office in the Northern district of Alabama. See case no's: 2:12-cr-297-KOB-JEO, and 2:15-CV-8043-KOB. Mr. Riggs thereafter dedicated his every waking moment to his study of advanced criminal procedure. Over the last five years he has become a skilled and treasured legal writer who assists underprivileged victims of the judicial machinery. He is one of the founding members of Release of Innocent Prisoners Effort: RIPE Inc. and has assisted over 750 federal prisoners, directly or indirectly, acquire their desired relief.

In the beginning of Mr. Riggs' service to his country he vowed to fight for those who couldn't fight for themselves. In this capacity, he, here now, vows to dedicate the remainder of his life to the fight for justice by bringing awareness to the American people through his fiction and non-fiction writing concerning the law, government, and injustice.

In 2011 he donated a kidney to a fellow soldier. The man was on dialysis and quickly losing his battle. he had a young child who needed his father. That in mind and imagining what my children would do without me prompted me to donate a kidney to a stranger.

Thanks for your interest in Freebird Publishers!

We value our customers and would love to hear from you! Reviews are an important part in bringing you quality publications. We love hearing from our readers-rather it's good or bad (though we strive for the best)!

If you could take the time to review/rate any publication you've purchased with Freebird Publishers we would appreciate it!

If your loved one uses Amazon, have them post your review on the books you've read. This will help us tremendously, in providing future publications that are even more useful to our readers and growing our business.

Amazon works off of a 5 star rating system. When having your loved one rate us be sure to give them your chosen star number as well as a written review. Though written reviews aren't required, we truly appreciate hearing from you.

★★★★★ **Everything a prisoner needs is available in this book.**
January 30, 201 June 7, 2018
Format: Paperback

A necessary reference book for anyone in prison today. This book has everything an inmate needs to keep in touch with the outside world on their own from inside their prison cell. Inmate Shopper's business directory provides complete contact information on hundreds of resources for inmate services and rates the companies listed too! The book has even more to offer, contains numerous sections that have everything from educational, criminal justice, reentry, LGBT, entertainment, sports schedules and more. The best thing is each issue has all new content and updates to keep the inmate informed on todays changes. We recommend everybody that knows anyone in prison to send them a copy, they will thank you.

* No purchase neccessary. Reviews are not required for drawing entry. Void where prohibited.
Contest date runs July 1 - June 30, 2019.

FREEBIRD PUBLISHERS COMING SOON...

- **THE PRO SE SECTION 1983 MANUAL**
- **THE HABEAS CORPUS MANUAL**
- **INEFFECTIVE ASSISTANCE OF COUNSEL**
- **POST CONVICTION RELIEF: SECOND LAST CHANCE**
- **POST CONVICTION RELIEF: THE ADVOCATE**

INMATE SHOPPER
LARGEST BOOK OF RESOURCES
ANNUAL ISSUE

THE BEST 500+
NON PROFIT ORGANIZATIONS
FIND WHAT YOU NEED FAST

PEN PAL SUCCESS
THE ULTIMATE GUIDE TO GETTING & KEEPING PEN PALS

PENPALS
A PERSONAL GUIDE
PRISONERS

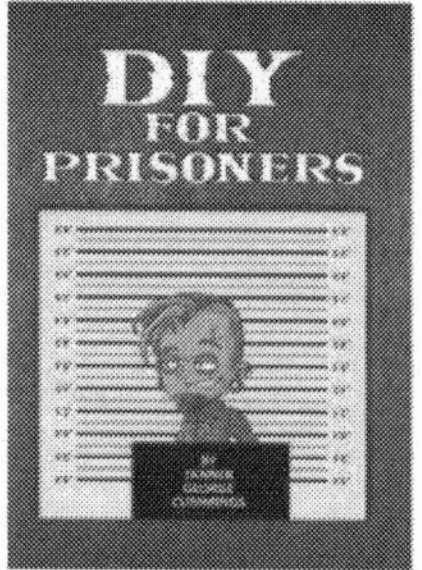
DIY
FOR
PRISONERS

Kitty Kat
ADULT ENTERTAINMENT RESOURCE BOOK
NON NUDE
BY MIKE ENEMIGO

CELEBRITY
FEMALE
STAR POWER
Josh Kruger

FREEBIRD PUBLISHERS
GIFT
LOOK BOOK

SEXY GIRL PARADE

PILLOW TALK

HOT GIRL SAFARI

Soft Shots

Fine Dining

The
CELL
CHEF

The
CELL
CHEF
II

FREEBIRD
PUBLISHERS

Made in the USA
Middletown, DE
25 February 2023